D0396889

THE PHILOSOPHY OF SUSTAINABLE DESIGN

The Future of Architecture

JASON F. MCLENNAN

FOREWORD BY BOB BERKEBILE

ECOtone LLC
publishing company

www.ecotonedesign.com

Ecotone Publishing
3187 Point White Dr. NE
Bainbridge Is. WA 98110

The Philosophy of Sustainable Design

Library of Congress Control Number: 2004091676

Library of Congress Cataloging-in Publication Data

McLennan, Jason F.

The Philosophy of Sustainable Design/Jason F. McLennan

Includes bibliographical references and index

ISBN 0-9749033-0-2

1. Architecture 2. Environment 3. Philosophy

First Hardcover Edition

Printed in Canada on Rolland Enviro 100, with 100% Post Consumer Recycled Content

Book and Jacket Design: Erin Gehle / softfirmstudios.net

About Ecotone Publishing
The Green Building Publisher

Ecotone is a new publishing company whose mission is to educate and provide examples of restorative design to people in the building industry. In nature, an ecotone is a biologically rich transition zone between two or more dissimilar ecosystems. In architecture we use it as a metaphor to help understand the richness of the boundaries between the habitats of people and the environment.

Ecotone Publishing—exploring the relationship between the built and natural environments.

For more information on Ecotone or to purchase other books please visit our website at: www.ecotonedesign.com

or contact us at:

Ecotone LLC
P.O. Box 7147
Kansas City, Missouri
64113-0147

Dedication

This book is dedicated to the loving memory of three incredible women from my family who supported me in countless ways. I owe much to each of them, certainly more than the dedication of this book. I only hope that it pleases them wherever they are.

This book is dedicated to my Grandmother Alexina Harvey whom I never met, but whose presence I have felt since I was a child.

This book is dedicated to my Grandmother Annie McLennan who believed in me and found ways to support my education and travels that helped transform me into the architect I am today.

And finally, this book is dedicated to my wonderful Aunt Rita Walter-Wittenheim who helped instill a life-long love of books and learning, and who read early drafts of the manuscript and offered much encouragement. Her recent passing is hard for us all.

Much love,

Jason F. McLennan

Acknowledgements

This book was written with the assistance and love of so many influential people. I am thankful for the support of each of them and regretful that a page of acknowledgements can only list a few. With that in mind, I would like to acknowledge those who did the most to help me complete the project.

First, I acknowledge my father, Dr. Fred McLennan, for helping to edit and correct my numerous errors and mangled sentences, as well as for his overall support and guidance through the whole project.

Along with my father, I acknowledge my wonderful family; my mother Sandra who is truly an angel on earth and my two sisters Melissa and Debbie, whom I love very much.

This book could not have been written without the knowledge I gained from Bob Berkebile, my mentor, colleague and friend. And to the dozens of green warriors, people like Pliny Fisk, Greg Norris, Kath Williams, Ron Perkins and Peter Rumsey who inspire me and lead me to think that change is possible.

I thank my team members at Elements/BNIM who teach me more each day than I could possibly teach them.

Without Erin Gehle, this book would not look as beautiful as it does, and without the guidance and support of Shannon Criss, Nils Gore and Mike Swann at the University of Kansas this book would not have had the rigor it does.

When I was frustrated with the process of writing almost 100 000 words and making them flow together with some semblance of order, I only had to spend a few moments with my two sons Julian and Declan, both of whom make me smile when nothing else can.

And finally, the most important person to the whole process, my wonderful, beautiful wife Tracy, who was the first to read most of the chapters and to give me critical feedback when it was most needed. Tracy was kind enough to put up with the countless hours I spent writing and who teaches me each day to be more patient, kind and humble. I am a better person because of her. I love you girl.

Chapter Outline

"In many ways, the environmental crisis is a design crisis. It is a consequence of how things are made, buildings are constructed, and landscapes are used. Design manifests culture, and culture rests firmly on the foundation of what we believe to be true about the world."

—Sym Van Der Ryn

Foreword

By Bob Berkebile, FAIA

One of my professors, Buckminster Fuller, maintained that we are all born geniuses but sadly we are gradually de-geniused by our parents and teachers. Generally I have discovered this to be true. But thankfully, I have found there are exceptions. Jason McLennan is one of the remarkable exceptions. We had received rave reviews from his professors at the University of Oregon before he joined the firm, but it was after his arrival that I began to appreciate his real capacity. As soon as he became acclimated to the office and comfortable with me—it may have taken about seven minutes—he unleashed a barrage of questions. These questions revealed that his parents, teachers and two very special aunts treated him more kindly than Bucky imagined was possible. They stimulated his inquisitive mind and nurtured his enthusiasm for life. Anyone who knows Jason will confirm that his passion for life and insatiable appetite for knowledge are inspiring.

Inspiration is critical, because from my perspective there are many reasons one could be pessimistic about the future. For two decades I have been exploring the impact of our lifestyles and community designs on human health and productivity, and on the vitality of our biosphere. During that time all of the key environmental indicators have declined. For example, the ten hottest years since we have been recording global temperatures (1880) have occurred during the last fifteen years, causing three thousand two hundred species from amoeba to zebra to move north at an unprecedented rate. It is becoming increasingly clear that American community designs have laid the foundation for the most consumptive, polluting lifestyle on earth. And it is clear that our behavior is the leading factor in The Union of Concerned Scientists' report that all the earth's life support systems are in a state of decline and that the rate of decline in every case is accelerating.

As this book is published, the future is not clear for the children in this year's kindergarten class; but by the time they graduate in 2020, the year of perfect vision, it will be. By then scientists will have overwhelming evidence as to whether or not the biosphere will continue to support human life through the next century. Many scientists are pessimistic about the outcome since much of the developing world is rushing to imitate our community model, a model which holds all the records for consumption, pollution and isolation. It's also a pattern, which, as it continues to spread, dramatically increases the challenge to the earth's carrying capacity and its ability to meet the needs of the 2020 graduating class.

But Jason sees it differently. He believes that we simply need better community and system designs and the will to execute it. And in spite of the significant changes we must embrace to make this possible, he is optimistic. He has seen it happen. He had the advantage of participating in a remarkable transformation as he was growing up in Sudbury, Canada. At the time Sudbury was, and still is, the nickel mining and smelting capital of the world. The extracting and refining of nickel was the economic engine for Sudbury and more. It was also the activity that destroyed the air, water and soil of the region. This practical experience of participating in and witnessing the results of a dramatic regional restoration fuel his optimism and inform his commitment to replace the long shadow we have cast on our children's future with designs that restore the balance between nature and human nature.

He has drawn from the best of our experiences with exceptional clients, communities and institutions who might generally fall into the category of change agents committed to creating restorative, pedagogical design solutions, from the best of his voracious reading, and most important from his creative thinking.

This is the time when the fate of the 2020 graduating class will be determined. In spite of the scientific reports about the decline in life support systems we have yet to be motivated to create a community that begins to restore the damage and add vitality to the social, economic and environmental systems. A significant shift in our worldview and behavior will be required for the graduates to be optimistic about their future. Jason knows that we have the capacity to change and he delineates some of the best thinking and activities that are leading to restoring natural systems and human potential in this book. He really believes that we can make the world a better place by 2020. If you and I embrace his vision, I believe the class of 2020 will find that he was correct.

Photo courtesy of Jo-Ele Wood

Philosophical Beginnings

*Will we be able to face our children and assure them that we did
not lack the courage to face these difficult questions, did not lack
the stamina to pursue the correct solutions?*
                                        —Pierre Elliot Trudeau

Preface

My past has taught me two important lessons; that we have an amazing capacity to damage the habitat of all living things while building our own, but we also have an ability to heal it through good design.

I spent the first nineteen years of my life in Sudbury, a small northern mining city in Ontario, Canada. Sudbury, otherwise known as the Nickel City, is at the southern edge of the vast, sparsely populated part of the province called northern Ontario, and in many ways serves as the gateway and nucleus for many of the communities over four hours drive north of the metropolitan city of Toronto. While being a typical Canadian community in a number of ways, Sudbury has a unique history dating back before any individual called it home.

Thousands of years ago, an ancient meteorite crashed into the Sudbury area creating a crater one hundred and twenty miles wide and forty miles long that Sudbury and many other smaller communities eventually nestled into. This crater, geologically unique, is one of the largest of its type in the world and would one day play a significant role in the development of the area. In 1883 Sudbury was founded by members of the Canadian Pacific Railway (CPR) looking for a suitable regional outpost in the vast CPR rail line that stretched four thousand miles from British Columbia to New Brunswick. The Sudbury outpost was not special in any regard until prospectors in the area chanced upon copper and then nickel ores in the rocks. From that point on, the history of the region would forever be altered as this small CPR outpost slowly transformed itself from a sleepy rail stop into a major international mining center, transforming the landscape and economy of the region. The early days gave little sign of the industry that would soon make Sudbury into the Nickel Capital of the world, at its height supplying ninety percent of the world's nickel from one community.

Over the ensuing decades, dozens of mining companies came and went in efforts to extract the precious ore from the ground. Two companies, the International Nickel Company (INCO) and Falconbridge, soon came to dominate the scene, providing thousands of jobs to the area over the next one hundred years. Sudbury would eventually support some one hundred thousand people in the city and about one hundred and sixty thousand in the region, making it the largest community in northern Ontario.

Over the years, the economic success of the mines began to reveal other less positive consequences to the region. In the early days, mining was an incredibly polluting industry and producing a ton of ore meant creating many more tons of air pollutants such as sulphur and carbon that ended up in the atmosphere, the soil, and the lungs of inhabitants. At that time, smelting[1] of the nickel ore was done in open pit mines that relied on intense fires to melt the ore. The fuel for these fires came first from local trees until the whole region had been denuded of its timber. Within a short time, the pristine landscape around Sudbury was altered forever and it would provide a telling lesson on the ability of human activity to create large-scale environmental damage.

By the sixties Sudbury had become famous worldwide for its lifeless landscape—stripped of trees and stained permanently black by the pollution created by the mining industry. By that time, the nightmarish air pollution responsible for this devastation had been tamed locally by the introduction of large smokestacks that sent the pollutants farther up into the atmosphere. In the twenties a five hundred and ten foot smokestack, "the tallest in the empire," was built, which itself gave way in 1970 to an even taller smokestack (the tallest in the world) constructed from continuous pour concrete equivalent to a one hundred story building. The building of the smokestack was not the end of pollution but it was good news locally, because it stopped the damage from getting worse and saved many lakes from becoming acidified. The pollution now was someone else's problem—those living downwind who had to face North America's single largest source of acid rain. Sulphur in large quantities has the ability to alter the pH of both soil and water, stunting plant growth, killing lakes and in many cases, as within a five to ten mile radius of the region's mining operations, killing off all trees. One can imagine the effect on human health. Unfortunately, the Sudbury response was part of a common attitude still in abundant practice all over the world today; that the solution to pollution is dilution, rather than responsibility. This common attitude suggests that we can just send our garbage and wastes "away" even though increasingly there is no more "away".

Stories of Sudbury's landscape were made more intriguing when Apollo astronauts paid the region a visit in 1971 in order to prepare for lunar landings. The region, it was believed, was as close to a "moonscape" as possible in North America and ideal for astronaut training. The geological remnants of the ancient meteor, combined with the impacts of the local mining, made parts of the Sudbury area eerily similar to a lunar landscape.

The truth was, however, that by the seventies, despite its scars, Sudbury was a good place to call home. During this time, in the dawning era of environmental responsibility, the region had begun to transform itself. In the seventies and eighties a massive re-greening effort took place as students, including myself, hauled bags of lime up hills to help restore a healthy pH balance to the soil and plant trees. C.M. Wallace, a local historian, recounts that the region transformed itself,

"Using local student labor during the summer months, the program, which entailed the liming of acidic soils, grassing, and tree planting, reclaimed more than 2500 acres of land within three years. Where there had been only barren outcropping of rock and thin, eroded soil, the newly planted grasses and bushes began to retain moisture and reverse the destructive cycle."[2]

Wallace also notes, "As part of image rebuilding in the face of worldwide criticism, the corporations demonstrated a community awareness previously unnecessary and initiated high-visibility projects such as Science North. The environmental movement generated a decade of activity by governments, companies, academics, and students that miraculously disguised a century of neglect."[3]

Literally, before my eyes, I watched the city transform itself from a barren moonscape to a livable, growing landscape that each year became healthier and healthier. By 1990, Chatelaine magazine even voted Sudbury as one of the ten best places to live in the country—a huge transformation from the little city known only for mining and environmental decay. For its efforts in environmental restoration Sudbury started to become known as a model of environmental recovery and even received a United Nations commendation. By the nineties the city had diversified and found a leading role within regional government, higher education, and the expanding service sector.

The message that was clear to me at the time was that, as a society, we had a role not only in degrading the environment but also in restoring it. The other message, full of hope and promise, was that nature, even severely abused, had the ability to rebound and life and order, so violently wrenched, could be returned. I was further encouraged by the knowledge, as I hauled bags of lime up hills and down valleys, that we could speed up the process of renewal with care and responsibility.

And yet, as Sudbury grew up from a simple mining town to a more mature urban center, I was equally disturbed by another trend, subtler, but no less devastating than the mining of the region. Sudbury, like so many communities in this country, developed in ways that ignored the cultural and geographical uniqueness of the place. It seemed with every new civic project that the community was working hard to create a land "where every place is like no place in particular, where cities are dead zones and the countryside is a wasteland of cartoon architecture and parking lots"[4] as it was so aptly put by David James Kunstler in his groundbreaking book, *The Geography of Nowhere*. Here was a community with a geological and industrial history unique to the world with a banal and ugly architecture that ignored its own uniqueness.

I found myself wondering why we were so busy repairing this place from the effects of industry when we were so quick to turn around and demean it with our architecture and our built environment. Growing up I witnessed some of my favorite climbing hills blown up and flattened, not for the nickel that was trapped inside, but to make room for shopping malls, cul de sacs and vinyl-sided houses. I witnessed wonderful wetlands and marshes getting filled in to become parking lots and strip malls, and I witnessed the destruction of historic buildings built in a time when architecture mattered, torn down and replaced with structures that did not look like they would last through ten Canadian winters.

If we just moved rocks to make way for ugly, inefficient buildings, how was this any different than what the mining industry had perpetrated in the first place? This was personal. I loved this place, with its black rocks, sparkling lakes, blueberries and stunted birch and poplars. Even before I could properly articulate it, I yearned for a regional architecture that would respect the unique qualities of the place. It deserved an architecture that emerged from the ground, made from local materials and designed to ride out long, cold winters and bask in the warm radiant energy of the sun It deserved an architecture that learned from our hard lessons on degradation and restoration and that took advantage of what the mining industry did not want and could not destroy.

And so I left Sudbury. I wanted to learn how to build buildings that embodied the lessons of this place, that not only lowered environmental impact, but also honored the spirit of the region. I was determined to unite these teachings into an understanding of how the built environment can honor the natural environment and elevate us in the process.

I went on to study architecture at the University of Oregon in Eugene, famous for its emphasis on sustainable design, solar buildings and place making. Eugene, at the beginning of the last decade, was a hotbed for sustainable thinking and it put me in touch with the first of many mentors who have helped shape my attitudes to the built and natural environments and widened my understanding of alternatives to conventional transportation, agriculture, industry and building.

It was in Oregon that Christopher Alexander proposed many of his ideas on place making including the groundbreaking *Oregon Experiment* that followed *the Pattern Language*.[5] At Oregon, I had the opportunity to study passive and active solar design under some of the original "solar rollers" who first explored these concepts during the energy crisis. Some of these professors such as John Reynolds, Rob Pena and Chuck Rusch were exceptional as teachers and always available to the students. They taught me that sustainable design was not an option but a responsibility for us as design professionals. They believed that sustainable thinking should be an integral part of the design process. Under their tutelage, I was able to build and test alternative materials with fellow students. For example, I helped build the first straw bale structure in the State of Oregon in 1992 and one of the first rammed earth and cob structures as well. As part of a student exchange program I spent a year in Glasgow, Scotland studying urban theory at the Mackintosh School of Architecture, applying my design knowledge to wider urban and community issues. Upon my return to Oregon to finish my degree I accepted a position as the director of the Solar Center where I helped disseminate information on many aspects of sustainable design. I spent my final two years in Oregon designing two passive solar houses and several remodels that used alternative materials. I also taught classes in sustainable design and architecture appreciation at the local community college.

In the early summer of 1997 I received a surprise job offer to work with Bob Berkebile of BNIM Architects in Kansas City, one of the founders of the green architecture movement in the United States. As part of my responsibilities, I was to research and design green buildings for the firm. Despite having never been to the Midwest, I moved to Kansas City to begin work on the Montana State University EpiCenter project, funded by the National Institute of Standards and Technology to be the most energy efficient lab building in the world. Working with Berkebile and a host of outstanding consultants from around the country on this and other projects proved to be a virtual Ph.D. program in understanding green technologies and materials and helped solidify my understanding of the tenets of sustainable design that I set forth in this book. Bob Berkebile continues to be one of the most important sustainable thinkers in the emerging green design movement that is starting to change all aspects of the building profession, and he, perhaps more than any other, has shaped my understanding of sustainable design. Many of the ideas discussed in this book can be attributed to Bob Berkebile, Ron Perkins, Pliny Fisk and others who I worked closely with on the Montana Project.

While in Kansas City I continued to teach sustainability as an adjunct professor at the University of Kansas and in 2000 I founded Elements, the sustainable consulting division of BNIM. Between 1997 and 2004, BNIM transitioned from a more typical Midwest architectural firm to a nationally prominent green design firm. At the same time, I witnessed the building industry following a similar path, as an increasing number of architects, engineers and developers around the country began to question the way they did business. This growing movement has just recently started to move beyond its infancy to define itself as something that is here to stay. For example, the US Green Building Council and the LEED rating system are currently helping to transform the building marketplace. In the coming decades green architecture will move from a fringe activity to become the dominant approach to design.

I wrote this book because I believe it is possible to change the way we design and build our buildings, communities and cities. I want to see each community discover what is unique to it, as I have with Sudbury, and to respect these unique qualities in the places we make. I believe it is possible for us to live in our environment, both natural and of our own making, in ways that are healthy, nourishing and restorative. Through this book I want to contribute to the advancement of the sustainable design movement. I believe in sustainability and I believe we have a choice to become truly sustainable in our design processes. As William McDonough has so aptly put it, "design is the first signal of human intention."[6] So what are our intentions? What kind of world will we leave to future generations? This book was written to arm those involved in creating our built environment with a philosophical basis. Architects, engineers, contractors and developers have a critical responsibility as the shapers of the places we inhabit.

It is my hope that each year, more and more of us embark on this journey to move to a sustainable future. Indeed, this book was written for the vast majority of architects, engineers, builders, interior and landscape design professionals, and building owners and managers who are in the early stages of their own journey to understand the sustainable design movement and how it affects their profession and way of doing business. It is my hope that this book can serve as a new primer and guidepost for people from a wide spectrum of backgrounds. The book examines the importance of design; indeed of good design, of responsibility and of opportunity. It discusses the roles different professions play in this movement, provides key definitions and outlines principles. Hopefully, it provides a framework for dialogue and transformation to occur. It examines barriers both real and imagined and discusses why this change to sustainable design is so critical.

This book is not about righteousness or laying guilt. Guilt is a poor motivator. Rather, it is about providing a basis for getting us to where we need to go regardless of our beliefs, because there are solid economic and social arguments for sustainability as well as moral and spiritual ones. You are reading this book for a reason—what is it? Perhaps you want to design your buildings differently, or just tap into this growing market for economic gain. Whatever the reason, I urge you to begin by examining your beginnings, and what brought you to this point. What are your attitudes, preconceptions and opinions about sustainable design? How have these notions shaped everything you do? Will you begin to make the change to sustainable design?

Along my own journey I have come to understand several key things:

- That we, as a society, cannot continue for long down the current path we are on, each year breaking records for the amount of energy, water and materials used and the pollution and waste created, without seeing widespread social, economic and environmental upheaval.
- That we in the building professions must bear a large share of the responsibility in redesigning the places and systems that we use to live sustainably, because many of the solutions to our environmental problems are design problems.
- That a sustainable future is possible and achievable within this century if we continue to remove the barriers to sustainability and apply appropriate technologies and the knowledge we continue to acquire.
- That most of the barriers to a sustainable future are not technological but fear and ignorance based.
- That each of us must begin now so that the treasures of today remain for future generations to enjoy. Each of us has a role to play.

Photo by McLennan

The Philosophy of Sustainable Design

An invasion of armies can be resisted...
But not an idea whose time has come...
— Victor Hugo

Chapter One–Defining Sustainable Design

Sustainable Design is an idea whose time has come. All over the country, indeed around the world, architects, engineers, developers and builders are all clamoring to understand how to market their services to reflect a new way of building and a new approach to design. Few firms in the country have not heard of sustainable design and realized, at least to some extent, that they must change the way they approach their business if they want to claim a portion of this rapidly growing market share. Those who have not heard the signals will soon realize that if they are to stay competitive they too must begin to understand what sustainable design is, and how it is transforming our buildings and the design professions.

And yet, despite the growing awareness and interest, few words in the design and construction industry have been so poorly used as that of **sustainable design** and **green architecture**. These terms have come to mean a lot of different things to different people, and many misconceptions exist that have created barriers to its adoption. This book will hopefully dispel some of these myths. Almost every architectural and engineering firm today claims, to some extent, that it practices sustainable design or at least has done a few green buildings, while in reality, most have little true understanding of the subject. The word "sustainable" has been applied to many buildings that do not deserve the designation, thus shrouding the few that do.

For many professionals a green building is something that merely incorporates a few recycled products or has good windows. This approach, as we will discuss, is not nearly enough. For the record, few buildings built today in Western society should even be called sustainable. A lot of buildings and building products get designated green or sustainable because they contain a few features that lower their environmental impact to some degree.[7] Sustainable design is not about features. While it is disappointing that this amount of misunderstanding exists among design professionals, it is encouraging that so many are first learning the jargon and then the meaning behind the words when a few short years ago the issues were barely discussed.

Part of the problem is that the term Sustainable design is wholly inadequate to describe the movement and philosophy behind it. In the dictionary the word sustainable is defined as something that is "able to be maintained,"[8] which doesn't accurately portray the need to change the way we relate to the natural world. Much better words could have been chosen such as *restorative* design to imply the challenge ahead or *ecological design*[9] to highlight the main focus of the philosophy. Many more adjectives could have been chosen that would have been more appropriate or compelling.

And yet, as Humpty Dumpty once said, "words mean what we want them to."[10] Most people in the sustainable design world want the term to mean much more than "maintaining" and so it has come to mean much more to them while others want it to mean much less. The challenge, of course, is to come to a common understanding of what we mean when we talk about sustainable design. This book attempts to help the movement come to this common understanding.

Another reason for the confusion surrounding sustainable design and the label of "sustainable building" is that people are trying to articulate a movement that is still in its adolescence-one that is actively defining itself, its principles, components and philosophy. Like any immature individual, sometimes it seemingly contradicts itself or seems unclear or even irrational. And with incomplete knowledge comes the spread of incomplete information. Another reason for its misapplication is that sustainable design has operated for a long time outside the mainstream of the design and construction industry, and so for a vast number of people it means a total shift in how their profession is viewed. For many, it means unlearning as much as it means learning new things. Old habits, as they say, die hard. It is for this reason that changes in philosophy tend to occur in generational timeframes rather than individual, and sustainable design is no exception. With the exclusion of a few pioneers, it will be the youngest generation practicing today and those presently in school who will bring about the most change.

This is not a how-to-book on green building. It does not contain a bunch of case studies or lists of materials for designers to use. This book is not about sustainability in the broadest sense, as defined by the Brundtland Commission, which defines sustainability as "meeting the needs of the present without compromising the needs of the future." Sustainability deals with all aspects of society including agriculture, transportation, industry and politics, and other than brief mention these issues are not dealt with here. These boundaries are not always solid, but necessary for the scope of this book. A lot of great books already exist on sustainability, green building techniques and general environmental issues, some of which are listed in the Green Warrior Reading List contained in the appendix. This book is about one slice of the sustainability pie...it is about **Sustainable Design**, which, as mentioned, is sometimes known by different names such as ecological design, green design, green architecture, eco-effective, holistic and environmentally friendly design, which should all encompass a similar meaning. For this book, only the terms sustainable design and green architecture will be used since these are the terms most commonly used in the industry.

Sustainable design is the philosophical basis of a growing movement of individuals and organizations that literally seeks to redefine how buildings are designed, built and operated to be more responsible to the environment and responsive to people. This movement is a powerful one, but still maturing and seeking to find its footing and vocabulary. Because of this maturing, a significant amount of disparity in understanding exists between its adherents and the definitions, terminology and jargon used to describe itself.

This book is intended as a stepping-stone in the maturing process, to firmly put forth the words necessary to define the movement and to share some of the great work and ideas of the many pioneers who for years struggled and still struggle against the barriers of change. As John Stuart Mill so aptly put it, "Every great movement must experience three stages: ridicule, discussion, adoption." [11] For sustainable design we are in the early transition phase between discussion and adoption. While just three years ago the attitude towards the movement was very different, no one today is ridiculing sustainable design. It is no longer viewed as a passing fad or the whims of a few environmental bleeding hearts. The next few decades will be momentous in the scale of change as sustainable design principles move from the fringe to the mainstream, in their wake changing every aspect of the built environment. Over the next few decades we will begin a new ecological age of design, first started just over thirty years ago. With this as a basis, we can define what we mean by the term sustainable design:

Sustainable Design is a design philosophy that seeks to maximize the quality of the built environment, while minimizing or eliminating negative impact to the natural environment.

This definition is useful because it highlights several important elements. First and foremost it establishes sustainable design as a philosophy. The philosophy of sustainable design is important because one of the earliest barriers arose because people viewed sustainable design as a stylistic endeavor, which it most emphatically is not. Sustainable design is an approach to design and not an aesthetic exercise and thus it can never go out of style or be discussed as a fad, as some critics have described it.[12] Secondly, because it is a philosophical approach to design, it can be used on any building type at any scale; indeed, it can transcend the design of buildings to include any object or project under design. There are no physical scale barriers to its adoption. It is a philosophy that simply asks, "What is the most we can do on a given project to enhance the quality of the built environment while minimizing or eliminating the impact to the natural environment?" However, for the purposes of this book, sustainable design will usually be referred to in the context of buildings and developments.

The next part of the definition is equally important because it establishes the fact that one of the major goals of the movement is to enhance quality. By quality, we mean creating better buildings for people, better products for our use and better places to inhabit. Early on, some people were concerned that the movement meant lowering quality and reducing comfort and well-being, when in fact the opposite was true. Sustainable design starts with the understanding that the purpose of our designs is to create physical artifacts that benefit people. This movement seeks to enhance that goal with a wider, more holistic approach.

The final part of the definition is the most obvious one. Clearly, one of the major goals of the movement is to reduce impact on the natural environment. What is not as obvious is that the ultimate goal, indeed, a necessity, as we grow from six to seven billion people and beyond is not only to reduce impact to the natural environment, but also to eliminate negative environmental impact completely through skillful, sensitive design. A project perhaps should not even be called sustainable or green until it reaches a high level of performance.[13] The most serious adherents of the sustainable design movement are not content with merely limiting damage—and from project to project continually look to up the ante, finding ways to enhance comfort while further raising the bar in environmental performance. As Sim Van Der Ryn discusses in his very important book *Ecological Design*, "In many ways, the environmental crisis is a design crisis." It is a consequence of how things are made, buildings are constructed, and landscapes are used."[14] Sustainable design is an approach that looks to the design process to heal as well as it has damaged. Bill Browning and Dianna Lopez Barnett also described it accurately in their *Sustainable Design Primer,* by reminding us that "it represents a revolution in how we think about, design, construct and operate buildings." [15] Sustainable design implies responsibility and it implies a far-reaching respect for natural systems and resources, respect for people and respect for the cycle of life. [16]

It is helpful to think about sustainable design in terms of the word **respect**. The opposite of respect is contempt. Our current system of construction, materials manufacturing and design are done in such a way that it may as well be contemptful of natural systems. If you respect something you honor it, you act as its protector, as a steward or parent. It is in this vein that we describe sustainable design. When you have contempt for something you abuse it, neglect it, ignore it and use it up. Of course, the truth is that it is not really contempt for the natural world or any big conspiracy that is behind most environmental degradation but rather it is a by-product of ignorance and the inertia of progress and politics. Nature, in most cases, is just in the way. In the twenty-first century we can no longer plead ignorance and innocence for our actions. Since we know that our buildings are a big part of the current crisis, inaction and resistance to the sustainable design movement can only be viewed now as contempt.

Sustainable design also implies intention—intention to seek the best solution that balances environmental concerns with comfort, aesthetics, cost and a host of traditional architectural or design concerns. While it implies intention, sometimes sustainable design can be an intuitive process among skillful designers who have successfully integrated the principles into their design process. Sustainable design should be thought of as a verb, not a noun, meaning that the act or process of sustainable design must clearly be separated from the product. As mentioned earlier, almost no buildings being built today are, in the truest sense, sustainable. This is not so much the failing of the movement, but the reality of changing the incredibly complex system that is the building industry. The sustainable design movement today has produced a lot of better, less damaging, more efficient buildings, but the buildings themselves cannot be called sustainable. It may be fine to label them as green buildings if necessary, but the word sustainable should be reserved for buildings that truly are sustainable. A truly sustainable building is one that has no negative operational impacts on the environment and few embodied ones as described in more detail in Chapter Ten—Shades of Green.

In many ways, sustainable design is simply **expanding the definition of good design** to include a wider set of issues. Traditionally, architecture dealt with several factors, but cost, schedule, functionality and aesthetics drove the decision-making process, or as the ancient architectural theoretician Vitruvius discussed—firmness, commodity and delight.[17] But sustainable architecture adds more layers and asks more questions—Is it good? Is it the responsible choice? What effect will these design decisions have on the environment? On human health? It reminds us of a wider set of issues that for too long have been ignored in the design process or, if not ignored, given a very minor role in shaping the designs of our buildings and communities—afterthoughts. As Bill McDonough, one of the pioneers in the green design movement asks, "Was Auschwitz a good design?" It certainly was efficient at what it was designed to do, but was it good? Of course not! While this is an extreme example, we can think of many others where the same process can be implied. If a building wins design awards, but suffers from sick building syndrome due to poor detailing and specifications, is it a good design? If a building was built on budget and on schedule and meets all programmatic requirements but does so by imposing an enormous ecological burden, is it a good design?

Sustainable design helps instill a sense of responsibility and higher purpose back into design. Designers who adhere to the philosophy are not merely providing a product or commodity, but they are providing a service that goes beyond the immediate client to other people, to other species and even to future generations. McDonough eloquently described this as "intergenerational tyranny" because the decisions and consequences we make today will be inherited by the innocent residents of the future. Sustainable design seeks to provide solutions that are "good for all species for all times." [18] For, as Edmund Burke wrote over two hundred years ago, *"Society is a partnership, not only between those who are living, but between those who are living, those who are dead, and those who are to be born."* [19]

Sustainable design is often used as an umbrella term to describe a set of strategies, components and technologies that lower environmental impact while in many cases improving comfort and overall quality. These categories include but are not limited to:

- Daylighting
- Indoor Air Quality
- Passive Solar Heating
- Natural Ventilation
- Energy Efficiency
- Embodied Energy
- Construction Waste Minimization
- Water Conservation
- Commissioning
- Solid Waste Management
- Renewable Energy
- Xeriscaping/Natural Landscaping
- Site Preservation

Many of these components are explained more fully in Chapter Nine–The Technologies and Components of Sustainable Design. And in many ways these components are the most tangible parts of the sustainable design movement as people can more readily understand things that they can point to and identify. As with any philosophy however, its true wisdom is in its principles, not its components and the sustainable design movement is no exception. Although immature, the sustainable design movement has for the last few decades been developing a set of tenets, or principles that guide sustainable design practitioners. These principles are documented for the first time in this book.

After discussing the Evolution of Sustainable Design in Chapter Two, the next few chapters will explore the philosophical underpinnings of the sustainable design movement.

"Philosophy must be a tool of realism which repeatedly permits us to rediscover ourselves and shed the linguistic obscurantism of whatever power structure is in place. In doing so, we alter or shed the structure itself." [20]

—*John Ralston Saul*

CHAPTER TWO

Photo by McLennan

The Evolution of Sustainable Design

"One reason we are in so much trouble is that our modern culture is paradoxically behind the times, still assessing the world the way it did in the nineteenth or even eighteenth centuries: as a place of inexhaustible resources, where man is at the pinnacle of creation, separate from and more important than anything around him."

—David Suzuki[1]

The Origins of Sustainable Design

In the last chapter, sustainable design was described as "a philosophical approach to design that seeks to maximize the quality of the built environment while minimizing or eliminating the negative impact to the environment." The design in question refers to our architecture, the structures we create to provide us with shelter.

For many people, the sustainable design movement started sometime in the early seventies as a response to the oil crisis, launching a movement concerned with all things solar and energy conserving. For others it was a decade earlier, coinciding with the publishing of Rachael Carson's landmark book, *Silent Spring*, believed by many to be the catalyst which launched the wider environmental movement. Others still believe that the true roots of sustainable design can be found much, much earlier, in indigenous architecture around the world, in vernacular forms such as the tee-pee, the igloo, and the cob house. These structures are cited because they provide shelter while treading lightly on the land.

The truth is that all of these beliefs are correct to some degree, for no movement or idea has just one start, but many threads of cause and effect that trickle down through the centuries. Each action creates a reaction, building somewhat imperceptibly until one day it becomes apparent. For some people, the moment when it is undeniably visible to all is the beginning, but for others, who can see the threads and the linkages, the beginnings appear much earlier. David Suzuki provides us with an example;
" When grains of sand are added to a sand pile one at a time, the pile grows until it reaches a critical point at which the addition of one more grain of sand causes avalanches, slides and massive changes. It is an apt metaphor for the way individuals can create sudden shifts in popular understanding and social action." [2]

At what point can it be said that the avalanche was started? Did it begin with the first speck of sand that appeared on the site? Did it begin when this speck was joined by other specks to create a pile? Did it begin when the first sand speck began to move? Or did the avalanche really begin once there was momentum and the slide was irreversible?

And so it is with the origins and history of sustainable design. The truth is that sustainable design has had many beginnings, and the story goes back further than we can remember or record. At the same time, as we will explore, the origins of sustainable design are very recent, in living memory of many who will read this book. History in some ways is story-telling; it contains truth, but is never the complete truth as it is limited by the perspective and experience of the historian. For every event, countless beginnings, countless versions of history emerge depending on who tells it and where it is told. For this book, a story will be told of a history with four beginning points or stages. Each of these stages can be thought of as a distinct evolutionary stage. The four stages include:

The Biological Beginning of Sustainable Design
The Indigenous Vernacular Beginning of Sustainable Design
The Industrial Beginning of Sustainable Design
The Modern Beginning of Sustainable Design.

Each of these stages has a different issue or component of the history to tell.

The Biological Beginning of Sustainable Design

Photo courtesy of J. Scott Turner.

Termite mound integrated with tree in Africa.

In many ways, the history of our architecture can be summed up as the ultimate pursuit of comfort. In extreme cases, comfort can be defined as security, and architecture through the ages has often been shaped by the need to defend and protect against enemies be they human or animal. But for the most part, comfort is defined in less harsh terms and embraces the pursuit of thermal comfort or shelter from sun, wind or cold temperatures depending on climate.

Our obsession with comfort conditions is no different than with any species. Genetically, we are all hot-wired to seek optimal conditions to breed, thrive and consume. Different species have different mechanisms that they employ in pursuit of comfort. Some animals will migrate great distances to find suitable comfort conditions, crossing oceans and continents as necessary. Monarch butterflies and countless species of birds travel thousands of miles in search of breeding grounds and winter havens. And yet, there is no doubt that the drive to migrate is a strategy that emerged out of the desire to seek comfort, not an innate need. It has been shown that if suitable comfort conditions can be provided migrating birds will forgo migration, as is the case with many ducks and Canadian geese that stay year round in places where they have been well fed and that provide them with some form of shelter from winter conditions.

Other species have found different strategies in the pursuit of comfort. Some have found physiological methods to deal with weather changes such as growing and shedding fur, hibernating or shivering. Others have found ways to create their own habitat, and thus temper the outside conditions to be more suitable. This group of species can loosely be called the "habitat builders".

Over thousands of years each of the habitat builders has perfected techniques to create as close to an ideal habitat as possible to ensure survival of the species (on the most basic level) but also to create the ideal comfort environment. The honeybee creates a hive for protection, comfort and to serve as a storage vessel for honey creation. The beaver, perhaps the most famous of the habitat builders, builds elaborate dams and lodges to control water levels and hydrology in a localized area in order to prevent freezing and for protection from predators. The beaver is, in many ways, the civil engineer of the animal kingdom.

Perhaps even more impressive is a species of the termite of the genus *macrotermes*, found in sub-Saharan Africa. The *Macrotermes* have perfected the art of making adaptations and creating habitat. They could be described as the relentless re-modelers of the animal kingdom. This particular species has developed a symbiotic relationship with a particular fungus that thrives in conditions of elevated carbon dioxide(CO_2) levels. If there is too little carbon dioxide, competing fungus species take over and the termites starve; too much carbon dioxide and the termites die through asphyxiation (although obviously they tolerate much higher carbon dioxide levels than we do). In this symbiosis, the termites work to provide the appropriate microclimate for the cultivation and expansion of the fungus and the fungus in turn helps to break down foraged wood and grass into more easily digested simple sugars (like a built-in composter). It is not always clear who is the master and who is the slave, as the fungus emits a chemical that seems to drive the termites into digging and working harder at habitat building and remodeling, "hijacking the behavior of the termites."[3]

In their quest for the right carbon dioxide balance these termites build elaborate structures that dot the African landscape, often reaching heights of several meters or more above ground and a few meters below. The above ground structures, made of sand, saliva and fecal matter and often as hard as concrete, serve as a natural ventilation chimney drawing air from above ground down deep into the underground structure that actually houses the colony. The distribution of carbon dioxide within the colony drives the movement of soil and the erection of these elaborate structures that over time are tuned to the specifics of the site and the needs of the work within. Mounds in open areas are shorter than mounds in tall grass, predicated by the access to winds that can flush the termite mounds as needed. If the termites build a chimney too tall, too much air enters the colony and unfavorable conditions emerge, driving the termites to remodel, plug holes and change the dynamics of the chimney. These ventilation chimneys must work all year round in various temperatures and with huge variations in wind speed and direction. Because of these variations, the termites are constantly remodeling and fine tuning their structure to work in multiple modes and climate conditions. Their habitat needs to be built in such a way that it is easily adaptable and flexible to respond to changing needs within the colony and externally to climate.

In still air the naturally moist, buoyant warm air rises up out of the top of the chimney in all directions through what is called the stack effect —the taller a structure the more suction that exists. On windy days, this mechanism changes and air is forced out by wind entering the chimney on the windward side and exiting on the leeward side. Overall the mound operates almost like a living thing itself—a giant lung to maintain comfort conditions for the termites and the fungus.

In many ways, the termites, the beavers and the honeybees are our brothers and sisters. We share a kinship with these creatures, because we too build structures that alter the environment for the purpose of providing comfort. Throughout history, using locally available materials, we have built structures to perform the same general function as that of the termite mound. It could be argued that the origins of sustainable design can be found in our biological beginning, as part of our heritage and connection to the web of life on earth. This could be described as the beginning of all

our history, including the knowledge that we are no different than the beaver, the termite and the honeybee and that our survival, like theirs, is tied
to the balance of multiple other processes and species. As David Suzuki
reminds us,

> Together, all species make up one immense web of intercon-
> nections that binds all beings to each other and to the physical
> components of the planet. The disappearance of a species tears
> the web a little, but that web is highly elastic. When one strand
> is rent the whole network changes configuration, but so long as
> there are many remaining strands to hold it together, it retains its
> integrity.[4]

Part of this knowledge comes with the understanding that we are no worse
than any other species, and should feel no guilt for *some* amount of impact
that is due all creatures. Every species on earth will seek optimal conditions and thrive until the point that some other natural processes such as
disease, a food shortage or a competitor puts the growing species in check.
But by itself no species, including homo sapiens, seems to regulate its own
growth. The system, through diversity, self-regulates.

All species and especially the habitat builders create an impact on their
environment that is beneficial for some, but not for others. No animal lives
in perfect harmony with its surroundings, but is merely part of an inter-
connected web of cause and effect. The beaver does not show remorse
when its dam floods an area and drowns a few dozen small mammals and
a few thousand insects. The termite cares little for trees that die to provide food and nutrients. Our history of expansion and growth is not part
of some unnatural process, just the case of a species that has been clever
enough to avoid most of the traditional checks and balances that nature
has so far thrown its way.[5]

Despite the fact that it may be natural, at some point this counterbal-
ance cannot be ignored because growth in a finite system can never be
infinite. This is a powerful lesson derived from our biological heritage, for
while we are no less intelligent than any species, we have to date proven
no smarter in this regard. There are no exceptions made for us. Ancient
history is filled with examples of cultures that grew and consumed until
a natural check occurred to end the culture. Striking examples include
the inhabitants of Easter Island who denuded their landscape of trees and

ultimately forced their demise, leaving behind giant statues as reminders of their folly.[6] The Sumerians similarly over-irrigated and taxed their land resulting in salinization and crop failure that spelled the end to that great civilization.[7]

We are reminded yet again of our place in the nature of things by David Suzuki who tells the story of the power of exponential growth using bacterium as an example. There is a close parable to how we, as a species, are acting.

> Imagine that we introduce a single bacterium (in a test tube) that will proceed to divide every minute. So at the beginning, there's one cell, a minute later there is two…at 60 minutes in this example, the test tube is full of bacteria and the food is gone. When was the test tube half full? …59 minutes. So at 58 minutes, it was 25 percent full, at 57 minutes, 12.5% full. At 55 minutes, the test tube was only 3 percent full.

> If at 55 minutes, some bacterial genius spoke up and said, I think we have a population problem, the less astute majority would probably retort, "what are you talking about? Ninety seven percent of the test tube is empty, and we've been around 55 minutes!" At 59 minutes though most bacteria would probably realize they were in trouble. Suppose they threw money at their scientists and begged for a solution. And suppose that in less than a minute those bacterial scientists created three test tubes full of food! Everyone would be saved right? Well no, at 60 minutes, the first test tube would be full, and at 61 minutes the second would be full, at 63 seconds all four would be full…[8]

It remains to be seen in our history, whether we prove "smarter" than the bacterium in this example. It took thousands of years for our population to reach one billion. It has taken less than a century for it to reach six billion. It has been projected by some that the population of the earth could grow to ten billion within the next century.[9]

Is this the full story of the history of sustainable design? Of course not! It is just the first beginning, a beginning that places us within creation. It provides the context for everything that is to follow. **It clearly states that we are no different than any other species in our relationship to the**

overall system. Since we now have the ability to live outside the original parameters for our species we have to find ways to self-regulate, before the system ultimately does it for us in ways that may not be pleasant.

Our Indigenous/Vernacular History—The Second Beginning

In the sustainable design movement today, many people idealize the designs and innovations of vernacular architecture that can be found in ancient cultures all over the world. They believe that the innovations of our ancestors were a high point in the development of a sustainable architecture, and comparatively, it has been all down hill since then. These people point out that many of the ideas discussed within the sustainable design field are not new ideas, but those that have existed for centuries. For many this explains why our vernacular history is the true start of sustainable design.

There is a lot of truth in this opinion. One does not have to look any further than the wide array of architecture that was developed within North America over the last ten thousand years to see some remarkable innovations in pursuit of comfort. The stunning ruins of Mesa Verde in New Mexico show the ingenuity of those who built this incredible village. The village was constructed out of stone and located at the base of a giant cliff outcropping. The attached diagram shows how the cliff was used to aid in providing comfort to the building inhabitants. In the wintertime, low angle sun penetrated into the cliff dwellings and provided heat to people and buildings. In the summer time, the high angled sun was kept away from the buildings and people stayed cool in the shade. The use of thermally massive stones with small windows further accentuated

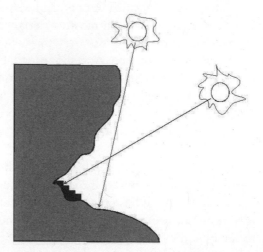

Section diagram of Anasazi cliff dwelling demonstrating knowledge of passive solar principles. The village was located within the shadow of summer sun yet open to low winter sun.

the benefits of the cliff location. Small windows let in enough air for ventilation, but not too much that drafts would become a problem. The heavy stonework served as a "thermal sink" to retain heat in the wintertime and to stay cool in the summer. It appears that this village was abandoned only when water supplies became too scarce in the area.

The Plains Indians developed a different architectural response to the need to provide comfort. As a nomadic society, their architecture needed to be mobile and so the tee-pee was developed from animal hides stretched over a wood structure. Over time this tent-like structure became very sophisticated in its ability to modulate localized temperature conditions. In cold weather the tee-pee could be closed tightly and a fire started in the interior. Smoke would rise through a small opening in the top, but due to the shape of the structure, heated air would remain inside longer. In warm weather, large flaps could open at the base of the structure, allowing people to remain in the shade, but provide them with access to breezes that could sweep through the tent.

These two examples underscore the emergence of some compelling ideas that shape sustainable design. The first is the idea of regionalism.[10] Architecture was designed with local materials and harnessed sun, wind and light for comfort. Design responses changed dramatically as one changed to a different biome or climate zone. Structures were built "of the place" and would return safely to the land when their useful life was over. The igloos of the north and the wooden longhouses of the Pacific Northwest provide more examples here in our continent. Numerous other examples can be found throughout the world.

The second idea is that of current solar income. Current solar income is a term used to describe the use of any energy source that is renewable and "currently" available. Vernacular architecture has always relied on current solar income and used the sun or the burning of biomass to provide heat. Doing so ensured that environmental impacts were small and limited to what the system was currently producing. To further clarify this second idea, financial income is used as a metaphor. Current solar income is comparable to a person living off salaried income or interest from an account. As long as this individual does not overspend he/she will have adequate money in perpetuity. Living off current solar income means getting energy or heat from the sun or from rapidly replenished biomass. The opposite is living off "old solar savings" or "savings of energy" as is the case with petroleum or coal usage. This is equivalent to an individual who overspends and uses savings to live, which eventually are depleted or worse still lives off of credit cards. When old solar savings are used, they are eventually depleted, but in the use process they release centuries of carbon dioxide to the atmosphere at a rate faster than the active system can accommodate. Herein lies the source of global warming.

The third idea is the concept of **looking to nature first to provide solutions for comfort**. As a species we have learned a lot from watching other species in order to be effective ourselves. Our ancestors were practicing bio-mimicry long before we were aware of it as a concept. Bernd Heinrich, biologist, ultra marathon runner and author of the book *Racing the Antelope* reminds us that, "Animals give us solutions to problems that are the product of evolution. They are the results of experiments that have been performed without bias or prejudice for millions of years." [11]

This is the bridge between the first beginning of sustainable design to the second. All around the world examples can be found that illustrate these ideas and can provide inspiration regarding how to harness nature for comfort in our buildings. And yet, is this really the beginning of sustainable design? Or is it just another partial beginning? It is accurate to say that it was the beginning for many of the strategies and processes of sustainable design, but not for the complete philosophy and reasons behind the movement. The indigenous cultures of yesterday were not trying to build a sustainable architecture. They were merely trying to provide comfort given the tools and technology that they had available. People built with local materials because they had to. They built locally because they were limited by the distances that people or animals could transport materials.

Some have tried to depict our ancestors as being ecologically superior to modern people because of their closer relationship with the environment. And again, while there is much truth in this statement, it is a very gross overgeneralization. Ecological superiority can be defined in a lot of different ways. In a sense it could refer to the relative impact that one individual has compared to another, or the awareness different individuals have of their local ecology. In these ways there is no comparison between the environmental footprint and awareness we have to that of our ancestors. However, if ecological superiority is viewed as requiring a conscious choice to not impact the environment for ecological good, even if it has some negative personal consequences, it becomes much less clear. In most cases, indigenous peoples did not limit their expansion because of ecological good. Instead, they were limited by tribal boundaries and competition within the species. They learned to protect what they had and to preserve it because it was often difficult and dangerous to expand outward. Within these cultures some resources reached the point of having religious significance and these resources were preserved for spiritual reasons not for fear of ecological collapse.[12]

In most ways, our ancestors could not have understood the link between their actions and global environmental problems, although certainly they were familiar with some localized ones through trial and error. In a sense our vernacular past could not have been the complete beginning of the sustainable design movement because there was nothing to react to, nothing unsustainable to improve upon. In those days, nature truly was boundless.

A notable point is that every major human migration, regardless of cultural background, has resulted in major shifts in the health and dynamics of the ecosystem in question. When the Maoris moved into New Zealand one thousand years ago, they decimated the local bird population, helping to make extinct such wondrous creatures as the giant flightless bird, the Moa. Similarly, the Polynesians who would become the Hawaiian people created widespread change in the islands of Hawaii.

> Native people altered the habitat so that it met their needs and comforted to their cultural expectations-so thoroughly that extinctions followed in their wake. Ancient Hawaiians cleared land with fire and diverted streams for irrigation, and crop plants and extensive grasslands took over what had been forested coastal areas. Fish ponds emerged where there had been mudflats. Hawaiians introduced dogs, pigs, chickens and—inadvertently—rats and reptiles that had stowed away on their canoes. As a result, well over half of the endemic bird species became extinct.[13]

Closer to home, but farther back in time, when the Bering land bridge linked North America with Asia, the Paleo-Indians migrated and within only a few centuries had forever altered the landscape of this continent and South America, decimating much of the mega-fauna that once roamed free.[14] This kind of impact continued through to the Native American population that the Europeans discovered a few centuries ago. The Europeans encountered a vast landscape that had been actively managed by fire for generations upon generations, in order to enhance the success of species that were beneficial for the native population but ultimately detrimental to many others.[15]

In general, the harder a place was to reach or penetrate by humans of any culture, the less environmental impact occurred. Places such as deserts, mountains and dense jungles were often safe havens for many species. Conversely, the greater the opportunity for migration or cross-fertilization by people of different cultures, the greater the environmental impact as people brought their technologies with them. Where people could migrate over long distances from similar climate zones the impact was most severe. In Europe and Asia expansion was easy because tribal groups could migrate across similar latitudes and climate zones and therefore environmental impact was highest. The easy mixing of cultures from east to west also meant a greater mingling of technologies (and also germs), further hastening the impact to environment in those continents.[16]

Ultimately, despite some widespread changes to the environment, the story of our vernacular past is less about environmental degradation than it is about environmental change. It wasn't until a few hundred years ago that certain key technologies began to forever change every facet of our existence. The third beginning to sustainable design's evolution can be found in the industrial age.

Industrialization—The Third Beginning

Over the last two hundred years we have made enormous progress in our quest for comfort. Numerous technologies have been invented that make it possible to achieve comfort at a level never reached throughout human history. While our ancestors modulated comfort through careful design and harnessing of the elements, we were never quite content with this relationship. Too much was dependent on variables out of our control, and despite clever vernacular forms, people were often just slightly more comfortable than they would have been without this modulated comfort. For a couple of thousand years this basic fact changed little around the world, even though great changes to architecture were often made. More substantial changes occurred as people abandoned a nomadic lifestyle for permanent settlement in more densely populated towns and cities. Although buildings were more permanent, the inhabitants still depended on the harnessing of nature for comfort and the living off of current solar income.

The technologies that came out of the industrial revolution were able to totally change the relationship between the climate inside and the climate outside. With modern technologies such as air conditioning and combustion heating systems it was now possible to be warm no matter how cold, and cool no matter how hot. Building design began to change to respond to the possibilities of the new technologies. Before the invention of electric lighting, buildings were designed to be narrow to allow as much daylight as possible to light interior spaces. Afterwards, forms changed and spaces were designed to celebrate electric lighting even when ample daylight was available. Before the invention of the elevator, buildings were rarely over a few stories and density was limited. New technologies, the elevator and the proliferation of materials like steel allowed the construction of ever-escalating high-rise buildings that now are a ubiquitous part of our society.

Technologies not directly linked to the building industry also significantly influenced building design. The steam engine and then the automobile erased geographic distances that once proved insurmountable. Materials and technologies could now be shipped all over the globe and the idea of building locally became a thing of the past. Building materials were no longer confined to the local stone, brick, wood or earth that was available and architectural character changed significantly because it was no longer limited by regional limits. As materials changed so did form, and building

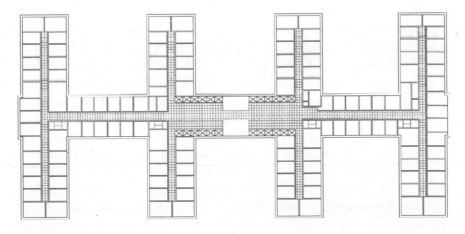

Pre-War buildings typically had narrow floor plates in order to allow for daylight and natural ventilation. With the proliferation of electric lighting and air conditioning floor plates became deeper.

designs were exported around the world regardless of culture and climate. Since technology could now take care of all comfort needs, regionalism was deemed by many to be irrelevant.[17] Buildings could now look the same regardless of whether they were located in Anchorage, Alaska or Hilo, Hawaii.

Alongside the advances in technology came intellectual ideas that would have as significant an effect on our relationship with the environment as did the car, elevator or refrigeration. The belief in "manifest destiny" got its start in the sixteenth and seventeenth centuries, picked up momentum over the eighteenth and nineteenth centuries and has continued until today. A common idea that emerged was that it was our God-given right and responsibility to harness and tame nature as we saw fit. The Englishman Francis Bacon was quoted as saying "that if we are to have the good life, nature's secrets will have to be forced from her."[18]

With these ideas and the proof of a staggering array of life-changing inventions that seemed to occur every few years, many people began to believe that we had the ability to do anything, or solve any problem with a man-made technological fix. This blind faith in the power of technology and human ingenuity grew to a point that the confidence in our abilities to invent technological solutions to any problem became almost a religion for many people. In their minds we could create a technological solution for any desire, and fix any problem that came up as well. In many cases technologies were used for the sake of technology, even when more passive or low-impact options were available. In our haste to move to the future that was our destiny to claim, western cultures staged a massive forgetting of the lessons and strategies learned over centuries by our ancestors. This paradigm shift, this new worldview, became so dominant by the nineteenth and early twentieth century that machine-like metaphors began to replace all others, even when it was biological processes being described. We believed we could regulate natural processes better than nature itself. Doctors compared people to clocks and, as one of the twentieth century's most famous architects once said, buildings became "machines for living in."[19] This belief in the power of technology to cure all our ills persists to this day, a nineteenth century idea still going strong in the twenty-first century.

The consequences of this unbridled belief in our ingenuity and our inventions have been known for some time and summarily dismissed and forgotten as people have repeated the mantra to themselves. Each of the major technological revolutions that occurred seemed to create a disproportionate amount of unintended pollution and health problems for people, consequences that were not intended or expected. With each problem a new technological fix was soon to follow which carried with it an additional set of man-made ills.

Author Wendell Berry has lamented, "The worst disease of the world now is probably the ideology of technological heroism, according to which more and more people willingly cause large-scale effects that they do not foresee and that they cannot control."[20]

By the eighteenth century many familiar environmental problems began to emerge throughout the world. London, at the time the world's most industrialized and advanced city, suffered terribly from air pollution caused by the burning of coal. Not surprisingly, it was a London physician who invented the word smog, which is a word combining smoke and fog.[21] By the close of the nineteenth century and the beginning of the twentieth, the environment was being assaulted by all sectors of human civilization, from industry to transportation to the buildings that gave us shelter.

By the beginning of the twentieth century coal-fired combustion in large cities like London was horrific. This factor, combined with the increased use of the automobiles devastated local and regional air quality. In the book, *Something New Under the Sun*, the author tells how "During the week of December 4-10, 1952, London suffered the worst recorded air pollution disaster anywhere, bringing early death to 4000 people. A few years later London had converted to oil."[22] For a thousand years before 1800, carbon dioxide levels in the global atmosphere varied around 270-290 parts per million (ppm). But around 1800 the level of CO_2 began increasing greatly, reaching about 295 ppm by 1900, 310-315ppm by 1950 and about 360 ppm by 1995.[23]

The typical solution to addressing environmental problems was not to deal with the root of the problem, but instead to find a band-aid solution that typically sent the problem further afield. For example, Sudbury, with its nickel mining, was North America's single largest source of acid rain. Its solution in the first three quarters of the twentieth century was to build the world's largest smokestack[24] and disperse its pollutants over a much wider area. It helped halt the decline of the region's environment, but sent the problem to other communities downwind. It wasn't until the last few decades that these mining operations truly began cleaning their emissions.[25]

At times it seemed that even single human beings were having global environmental impact. In 1930, Thomas Midgley invented Freon, the first CFC, [26] which was thought to be harmless at the time, but is now known to be largely responsible for stratospheric ozone depletion that threatens all life on earth. The ozone hole over the Antarctic is now larger than the United States and extends over inhabited land in South America. What is remarkable is that this same person also invented leaded gasoline, which was originally designed to enhance the engine performance of cars. We now know that leaded gasoline ends up in the blood stream of people and animals all over the world, causing cancer and birth defects. Midgley was born in 1889 and also worked on the design of aerial torpedoes. A prolific inventor, he held numerous patents and was one of the most celebrated scientists of his time. He is perhaps now the holder of the dubious record of having started a chain of events that has caused more environmental harm than any other person in history. His story has overtones of "dealings with the devil" with a meteoric rise of fame and innovation ending in tragedy and bizarre death. The author of *Something New Under the Sun* recounts how Midgley had "contracted polio in 1940 and designed a system of ropes and pulleys to help him in and out of bed. In 1944 he died of strangulation, suspended above his bed, entangled in his network of ropes." [27]

The third beginning to sustainable design began in the Industrial Age because a large number of people began to take notice and disagree with the effects of progress that they now had to live with. In essence, it was necessary for some level of environmental degradation to occur before people could react to it. Sustainable design is a conscious reaction to the consequences of unsustainable practices. The first reactions to environmental pollution were centered on concern for personal health. Industrialized cities were dangerous places to live in due to poor air quality, with a majority of people suffering from some type of upper respiratory disease. The city of St. Louis led the way in the United States in smoke reduction activities that soon spread to other industrialized cities. [28] Efforts began to switch from polluting coal to less polluting oil, and to the creation of zoning that separated where people worked and lived.

Other ideas such as the City Beautiful Movement, whose focus was to improve the quality of the built environment and bring nature and life back to our communities, emerged within Europe and North America. Frank Lloyd Wright, one of the architects who spoke up about a more healthy connection to nature, stated, "I believe we were designed to give the beauty and freedom of the green earth as a heritage." [29] Unfortunately, people like Wright also advanced planning ideas that unwittingly would have negative long-range impacts to the environment due to increased transportation. [30]

The third beginning to sustainable design started because people from all walks of life were now **making the connection between modern activities and the health of people and the environment**. The late nineteenth century saw the emergence of groups like the Audubon Society and the Sierra Club which were dedicated to preserving places of beauty. In the first half of the twentieth century Teddy Roosevelt created the National Park System and a formalized means of protecting the environment in the United States resulted.

Despite this auspicious start, the reaction to environmental degradation rarely challenged the larger issues of technology and our fundamental place in nature. The design of our buildings and transportation systems often went unnoticed. We continued to shape our buildings based on the use of technology rather than on the basis of place and climate and, in so doing, used more and more energy. In many cases, while people admitted that certain technologies had indeed caused harm, they still blindly believed in the next technology that would fix the problem. We often cleaned up localized problems such as air pollution, but started creating more diffuse global problems that often were not discovered for another fifty years. The dominant paradigm of expansion and exploitation continues to this day.

The Modern Sustainable Design Movement—The Fourth Beginning

The Environmental Backdrop

While the environmental movement had its first beginnings at around the turn of the nineteenth century, it was not until the second half of the twentieth century that the modern environmental movement emerged. The rise of the modern environmental movement came with the realization that we must change our ways, not merely for the vague concept of saving the earth but for saving our own species! In the early nineties an unprecedented list of Nobel laureates signed a declaration of warning to humanity that told us that we had only a few decades to change the course we were currently on. An excerpt from this document stated that:

> If not checked many of our current practices put at serious risk the
> future that we wish for human society and the plant and animal
> kingdoms, and may so alter the living world that it will be unable
> to sustain life in the manner we know. [31]

Despite the historical nature of the document, signed by the most respected list of scientists from around the world, it was almost entirely ignored by the media.

A decade has passed already. David Suzuki explains that, "human observation tends to be directed at events that are big and dramatic, or events that go on over a course of a year, like a major drought. But events that induce profound changes for the earth and for human prospects, and that stretch over periods of two to three decades, are judged as speculative." [32]

In the first decade of the twenty-first century the health of the natural environment is in dire condition with "all living systems in decline, and the rate of the decline increasing." [33] The annual number of species added to the red book, the list of endangered or threatened species worldwide, is growing at an alarming rate. Even more troubling is the list of species disappearing worldwide as habitat destruction is intensified. It is a sad thing to realize that our children and grandchildren will never know what it is like to see certain birds, plants, insects and animals. We are living through an age of man-made extinctions that rival in magnitude the greatest extinctions of the past. To make matters worse, the country that is the most emulated around the world, the United States, holds all the records for consumption and environmental impact. We are responsible for a disproportionate share of the environmental problems we face today.

> We use one-third of the world's paper, despite representing just
> 5% of the world's population. Similarly we use 25% of the oil,
> 23% of the coal, 27% of the aluminum, and 19% of the copper.
> An average American uses twice as much fossil fuel as the aver-
> age resident of Great Britain and 2.5 times as much as the average
> Japanese. We consume over 3.25 pounds of boneless meat, 1.5
> times as much as the average Briton or Italian and more than 2.5
> times as much as the average Japanese. [34]

Natural Capitalism puts this consumption in perspective; "For all the world to live as an American or Canadian, we would need two more earths to satisfy everyone, three more still if population should double, and twelve more earths altogether if worldwide standards of living should double over the next forty years."[35] What happens as the population of China, India and others begin to adopt the industrialization and lifestyles that we have enjoyed?

We are continually encouraged to consume more, as if our current habits were not enough. "The average American is exposed to about three thousand advertising messages a day and globally, corporations spend over $620 billion each year to make their produces seem desirable and to get us to buy them."[36] We seem to suffer from the affliction that Will Rogers so aptly described, "Too many people spend money they haven't earned, to buy things they don't want, to impress people they don't like."[37]

At the same time there is growing proof that our increased levels of consumption are no longer improving the standard of living for most Americans. Background levels of environmental pollution are beginning to have a negative effect on health. For example, since 1980 there has been a huge increase in asthmatics (forty-two percent for males and eighty-one percent for females) with almost seventeen million Americans suffering from this illness. Thirty-eight percent of Americans now have allergies.[38] The percentage of people suffering from cancer is also rising. Despite records of consumption and wealth Americans are not the healthiest of nations, or the happiest. Will we find ourselves in a position to make positive change?

With this environmental backdrop, we now explore the rise of the fourth beginning, the modern sustainable design movement.

The Seventies—The Green Design Toddler

Sustainable design is a sub-set of the modern environmental movement and it is the building industry's reaction to the realization that *how* it does business is a large contributor to the environmental problems we face today. According to the US Green Building Council, buildings account for almost forty percent of the energy and twenty percent of the water used in the United States today. In the period between the sixties and the nineties, the Four Stages or "strands" of sustainable design merged to form the start of the modern sustainable design movement. During this period, a growing number of people became conscious of our biological heritage as it relates to creating habitat, realized the virtues of indigenous design solutions, and accepted that man-made technologies carried risks and limitations.

In the sixties it was the publishing of *Silent Spring* that galvanized action for the broader environmental movement. For the sustainable design movement, the major lever for change occurred a decade later with the energy crisis. The escalating price of oil in the seventies energized a lot of designers to begin to look at how buildings could be designed to reduce energy demand and be more cost efficient. All over the country architects began to rediscover vernacular strategies and forgotten lessons. The era of passive solar houses was in its infancy. People began experimenting with ways to use the sun for heat and electricity and often tried elaborate experiments to achieve comfort with few conventional systems. Many of the most influential leaders in the sustainable design movement such as Sym Van Der Ryn, Amory Lovins, Steve Strong and Pliny Fisk got their start at this time. Countless others experimented with energy conservation and solar energy strategies only to abandon them to more conventional methods when the cost of energy dropped significantly. Some important events emerged during this infancy stage.

1. Architects and engineers revived passive, climate responsive, bioregional strategies, which still form a foundation for sustainable design.

2. Architects and engineers adopted appropriate technologies into architecture. Designers began experimenting with the integration of alternative energy and waste technologies into their buildings. Solar panels and wind turbines made their common debut. People like Michael Reynolds began experimenting with other building materials such as scrap tires and bottles to build "earthships". Many of these experiments failed while a few, like photovoltaics, crept forward slowly.

3. A public perception formed regarding what energy conservation design looked like and how it functioned. Unlike the previous developments, this perception was not positive. For many the green architecture of the seventies was an eyesore at best and an uncomfortable fad at worst. The perceptions formed during this decade would hurt the movement for the next twenty years.[39] The experimental nature of systems and materials kept the movement at the fringe.

4. Many of the leaders in sustainable design experienced their sustainability initiations.[40] Sustainable design leaders are defined as individuals whose ideas are helping to shape the way we design, construct and operate our buildings. Some of these individuals should be regarded as our environmental heroes because they continued to develop the ideas and strategies when sustainable design wasn't popular. Many of these individuals will be introduced in Appendix B.

In many ways the movement in the seventies was like a toddler, first learning to walk and to do the basic things needed to survive. The movement itself was called Energy Conserving Design, not Sustainable Design, revealing a bias towards energy. This bias could be described as an immature understanding of the interconnectedness of all the issues germane to the movement. Uncertain and moving in often-conflicting directions, the time was not yet ripe for large-scale change to occur. By the end of the seventies, those who would be the most committed to the ideas of sustainable design continued to practice, using the principles of sustainable design, while others disappeared into the rank and file of the professions ignoring the lessons they briefly flirted with.

The Eighties—The Neglected Green Design Child

By 1980 the green building movement was just starting to get organized. Two important industry groups were formalized in 1980 to continue to support the ideas galvanized in the previous decade; the American Solar Energy Society (ASES)[41], and the Passive Solar Industries Council (PSIC). Beyond that, there were few bright spots. The movement was starting to get organized but had a long way to go.

Energy was cheap again and people saw little need to conserve. The decade saw very little growth in the interest and ideas formed in the seventies. New members stopped flocking to the movement and the design schools, for the most part, stopped teaching the basic principles. This reality, of course, mirrored the trends in society at large. The eighties were a decade of decadence and consumption, politically backward in terms of the environment. The mantra was more was better and "less is a bore".[42] The architectural style of the day was postmodernism, a throwback to the idea that buildings could and should be built the same regardless of place, climate and culture, albeit this time with a costume of faux architectural forms ransacked casually from history. Green was no longer cool. Sustainable design proponents faced additional barriers. Good information was scarce. Green materials were few and almost always more expensive. Design mistakes continued to be made by people with good intentions, but with little knowledge. This combination of factors was not a formula for rapid growth!

The movement also suffered a few setbacks when many of the buildings designed to be energy conserving in the seventies turned out to be sick buildings as well. Many of these buildings were designed with very tight envelopes and had reduced air changes, causing build ups of carbon dioxide and indoor pollutants from off-gassing of interior finishes and furnishings. Proponents of sustainable design learned that they too had to consider a wider range of issues when designing.

Those who practiced green architecture at this time did it only for the right reasons. Few made money. New recruits were scarce. However, some important things did occur. The first is that what the movement lacked in sheer numbers of supporters it made up in quality. People like Bob Berkebile, Randy Croxton, Greg Franta, Gail Lindsey, Bill McDonough, and Gail Vittori joined their considerable talents to the cause. A few conferences, with the biggest being the Annual Solar Convention, were held but attracted only small numbers of attendees.

By the end of the eighties, little had been accomplished across the country in terms of environmental impact and buildings used more energy than ever. However, key people and ideas came together and would, in just a few years, make significant change.

The Nineties—The Screaming Green Pre-teen

The first few years of the nineties looked little different from that of the eighties. Support was low from the mainstream of the industry and good information was scarce. And then, little-by-little, things began to change. Here and there more supporters joined the movement, perhaps as a reaction to the decadence of the previous decade, but also as a reaction to the visible decline in environmental health being documented world-wide. 1992 marked the year of the Rio Earth Summit, and people around the globe began to pay more attention to the state of the world. That same year, *Environmental Building News* was first published, offering the industry access to unbiased professional information on green design choices.

Alex Wilson, Nadav Malin, and a small group of supporters published the journal without advertising money and the potential bias it brings. This magazine and its spin-off products remain the industry's most important source of information.

In 1990-1991, under the leadership of Bob Berkebile, the American Institute of Architects formed its first Committee on the Environment. Funded initially by the EPA and the DOE, the group began important research to understand how the construction industry affected the environment. And this time, energy was not the only issue. The committee began to look at material selection and resource conservation as well. The movement, still small, was starting to mature. In 1996 the Environmental Resource Guide was published, the first attempt to quantify the life cycle impacts of building material decisions.

Leading green practitioners and sustainable design philosophers began to widen the issues that fell under the purview of the movement. Concern for energy was joined by concern for materials and resources and then finally concern for human health and productivity. Most notable were issues of indoor air quality and human health. People were beginning to research and test the link between health and the materials used in construction. Just like a pre-teen, the grown-up personality and interests were beginning to form. As it did so, the circle began to widen and the rate of buy-in began to grow.

In the mid nineties two men, David Gottfried and Mike Italiano, began attending the AIA's Committee on the Environment meetings and raised questions and issues. They believed that for the movement to grow further a more inclusive approach, one not necessarily led by architects, needed to be established. Their vision was of a volunteer committee led by representatives of all aspects of the profession, including engineers, builders, landscape architects, interior designers, academics, industry reps and architects. This inclusive approach proved to be one of the most significant moves in advancing the building industry towards sustainability.

In 1993 The US Green Building Council(USGBC) was formed and comprised of a diverse array of individuals as envisioned by Gottfried and Italiano. The formative effort was buoyed by the support of most of the early green warriors from the seventies and eighties who saw the potential for the effort and lent their considerable intelligence and experience. The first meeting of the council was held at AIA headquarters in Washington, DC in April of 1993 with only a handful of people in attendance and an operating budget of no more than thirty thousand dollars. Within only eight years the council's membership grew to several thousand and its operating budget to a few million dollars.

A few years after its first meeting, the council launched its flagship product in pilot form, with a green building rating system that helped determine how green a particular building was. This system, called Leadership in Energy and Environmental Design (LEED) helped the designer with a structure of designated points in several broad categories including energy, water, materials, indoor environmental quality and site design. By collecting enough points, a building would warrant one of four levels of certification.[43] For the first time there was a more rigorous way of determining whether or not a building had good environmental performance, as opposed to just having a list of supposedly green features.[44] In a short time this tool would achieve widespread attention among all branches of the building industry.

Simultaneously with the rise of the USGBC came the creation of a host of regional and national conferences that served to bring people, ideas and materials together. With speakers as eloquent as McDonough and Berkebile inspiring change, a whole new generation of advocates was born. These conferences proved essential in getting the word out about the USGBC and its LEED rating system and about sustainable approaches and materials in general. Some of the more prominent conferences included the EnvironDesign, founded by Interior Sources Magazine in 1999, Greenprints, founded by the SouthFace Institute in 1997, and the continuation of the National Solar Conference started in the previous decade. Many regional conferences brought the message home to other more localized markets.

Almost as powerful as the creation of the US Green Building Council itself were the improvements that were happening to the built examples of sustainable design. Buildings were better designed both technically and aesthetically. In the nineties, buildings started to be built that were successful no matter what criteria for judgment was used. New buildings like the Deramus Pavilion in 1995, the Wildflower Center in 1998 and the Chesapeake Bay Foundation in 1999 were widely published and admired on architectural terms as well as on environmental ones. The AIA Committee on the Environment, now with a slightly diminished role due to the creation of the USGBC, struck back with an annual awards program called its "Top Ten" to recognize the ten best projects that reached a high level of both environmental performance and artistic design. Even more exciting was the number of architects like Richard Rogers and Renzo Piano, known originally for the quality of their designs, who were now verbally championing the benefits of a sustainable design approach. With each passing year in this decade, the movement matured. With each year, the rate of growth of those practicing sustainable design also increased. As more was built, the industry started to learn what worked and what did not work. Individuals describing the movement even began to change the way they spoke about the topic. The hard line message of guilt for "building the wrong way" began to be replaced with more persuasive arguments of the benefits of designing differently. Issues such as productivity and life-cycle economics began to surface. The Rocky Mountain Institute began publishing documents such as the groundbreaking *The Greening of the Bottom Line* and people like Bill Browning, Ray Anderson and David Orr became articulate messengers of the wider issues that were allied with sustainable design.

As with most things, success begat success. New magazines such as *Environmental Design and Construction* and *Green@Work* emerged to serve the growing army of supporters. *GreenClips*, an electronic newsletter created by Chris Hammer, got widespread notice. Even the more traditionally conservative journals such as *Engineering Record*, *The Construction Specifier*, and *Architectural Record* started publishing articles on the topic. At the beginning of the decade, Sustainable design was a fringe movement. By the turn of the century, "Green" became cool.

The 2000 Decade—The Temperamental Teen

The first decade of the twenty-first century looks promising for sustainable design. The trends in growth and buy-in have continued and perhaps even intensified. The movement is quickly approaching maturity in terms of how it describes itself and by the work of its leading practitioners. In 2002 the USGBC held its first annual Green Building Summit in Austin, Texas. The conference attracted nearly four thousand attendees and had to close registration and turn people away a week before the conference began. The conference was a sign of the arriving of green into the mainstream of architecture. By the next year, the conference grew to five thousand participants.

This decade will likely be known as the decade that green became mainstream, as people from all walks of life and from all backgrounds began to adopt the principles of sustainable design. At the time of this book's writing, several cities and government entities have adopted the LEED rating system as their minimum standard of building. Green is becoming policy. By 2003, approximately four percent of all building construction in the United States was pursuing a LEED rating.[45] Most importantly, the perceptual barriers to green design seem to be falling away. People are starting to believe that sustainable design results in better buildings that are healthier and more cost effective in the long run; in some cases, even cheaper in the short term. A growing list of productivity studies by people like Judy Heerwagen and Vivian Loftness are beginning to prove to a skeptical industry that green can have immediate and substantial paybacks due to increases in workplace effectiveness and decreases in absenteeism, sick days and comfort complaints. Studies such as the Packard Matrix, explained in more detail in chapter thirteen—Green Economics, show a full range of positive outcomes as people set their targets higher and higher in terms of environmental performance.[46] Green architects like Glenn Murcutt are winning the Pritzker Prize for design, awarded to the best designer of the year by the AIA.[47] In this decade, many are now going green because they see economic rather than moral reasons to do so. This is the mark of success for the movement.

The Principles of Sustainable Design

Respect for the Wisdom of Natural Systems
The Biomimicry Principle

"For a long time we thought we were better than the living world, and now some of us tend to think that we are worse...but neither perspective is healthy. We have to remember how it feels to have equal standing in the world, to be "between the mountain and the ant...part and parcel of creation."

—Janine Benyus

35

The Principles of Sustainable Design

In the first chapter, sustainable design was defined as a philosophy. The most basic definition of a philosophy is that it is a way of seeing the world through a particular thought pattern or doctrine. To provide an example we turn to the great Taoist tradition founded in China. In that belief system, The Tao is described as a "way of life that sustains you, guides you, and leads to innumerable rich experiences." [1] It is a way of life that asks that you follow a life according to the principles of Tao, which often has to do with simplicity, awareness and discipline. It asks that you follow the current of life, rather than fighting it.

As in the Taoist tradition, all philosophies typically include a set of basic principles or concepts that underlie the particular sphere of knowledge. Sometimes these rules are written down in complete texts like *The Upanishads* or *The Tao Te Ching*. At other times they take the form of uncollected and ever-evolving beliefs such as found in the cultures of some indigenous peoples – told as stories passed down through generations. Sometimes these philosophies and principles form the basis of religions depending on whether the authorship was viewed as being from a divine source. At other times, philosophy forms the basis for great political and economic movements. Some philosophies such as those expressed in Adam Smith's *Wealth of Nations* or Karl Marx's *Das Kapital* change the course of history through the power of their ideas.

In many ways, the sustainability movement, of which sustainable design is a part, has things in common with each of these belief systems. While it cannot, and should not be viewed as a religion, it does imply a moral code of responsibility and a structure in which to guide a change in behaviour. Many believe that sustainability is such a powerful philosophy that it will soon change the course of all aspects of our life on this planet. Its adherents are growing quickly and are comprised of people from all walks of life. Many of these individuals are not yet aware that there is an organized worldview emerging, while others are distinctly aware and helping to spread change. The sustainability movement has at its core two fundamental beliefs:

1. That our lifestyles, technologies and sheer numbers are having a negative impact on the environment, putting at risk the viability of the planet to support our continued existence, and the existence of

many of the animals and plants that we share the world with.

2. That we have a responsibility, as caretakers or stewards of the earth, to craft our societies and the technologies in it in a way that allows for the continued survival of our species and those that we share it with—regardless of their perceived direct value to us.

Those who finally understand and accept these two basic beliefs are those who have begun the sustainability journey. Sustainable design, as the design component of the sustainability philosophy, is comprised of a growing number of people who understand and accept the sustainability premises. Since the seventies, sustainable designers have realized that these foundational principles must apply to the design of our buildings and communities specifically and, working one project at a time, have begun to define a set of principles or tenets that guide the sustainable design process, albeit in an unconscious and organic way. Unlike with many philosophies, sustainable design principles are not invented but **discovered** by individuals or groups. The true principles, for the most part, have existed in some form in nature already.

It is important to mention that the sustainable design philosophy, unlike some philosophies, does not have one author, nor a divine source and is continuing to evolve and develop. Indeed, as mentioned earlier, it is still in the early stages of its development. It is the work of hundreds of individuals often fighting the status quo and modernist worldview of how things should be done. It recognizes that we are on a path towards a sustainable future, and that as much as some of us would like it to be different, we cannot instantly get there because of perceived barriers that may as well be real, and also because of some very significant economic, political, religious and technological barriers. The sustainable design movement realizes that in the present we need vibrant places to live and work in, and for now we must do our best to move towards sustainability in our designs. As an approach, it does not accept the status quo and actively looks to eliminate both real and imagined barriers to its development. Sustainable designers hope that this process of change will not take too long, as we are quickly learning that the earth is not an infinite system that can continuously handle our abuses.

Six major principles of the sustainable design movement have emerged to date. Within these major principles are numerous sub-principles that flesh out the tenets of the philosophy. For the most part these six principles deal specifically with sustainable design. Nevertheless, many of these principles overlap with those of sustainability in general, as it is hard to separate them fully. Those that do overlap with sustainability are described from the standpoint of their relevance to the sustainable design movement. Some of these principles will be credited to individuals who have done the most to advance their "discovery" within the industry, although most, as mentioned, have multiple authors. Once again, the word respect is used as the guiding framework of each of the major principles as it conveys an overall attitude of reverence and responsibility for the principles described.

The Six Governing Principles of Sustainable Design are:

- Respect for the Wisdom of Natural Systems – The Biomimicry Principle
- Respect for People – The Human Vitality Principle
- Respect for Place – The Ecosystem Principle
- Respect for the Cycle of Life–The "Seven Generations" Principle
- Respect for Energy and Natural Resources – The Conservation Principle
- Respect for Process – The Holistic Thinking Principle

Principle 1—Respect for the Wisdom of Natural Systems
The Biomimicry Principle

I do not see a delegation
For the four-footed
I see no seat for the eagles

We forget and we consider
Ourselves superior.

But we are after all
A mere part of Creation

And we must consider
To understand where we are

And we stand somewhere between
The mountain and the ant.

Somewhere and only there
As part and parcel
Of the Creation

—Chief Oren Lyons

In 1996 Janine Benyus, a biologist and science writer, published a book called *Biomimicry* that described the re-emerging science and philosophy of learning directly from nature. Benyus coined the term *Biomimicry* from the Greek word bios, meaning life and mimesis, meaning imitation. In her book, Benyus has described the science as having three major components:

1. Nature as model – taking inspirations from the designs of nature
2. Nature as measure – using an ecological standard to judge the rightness of our innovations
3. Nature as mentor – valuing what we can learn versus what we can extract

She went on to describe that all of nature's innovations, on land, in water and in the air have nine things in common:

- Nature runs on sunlight
- Uses only the energy it needs
- Fits form to function
- Recycles everything
- Rewards co-operation
- Nature banks on diversity
- Demands local expertise
- Curbs excesses within
- Taps the power of limits

These components stand in stark contrast to the way we, in industrial society, do things, with our energy wasteful, throwaway oil economy that diminishes diversity and all things local. The idea of respecting the wisdom of natural systems is described as re-emerging, because in many ways this idea is not new, because we have been using nature as a mentor and model for as long as we have walked on the planet. But in the modern age of the last two hundred years we have seemingly forgotten this history and connection and progressed as if the opposite were true—like only humanity is capable of innovation, a negative side effect of the reductionist scientific process that separated us in many ways from the reality around us.

We have only just recently begun to turn our thinking back to the source of all of our innovations—nature itself. Since the industrial revolution, and perhaps much, much earlier, we have acted in some form of collective denial, so convinced were we that we were not only separate from but above nature and that we had to make our progress and inventions in a vacuum. All that nature had to offer us was the raw goods to supply our ingenuity and bravado, there for the taking, to be burned, used and thrown away as we saw fit. We did not see or did not want to see that this behavior could not continue in perpetuity. We did not see and sadly many still do not see that we could not change the rules that have been so elegantly crafted for us by nature. Respecting the wisdom of natural systems revolves around the idea that nature is already doing everything we could possibly dream or want in some form, somewhere on the planet. This principle recognizes that even nature's seeming failures—things that do not appear to work— are still available for our edification. As Bill Browning likes to say, "In nature, anything that did not work was recalled by the manufacturer."[2]

Delta Willis, the author of a similarly inspired book, *The Sand Dollar and the Slide Rule* recalls that the "Wright brothers devised stabilizers after the way a turkey vulture employs its primary feathers to reduce turbulence at low speeds. The cockpit of the supersonic Concorde was designed to be lowered on approach, like the head of a swan."[3] Our lessons in flight continue to this day as currently, the United States Air Force is studying the flight formations of geese in order to improve efficiency and fuel economy.[4] The V formations of geese and other species, as it turns out, has less to do with pure drafting as was conventionally thought, then it does with the creation of tiny vortexes that spin off the wings of the birds as they fly. These vortexes help pull the other birds forward, provided that the bird flies just behind and beside the wing of the bird in front of it, hence the V formation. Fighter planes, and even commercial aircraft, themselves patterned after birds, create these same vortices.

Indeed, almost all of our major discoveries in engineering and medicine owe their beginnings, and sometimes everything, to lessons culled directly from nature. It would be difficult to find examples of anything we enjoy today that did not have a nature-born inspiration—we yearned to fly by watching the birds. Velcro, one of the most direct nature-inspired inventions is a carbon copy of the way seeds stick to animal hair, devised through natural selection in order to aid in spreading the plants' genetic matter. Spider silk has done much to teach us about composites, as ounce per ounce it is five times stronger than steel and five times tougher than the Kevlar we use in our bullet-proof vests.[5] At the same time, it is elastic in nature, able to stretch and maintain its integrity after impact. Properly scaled, it could catch a 747 in flight, and then stretch and bounce back to its original shape. Our technologies have not even come close to this feat of structural and chemical engineering. In *Biomimicry*, Benyus makes the humorous observation that "The spider manages to make an equally strong and much tougher fiber at body temperature (than Kevlar), without high pressures, heat, or corrosive acids. ...They take flies and crickets at one end and process a high-tech material at the other end."[6]

Innovations in medicine have also come to us the same way. A substantial amount of our painkillers and anesthesia that help us sleep painlessly through operations have been the gift of tropical plants and animals such as the curare vines and tree frogs that produce chemicals naturally that can suppress pain. Mark J. Plotkin, another biologist and science writer, reports that:

> a recent study of the 150 major pharmaceuticals showed that 100 percent of the drugs employed for dermatological, gynecological or hematological purposes; 76 percent of those used for allergy, pulmonary, and respiratory purposes; 76 percent used to treat infectious diseases; and 75 percent employed for general medicine and analgesic purposes are derived from or based on natural products.[7]

Plotkin goes on to say "how ironic that, just as we develop the tools for unlocking some of nature's secrets—secrets that have the potential to cure our ills, feed the hungry, and create employment—we are destroying the resources we are increasingly capable of utilizing."[8] Almost all of our knowledge of natural medicines began with ancient local sources of knowledge—knowledge which is now disappearing. Plotkin reminds us that one quarter of the world's six thousand languages, mostly from indigenous tribal cultures, are dying and will likely disappear this century, and with them the knowledge learned from nature.

Respecting the Wisdom of Natural Systems is now starting to spread to every aspect of human society. It is increasingly being used to describe economics and business as in Jane Jacob's *The Nature of Economies* and in the groundbreaking *Ecology of Commerce*, authored by Paul Hawken and *Natural Capitalism*, co-authored by Paul Hawken and by Amory and Hunter Lovins from the Rocky Mountain Institute.

It is time that designers of our buildings, communities and personal habitats employ biomimetic principles as the foundation of their design process. In some cases this would mean applying biomimetic technologies like photovoltaics and fuel cells that will play a large role in the energy-generating capacities of all our facilities in the coming decades.[9] Both of these technologies are biomimetic in that they generate electricity cleanly, without odious by-products and pollution and use only sunlight and water as inputs. In other instances it does not involve technology as much as it requires understanding how to apply natural principles properly such as with daylighting, passive solar heating and natural ventilation. What could we learn about comfort if we more closely studied other habitat builders in their own environments? What does the beaver and the termite have to teach us about architecture?[10]

It is very possible that in the coming years **Respecting the Wisdom of Natural Systems** will become the most important principle of the six outlined in this chapter, as in some ways this principle can be said to encompass the other five. In essence this is the master principle behind the sustainable design movement, for within it is an approach to site design, including an attitude towards climate and place, the use of energy and materials and ultimately our own comfort and well-being. At the heart of this principle is the rejection of the modern metaphor of the machine, and its replacement with nature itself. Our buildings, communities and built environment need to emulate natural systems.

Paradoxically, while this principle may be the master principle, it is the principle that is the least familiar to the sustainable design community at the present time. It is also the hardest principle for some to come to terms with because it completely opposes what conventional society teaches, rewards and recognizes. The biomimicry principle is no less than a replacement of a worldview—of how we fit into the scheme of things, our own limitations, and the limitations of the world around us. Acceptance of this worldview for the designer demands that we change how we approach every step of the design process and for most, to begin the humble process of unlearning and relearning everything that we do.

Nature has the power to teach us everything we need to know as designers. Somewhere on this planet is a creature or natural system that provides a clue as to how to create a completely non-toxic, non-ozone depleting, energy-efficient refrigerant that would revolutionize the air conditioning industry. Or, an organism that can teach us how to more effectively dehumidify air without causing pollution. We just haven't found it yet! Hopefully, we will find and protect it and many others like it before we make it extinct. Nature wears many of her secrets on her sleeve, yet we have been too blind or arrogant to look. As Benyus concludes, "At its best, biomimicry should take us aback, make us more humble, and put us in the learner's chair, seeking to discover and emulate instead of invent." [11]

The Principles of Sustainable Design

Respect for People
The Human Vitality Principle

"The biggest tragedy is not the waste of natural resources, though it is tragic The biggest tragedy is the waste of human resources."

—Oliver Wendell Holmes

Respect for People—The Human Vitality Principle

A quick survey of most North American communities reveals a great deal of design infrastructure that is poorly designed and unfriendly. In many ways the architecture of the twentieth century has failed people. It is as if people and their most basic needs were somehow forgotten. The second sustainable design principle honors the notion that the whole point of designing and constructing buildings in the first place is to create habitat for people. It seems that along the way we have instead created habitat for automobiles and the other things in our lives, and it is coincidental if our buildings and communities also happen to work for us as well. Sustainable design endeavors to create the healthiest, most nourishing places possible for people without diminishing the ability of nature to provide nourishing places for the rest of creation and for our own species in the future. It does not give greater standing to the rest of nature, nor does it give less.

The word respect is essential to reinforce the dichotomy that exists between the types of places we have today and what is possible. We exalt our automobiles more than we do our neighbors. We design hospitals that do nothing but make people feel more sick. We design housing projects that erode the sense of community for individuals. We design schools that make the act of learning more challenging than the ideas being taught within them. Sustainable design aligns itself with the humanist architectural traditions that seek to create great places for people, and in this sense can be seen as a natural extension of what should just be considered good design. The philosophy of sustainable design is wholeheartedly about respecting the unique needs of people. It is about honoring diversity in individuals and giving control back to people for their environments and personal comfort. It is a surprise to many people first learning about sustainable design that the movement and philosophy is as much about people as it is about the environment. This lack of understanding is forgivable because of the way the media and corporations have often inaccurately framed the larger environmental debate as a contest between people and the environment or, more to the point, jobs versus the environment. This debate cannot help but spill over into the design world as well.

And yet, as John R.E. Bliese, in his book, *The Greening of Conservative America* informs us, "there is a consistent myth that cleaning up the environment and protecting the earth hurts the economy..."[1] when in fact, according to a large international study done by MIT "States with stronger environmental policies consistently out-performed the weaker environmental states on all the economic measures."[2]

People tend to forget that it is possible to elevate the concerns of other species without debasing our own. People also forget that most environmentalists do what they do because they love people and hope to leave the world as a better place for future generations to enjoy – future generations of people that is! Most environmentalists are doing what they do for their children and their children's children, and viewed in this way they should be seen not as mere tree huggers who love owls more than loggers, but as champions of humanity, fighting to protect the very lifeblood that sustains all of us. The misconception about people versus the environment extends to sustainable design directly because in the beginnings of the sustainable design movement early practitioners did not seem to be as concerned with human well-being as they should have been. Indeed, early practitioners often put more emphasis on technology and energy than whether they were creating good buildings for people. To the outside observer, saving energy seemed to be their only concern. Many poor energy-conserving buildings were built in the seventies and eighties that seemed to reinforce this perception.[3]

The emergence of sick building syndrome, as an unfortunate side effect of some energy efficiency measures, did not help either. Sick building syndrome is defined as a sustained state of unhealthy indoor environmental conditions. It is caused by the presence of prolonged unhealthy air quality that can come from a variety of sources including the chemical off-gassing of materials, mold and mildew growth, and elevated carbon dioxide levels caused by poor ventilation. Sick building syndrome occurred when buildings became tighter because these tight buildings trapped indoor pollutants inside at greater concentrations, ultimately making people sick. The older, less energy-efficient buildings avoided this, not because they were intrinsically healthier (they often had significant problems of their own) but because greater amounts of air in the form of leaks and drafts (known as infiltration) diluted the problem.

Since sick building syndrome was identified, the green building industry has done more to make our buildings healthier for people than any other movement in the building industry. The sustainable design movement has actively supported standards for reducing Volatile Organic Compounds (VOCs) found in so many of our building products including paints, stains, furniture, carpet and other finishes. Improved air quality is the result. Over time the industry has rid itself of asbestos and lead (in new construction at least) and it is likely that vinyl and certain types of arsenic and chromium treated wood products are next. It is important to mention that building practices that are toxic for other creatures are also very toxic to us, and strategies that are designed to lower environmental impact often have a way of working out better for people as well.

The sustainable design movement has also done a great deal to improve thermal comfort, lighting and other environmental factors to the point that many green buildings are expected to have healthier, more productive occupants than their traditional counterparts. This new understanding turns on its head the old myth that environmental responsibility means being less comfortable and doing without. We are now learning that properly designed green buildings are more comfortable and more pleasant to occupy than other buildings. The sustainable design philosophy has embraced the notion that we can do better with less. This trend is discussed further in chapter eleven which deals directly with productivity and well-being in green buildings. The issue of creating healthy places for people is very much ingrained in the US Green Building Council's LEED rating system. This system offers a large portion of its points to building features such as indoor air quality, daylighting, thermal comfort, connection to the outside, and general user control that all enhance indoor environmental quality.

While all of the factors mentioned so far deal with physical comfort issues, the sustainable design movement has also found ways of integrating psychological and spiritual well-being into the heart of its principles. On a philosophical level sustainable design focuses on how to produce architecture that is humane and properly scaled. It asks several fundamental questions about our relationship to the built environment as living creatures. What makes people happy? Productive? What factors in the built environment allow us to perform our work efficiently and with gusto? What factors inhibit such behavior? Sustainable design has, through much research and trial and error, found good, but not final answers to each of these questions.

Sustainable design also honors the need for beauty and artful design in our homes and places of work as a subset of this principle. This subset is discussed in greater length in Chapter Fifteen—The Aesthetics of Sustainable Design.

From a spiritual level, the same questioning process is also fundamental.

What nourishes people? How can our design decisions uplift the human psyche and connect us to things greater than ourselves? What are our moral obligations to producing architecture that does more than serve narrow economic interests? The deeper we delve into the sustainable design world, the more we realize that it has a profoundly spiritual dimension. The reason why many in the design professions are finding ways to introduce the sustainable design principles into their practices is because on some level they know that it is the right thing to do. When this kind of care and purpose gets introduced into any art form, as architecture should be considered, it cannot help but become elevated in the process.

Former Vice President Al Gore said it best in his book *Earth in the Balance*:

> The more deeply I search for the roots of the global environmental crisis, the more I am convinced that it is an outer manifestation of an inner crisis that is, for lack of a better word, spiritual...what other word describes the collection of values and assumptions that determine our basic understanding of how we fit into the universe?[4]

Sustainable design is a reaction of those in the design professions to this inner and outer crisis. Unfortunately, by itself this spiritual dimension is not enough of a motivator for many in our materialistic society but it is having an impact and, coupled with our greater understanding of the economic benefits of sustainable design, it is helping to make widespread change.[5]

As the sustainable design movement continues to mature, Respect for People will likely emerge as the most important principle for ensuring adoption of all aspects of the philosophy. People pay attention when health and well-being are involved even if they ignore the environmental reasons. The next evolution for sustainable design lies in better understanding how to honor the diversity of people and their roles in the physical environments.

CHAPTER FIVE

Photo courtesy of Dewees Island

The Principles of Sustainable Design

Respect for Place
The Ecosystem/Bioregion Principle

*"Can we not create, from a beautiful natural landscape, an
environment inhabited by man in which natural beauty is
retained, man housed in community?"*

—Ian McHarg

51

Respect for Place—The Ecosystem/Bio-Region Principle

Any trip through the countryside in Europe or other regions where the remnants of pre-industrial civilizations are still present will show vast differences between building technologies, architecture, food, dress and music within short distances. These diverse aspects of culture were for the most part inspired by place. Place is used as a word to describe the complex interplay of climatalogical, biological, geological and topographical features that create the differences we see around us. Our cultural legacies, born from these unique features, further heighten the distinctions between what is "home" and what is "away". Our buildings, as the largest physical artifacts of our culture, have the most to draw from and respond to the uniqueness of place. As described in the second chapter, for thousands of years, we built our structures with materials locally available, and adapted our architecture to the climate to maintain conditions as comfortable as possible throughout the year. Our negative environmental impact throughout this entire period, while rarely zero, was but a mere scratch compared to the wounds we inflict on the planet's health today with our more global and international approach to design and construction. It can be said that we have lost our respect for place.

In our unwavering search for greater comfort and security, we have, over the last two hundred years, developed technologies and philosophies that have taken us further and further away from the way we used to build and from our interaction with place. With the development of air conditioning, central heating, the elevator and industrial production processes, we were suddenly able to create conditions that were comfortable regardless of how hot or cold the region. All that was needed was a greater input of energy—energy that could be found by commandeering resources from as far away as necessary. We no longer were confined to building with locally available materials. Cultural traditions aside, we now imported materials from around the globe. Indeed, since the industrial revolution, we have carried forth this approach with zealous intensity. It is almost as if we have resented our connection to nature, to climate and to place. So smitten were we by our newly formed technological prowess that we discarded old building strategies and ways of living that had worked for centuries—even if they worked just as well or better than the new technological fixes. In the last two centuries we have seen the indiscriminate and asinine abuse of technologies in all areas, from architecture to agriculture. We have lost the ability to look holistically at both the intended and unintended consequences of our inventions and to find solutions that maintain ecological and cultural diversity and health.

A simple look at most of our communities being built today shows that we have indeed lost our respect for place. We seek our cultural development in sensationalism and misplaced individualism and technology for the sake of itself. It used to be that our places defined our architecture, but with a lot of modern urban design and architecture, place has become irrelevant, or worse, scorned. With every new subdivision laid out in America, we seem to be in a hurry to destroy the very things that in the past defined us as a people and made our communities distinct, "for this is the pattern by which those who escape to the country are encased within a faceless suburb, no-place, somewhere USA." [1]

Sustainable design asks us for something completely different. It does not ask us to return to the old ways of living as pure romantics, but it does ask us for the responsible, long-term use of technology and design. Sustainable design is built on the idea of regionalism. It honors the differences that exist between places, both on the macro level with climate regions, and on the micro level with topographical and biological differences. The philosophy of sustainable design rejects the notion that our buildings should look the same and be built the same in any region regardless of whether we have the technological know-how and resources to do so. Indeed, it demands that our buildings respond to place in fundamental ways—from the level of the site to that of climate and bioregion.

Sustainable design suggests that technological fixes be applied only after natural ones have been used to the fullest extent. An example of this would be to design a building to harness breezes for natural cooling when climate conditions are favorable, instead of ignoring orientation and relying on air conditioning. With this approach the design would have to take into account prevailing breezes and how they are affected by site features such as trees, adjacent structures and topography, and then locate air intakes and outlets to further improve the natural cooling effect. Sustainable design requires learning what is unique about a given place and how those unique characteristics can be celebrated and protected. It relies substantially on the qualities of a place to inform the process of design itself.

Architecture and landscape design that maintains a dialogue with its surroundings, and teaches us about the places we inhabit, enrich our experiences on all levels. The discourse between site, climate and ecology elevates the design object itself to a higher plane. A sustainable designer treats all sites with respect and reverence, no matter how uninspiring or degraded it may seem to be. Even the most degraded site can be restored and repaired under skillful hands; it is our duty to do so. The questions should then be: What does the site require? What can it become?

A sustainable designer understands that there is something sacred and profound in all places. This idea is more easily understood in more dramatic settings like the Rockies, but is no less true in the most mundane of surroundings. The difference lies only in our skills as designers and our ability to perceive that which is not yet visible. The truth is that every place, every community has something unique to it. It is the job of the sustainable designer (indeed of all design professionals) to uncover it and of all citizens to demand that it be honored and revealed. In Sudbury, those very same rocks that had been blackened and blasted for so many years had in fact created an environment unique on the planet. With every structure built, an opportunity presented itself to make Sudbury a place like no other—an opportunity continually missed by the developers and planners of the community. When we neglect to bring forth that which is unique and beautiful in our surroundings, we degrade ourselves and diminish our potential to communicate that which is unique and beautiful in our culture.

There is an inherent need in all of us to "come from somewhere", to know where home is, and to feel in some way that our home is special—indeed that we are special because of it. We are in many ways defined by our surroundings. We identify with place. Historically this identification was purely nature based. But, as the built environment has become so pervasive it now exerts an even stronger force on our cultural identities. If our built environment is disconnected from place, then what hope does our culture have? Culturally, someone from northern Minnesota should be very different from someone from southern Florida because of the extreme difference in climate, geology and ecosystems (and therefore its built environment as well). But as our built environment gets homogenized, so to do our cultural traits. Are we not diminished by this sameness?

The often used quote by Winston Churchill "we shape our environments, thereafter, they shape us".[2] is very true. Human culture itself has consistently sprung forth as reactions to the surrounding environment. Cultural diversity was enriched by the creative use of the foods that were available, dress that was designed to complement climatic conditions, and architecture shaped to maximize comfort based on what nature could provide. For Frank Lloyd Wright this was very much true of his home—the prairie, for many not as visually dynamic as other places in the United States. And yet to Wright it spoke volumes about how we should live and how we should build. His prairie style houses were characterized by low, vertical forms that mimicked the landscape. He believed that designers should intuitively understand the spirit of a place before they were to be trusted to design something placed on it. His belief in this principle was so strong that he urged his students to sleep outdoors at the place where their buildings were to be built, to work the land and to feel the passing of the seasons before design was started. Without such immersion, he believed, it was impossible to learn the subtle cues that lie all around us.

"If we build in the desert, let the house know the desert and the desert be proud of the house by making the house an extension of the desert, so that when you are in the house the desert seems the house's own extension.... The same thought, in the same feeling, goes for whatever we build, wherever we build it."[3]

For Frank Lloyd Wright this philosophy was translated literally into a building style that he called "organic", which implied creating built forms that sometimes mimicked the naturally occurring ones. While this is one interpretation, it is a stylistic bridge, unnecessary for sustainable design. A modern expression of local materials and response to climate is entirely possible without resorting to mimicking forms. Indeed, some of the other early modern masters like Alvar Aalto understood this completely and produced buildings that fit as well as Wright's did, but in a more modern, abstract lexicon.

A respect for place demands that our built environments differ from region to region and community to community. Sustainable design picks up not only on place but also on culture and individual differences. Subtly in places that are near, and dramatically in places that are far. A building in a hot humid climate should be designed and built very differently than a building in a cold northern one. Its landscape should differ, its site development should differ, and its relationship to other structures and construction should differ. A sustainable designer should draw a significant portion of his or her design information from the place it arises; from topography, watersheds, local hydrology, foliage, site biodiversity as well as from historical human culture and urban context. A sustainable designer attends to development in such a way that the health of these factors is improved.

To a sustainable designer, few things are as important as understanding orientation. Most buildings being built today were designed as if the sun and everything it brings such as warmth, daylight and ultra violet radiation did not matter. Buildings are built in hot climates with whole facades of glass, on all orientations that allow huge amounts of uncontrolled heat and light into the building, requiring an even larger amount of energy to keep the building somewhat comfortable—a burden self-imposed by the ignorant design team.

If there were only one thing that sustainable designers could drive home to the design community at large, it would probably be the understanding of solar design principles. It is a simple and unwavering fact that the sun changes its path over the course of the year, rising and setting later in the summer while traveling higher across the sky and lower and shorter in the winter. Buildings should be designed to respond to these entirely predictable changes in the sun's path. Our buildings in general should be designed to keep out direct sunlight when we do not need it, and to let it in when we do. Our buildings should respond differently on different sides of the building, and on virtually no occasion should the north, south, east and west look and perform the same. It is not always possible, especially in urban settings, to select the ideal orientation for a building, which for the record in the northern hemisphere is almost always a site with its long face to the north and south. And yet, the sustainable designer should still be responding to place to let sun or diffuse daylight in when it is needed and to keep it out when it is not needed. Too much light produces glare that causes visual discomfort; too little, a potentially gloomy interior. In sustainable design the power of orientation is critical because it affects so directly the environmental performance of the building, and also on the quality of the built environment for people. Nothing else is so critical to so many parts of the sustainability umbrella than orientation.

The same idea holds true for harnessing prevailing summer breezes for cooling and sheltering the building from winds in the heating season. Shaping a building to take advantage of nature's inherent ability to provide heat, coolth[4], and light is always a top priority, something understood for thousands of years by every cultural group on the planet and now so universally forgotten and ignored. Heating and cooling is, in many cases, provided for free from nature—provided a person knows how to harness it. Nothing is more efficient than that. As leading mechanical engineer guru Eng Lock Lee likes to say, "efficiency is free, ask for more."[5]

Typically, our environmental impact grows as we build our buildings. However, the end result of understanding and respecting place is that our environmental impact diminishes greatly. We harness free energy instead of relying on fossil fuels, and we can turn off lights because our windows let in the amount of light that we need. But even more important than this direct connection to environmental impact is the psychological one. Without this feeling, this connection to nature and place, we lose the compassion to protect and save the precious areas around us. Without its apparent utility, many lose sight of its true importance.

During war, the military makes it a point to try and dehumanize or make strange the enemy, as it is always easier to kill a stranger than a friend. As a society, we have done the same thing with the wild places that remain. So many of us are foreign to our own natural surroundings that it means nothing when we damage it. We certainly would not go out of our way to protect that which we do not know. Most individuals today cannot even identify more than two or three bird species from their area. Most cannot tell what plants are edible or poisonous. We have, even among our most educated, lost our ability to determine where true south is and we can not tell time on a sunny day, which is actually very easy as long as we are not worried about exact minutes.

We are disconnected from place, and this disconnection starts in our homes and carries through to our air-conditioned offices, theatres, shopping malls and museums. As a society, over ninety percent of our time is spent indoors. One cannot develop a knowledge and respect for place inside concrete and steel boxes. Once we disconnected our buildings from place we began the more insidious process of disconnecting people from place as well. Our disconnect with place has grown as our childlike belief in the ability of science and technology to solve our problems has grown.

It is this same disconnect that leads some people to think that global warming could be a good thing, so foreign to most people is the role that a stable climate plays in our economy and life support systems. What does it matter how hot it gets if you have an air conditioner? This disengagement is extremely unfortunate, because one could imagine that our technologies could be developed to give us a greater appreciation and understanding of our surroundings. Of all our technological inventions, it is perhaps the automobile that is the most to blame for the separation. In the past, getting from place to place required an intimate dialogue with climate and topography. Now, thanks to the automobile and the incredible infrastructure that supports it, we travel from one climate-controlled space to another, and at speeds where things outside our window are mere blurs. The faster we drive on our highways, the less the journey and the places we travel through matters. Americans use cars for eighty-two percent of their trips…a percentage that is growing quickly. There are more than two hundred million cars in the United States today with infrastructure that covers ten percent of the arable land and thirty percent of our cities and towns.[6]

With the sustainable design philosophy, there are no bad places, no sites unworthy of restoration and respect. But while there may be no bad places, respect for place reminds us that there can be poor places for us to choose to build. As modern developments bear witness, the prevailing attitude seems to be that nowhere is too sacred or special to build on. Anything is fair game. We level mountains, drain swamps, and clear forests to lay tracts of the same suburban housing developments like legos across the landscape. The philosophy of sustainable design takes the attitude that some places are not appropriate to be built on, paved over or harnessed indiscriminately for our use. The reasons for this belief are many. These reasons include:

1. The land has much greater use for humanity
2. The land is dangerous or unsuitable for human use
3. The land is too delicate and sensitive for human use
4. The land is being used already by other animals that cannot co-exist successfully with us

We should not be building on prime agricultural land. It is a crime against future generations to degrade topsoil and pave over farmland that could be put to use providing food to the growing billions. It is wrong to put golf courses and soccer fields in ranch country and pump water needlessly from receding aquifers for the temporary benefit of the few and the future impoverishment of all. Arizona and southern California should not be covered with green lawns, pools and driving ranges that need tons of water that the area cannot provide on its own. Development should be done appropriately, within the carrying capacity of the region. Too often, communities are built in areas that are prone to natural disasters, causing devastation to people and costing society millions, if not billions of dollars. The most common example of this inappropriate development is the propensity of people to build within the floodplains of our nation's rivers and streams. Each year hundreds of homes are flooded in the United States. In many cases the same homes were flooded only a few years previously. We do not learn from our mistakes. Sometimes whole cities are built in low lying areas prone to flooding and disaster. In 2001 the City of Houston was hit by tropical storm Alison that unleashed fourteen inches of rain within just a few hours in the heart of the city and the Texas Medical Center area—an urban campus that contains a few dozen research hospitals, intensive care units and medical schools. The devastation was close to five billion dollars, with twenty-two people killed and hundreds of research animals drowned, along with the research they were tied to.[7] This same area, built in a former swamp with a creek (now in a pipe) running directly underneath the campus, had previously flooded to some degree several times within the last twenty years. Numerous houses had been flooded multiple times. Each time FEMA (the Federal Emergency Management Authority) bailed out the institutions and the local homeowners to some degree. In every case people simply rebuilt, but in most cases without taking further precautions. Finally, after Alison, which was the worst flooding event in the nation's history, FEMA bought out several houses that had been hit several times and strongly cautioned all the institutions to take more serious steps to prevent damage in the future if they wanted to receive federal funding.

Flood damage is, of course, only part of the problem. In many places people build in areas prone to mudslides. We scream for compensation from the government and from the insurance industry and then rebuild in the same place. This is not respect for place. In parts of California homeowners have watched their houses slide down the hillside, only to rebuild in the same area after receiving their insurance money. Others in Colorado wonder why their houses burn down as wildfires sweep through the incredibly dry area where they have been built. People build close to the few wild areas that remain in America, and then complain when that wildlife strolls through their property—in the case of bears and wolves, often resulting in the killing of the animal. Construction in some areas creates inordinate amount of ecological havoc. Buildings should not be built on steep slopes that will create excessive amounts of soil erosion, or in areas that harbor threatened or endangered species. We need to leave alone the few healthy swamplands that remain. For wild places to endure they need to remain undisturbed, and they need to remain in sizable chunks that can support functioning ecosystems. For example, a single male bear needs one hundred acres of land to support itself in the wild. A healthy population of at least a thousand bears is needed to ensure genetic diversity and continued survival of the local population. For their needs alone one hundred thousand acres are needed. The bear is only one example, but open space needs to be of a certain size to be useful to all. Wildness does not exist in the strips of grass between shopping malls and mega theatre complexes.

Ian McHarg, the grandfather of ecological design sums this point up masterfully in his treatise on landscape design, *Design with Nature*,

> Consider that if you are required to design a flight of steps or a sidewalk there are clear and stringent regulations: there are constraints against the sale of cigarettes and alcohol to minors, society reacts sternly to the sale or use of narcotics and there are strong laws to deter assault, rape and murder. And we should be thankful indeed for these protections. But there is no comparable concern, reflected in law, that ensures that your house is not built on a floodplain, on unconsolidated sediments, in an earthquake zone, hurricane path, fire prone forest, or in areas liable to subsidence or mudslides.[8]

For the most part, we should no longer be building on virgin land, and looking to locate our homes and offices at the edge of town. So much underutilized and abandoned infrastructure exists within the fabric of our communities that could be re-used, revitalized and made to thrive. It is a shame to throw away the investments that we and the environment have made that could be given another life. In almost every case, revitalizing the places we have already developed results in greater cultural richness as well. Storm Cunningham calls this the Restoration Economy, and he believes that in the coming decades it will dominate all development.[9] When we consider that eighty percent of the buildings that will exist in twenty years have yet to be built it is a scary thought. If we keep promoting leapfrog development instead of preservation and redevelopment there will be no wild places left anywhere. It is not respect for place to use the land, throw it out and seek a new place.

Unfortunately, there is a trend to build schools on the edge of our communities rather than rebuilding them at the heart (a sound metaphor for how far we have drifted in our educational practices as well). The result is that we promote further development at the edges, stick kids in buses with no options to walk or bike to school and further remove our children from making a connection to community, to climate and to place. We do this because we think it is cheaper to do so. But its effects are the opposite. It cheapens us and costs us all a lot more money. Increased driving time steals time from children and parents, makes parents into chauffeurs and erodes the social institutions in place with neighborhood schools. Developers sometimes use the construction of schools as a catalyst for their developments, promoting leapfrog development that makes infrastructure more expensive and more environmentally damaging. Green designers should be willing to walk away from and, indeed, try to stop development that encourages the destruction of our natural and cultural heritage.

Once a building is being built however, it is the responsibility of the designer to build on the part of the land that is the most degraded, rather than on the parts that are the most pristine. So many buildings have destroyed the very reason people were building in the place to begin with. Sustainable design seeks to preserve the character of both natural and man-made features of any site. Construction should be done in a way that preserves as much of the site as possible; saving trees, stopping erosion and minimizing the areas where dirt is compacted by heavy machinery. In fact, the question should be "how can we leave the site in a better condition than we found it?" as Bob Berkebile continually asks on all his projects. "How can we be restorative?"[10]

In nature, the areas with the most diversity are usually those that occupy a transition zone between two distinct ecosystems. This transition area is called an eco-tone by biologists, which means "a biologically rich transition zone between dissimilar areas." This idea should permeate the designs of our built environment. The design of the built environment gives a great opportunity to produce wonderfully rich edges or eco-tones. Can we restore or enhance the site's fecundity? Can we restore the health of soil and native plants that purify site runoff and even improve the local microclimate by minimizing hard surfaces and maximizing tree shade where appropriate? Can we keep rainfall on site, rather than washing away nutrients? This respect for place crosses over into the human dimension as well. Can we promote development that improves the long-term vitality of the community and provides amenities for the community? Can the project decrease traffic congestion and free up time for people? The scope of impact should not be confined to the boundaries of the site. Can the project improve the vitality and fecundity of the community at large?

But creating an eco-tone with every project reminds us that to do so requires boundaries. There can be no transition to dissimilar systems if they are all the same. The principle, Respect for Place, encourages the idea of boundaries like those in Portland's Urban Growth Boundary that forbids most development from continuing outside of a predetermined area. This boundary protects farmland, timberland and nature itself from the encroaching path of progress. It ensures that all residents will continue to have access to the natural world that many of them moved to Oregon to enjoy. Without a boundary there cannot be an eco-tone. Indeed, the boundary is the eco-tone. Every organism in nature has a boundary and when that boundary is compromised the organism dies. Too often we destroy the very thing we love. There is a joke in the environmental movement that developers name their subdivisions after that which they have destroyed, such as Oak Hollow, a development that no longer has any trees over six feet still standing, and no oaks among them.

Too much of our development occurs as if there were no boundaries, no beginning and no end to place. We treat our planet as a continuous connection of building opportunities. Without a boundary between the developed and the wild, there is no wild. Our roads, the first wave of development, have become killing fields for thousands of raccoons, possums, cats, dogs, deer and others animals trying to peacefully cross boundaries that no longer exist. Only where nature is at its most abrupt and forceful do we halt our helter-skelter pattern of development. On steeply sloped mountains, dense swamps and arid plains we sometimes admit that there is a boundary, a place where we should not build. But this too has proven to be a temporary barrier as we blast rock to make way for winter ski villages, drain swampland to create suburbs and theme parks, and pump water from the aquifer to turn desert into golf courses and suburban yards. With no boundaries, development happens everywhere and once wild areas are reduced to mere parks. And then we have to feed the bears.

It is these same boundaries that create the next principle, The Principle of Respecting the Cycle of Life.

CHAPTER SIX

Photo by McLennan

The Principles of Sustainable Design

Respect for the Cycle of Life
The "Seven Generations" Principle [1]

> "Injustice anywhere is a threat to justice everywhere. We are caught in an inescapable network of mutuality—tied to a single garmet of destiny—whatever affects one directly affects all indirectly."
>
> —Martin Luther King

Respect for the Cycle of Life—The "Seven Generations" Principle

"All things in this creation exist within you, and all things in you exist in creation: there is no border between you and the closest things, and there is no distance between you and the farthest things, and all things, from the lowest to the loftiest, from the smallest to the greatest, are within you as equal things."[2]

Of all the principles, Respect for the Cycle of Life is perhaps the most difficult to fully grasp and yet, at its heart, it is perhaps the simplest. Respecting the Cycle of Life deals with the indisputable truth that we are but a mere part of a larger cycle of birth and death that has carried on for millions of years on this planet. It is about understanding that we have a part to play in this cycle and, with the stewardship of this process, a responsibility to see that the things we create and surround ourselves with also continue. Ultimately, it acknowledges that when we interfere with this cycle, we create profound problems for the environment and ourselves. We have a connection to nature that is inherent and essential to us. When we deny it, we deny a part of ourselves.

Bill McDonough and Michael Braungart remind us that "Nature operates according to a system of nutrients and metabolisms in which there is no such thing as waste,"[3] or as described by Paul Hawken **waste = food**. In nature, nothing is ever wasted but becomes a key part for another organism or another system. One animal's waste is another's food. And so on. Even within the inanimate world, this cycle of birth and decay and rebirth carries on in an endless cycle, but always in ways that are life giving and sustaining.

Ian McHarg, the grandfather of ecological design, eloquently describes the hydrological cycle—a key part of the cycle of life that sustains this planet.

A single drop of water in the uplands of a watershed may appear and reappear as cloud, precipitation, surface water in creek and river, lake and pond or groundwater; it can participate in plant and animal metabolism, transpiration, condensation, decomposition, combustion, respiration and evaporation. This same drop of water may appear in considerations of climate and microclimate, water supply, flood, drought and erosion control, industry commerce, agriculture, forestry, recreation, scenic beauty, in cloud, snow, stream, river and sea. We conclude that nature is a single interacting system and that changes to any part will affect the operation of the whole.[4]

He reminds us of how fragile and wondrous our planet really is, and the risks we face when we poke, prod and wrench it as we have been doing for the last two hundred years. The planet earth, unlike any in our solar system, sustains life within a narrow range of parameters that, but for a few exceptions, has remained remarkably stable for millions of years. The earth's atmosphere, for example, is twenty-one percent oxygen and a fairly constant 1.7 parts per million of methane. The methane in the atmosphere reacts with sunlight to form carbon dioxide and water, essential to life. To remain at this constant rate it needs to be replenished by living organisms—that which the methane makes possible at a rate of five hundred million tons a year (as a *waste* product of life!). If we had an atmosphere with slightly more oxygen we would burn up, with less we would choke and shrivel. If there were no living organisms on the planet the methane and numerous other chemical compounds would react until no more existed—the earth would turn into a waterless, dead planet.

The Gaia theory, advanced by James Lovelock, suggests that the earth acts like a giant, dynamic living organism that self regulates to maintain conditions conducive to itself: temperatures, humidity, gases and precipitation. The Gaia theory does not suggest that the planet itself is alive, but that it functions as if it was. How gloriously wonderful life is on this planet. The hydrological cycle described so eloquently by McHarg is tied intimately to plant life on the planet, a seeming chicken and egg scenario in which one is necessary for the other to exist; the mild temperatures of the earth tied to the continual cycle and balance of carbon released into the atmosphere or sequestered by plants and stored within the soil. In all cases the health of the whole system is tied to a web of diversity that operates in incredibly complex ways—complexity that we cannot, with the most sophisticated computers, comprehend. What happens when we upset this balance, when we continually cut the strands that sustain us? When we replace diversity with sameness? And create experiments to climate on a global scale? We are not exempt in any way from this overarching interconnectedness principle. And yet, curiously and arrogantly, we act like we are.

Waste = Food

In nature, as discussed, everything has a place or is food for something else. That is, except with the things modern society produces. What stupidity is it that compels us to design packaging that lasts for a thousand years when the food contained in it is meant to last for a few days? As Benyus writes, "Our greatest sin is this over engineering—we may not be able to live forever, but we make darn sure that our waste will." [5]

We are guilty of an irresponsible, over-engineering tendency in numerous aspects of our industrial economy while at the same time encouraging the throwaway consumption of these materials. We make things to last, literally forever, but only use them for brief moments. Most noticeable are the styrofoam and plastic containers that we use to hold everything from food to building materials. These are items that are meant only to transport another item but create an incredible amount of waste. In juxtaposition to this over engineering is our tendency to under–engineer things that are meant to have long life and use. Most household items and building components are designed with planned obsolescence in mind. Think of the millions of tires, dishwashers, radios and computers thrown away every year. Huge amounts of energy and resources are used to create objects that should be useful for decades, but instead, like their over-engineered counterparts, end up in the landfill in short order.

Respecting the Cycle of Life means creating an appropriate fit between the life expectancy of an object and its use, be it an appliance or a whole building. It means understanding that materials that are meant to be thrown away can quickly be used as food for another organism as part of the cycle of life, rather than something that takes thousands of years to degrade. McDonough and Braugart, in their new book *Cradle to Cradle*, tell of a new biodegradable milk carton that contains tiny flower seeds in its construction. When the carton is thrown away, it becomes nutrients for the life that springs forth from within. From container to garden and so on. McDonough and Braungart also talk about their line of fabrics called the McDonough collection that contains no substances that are carcinogenic, mutagenic or disrupt the endocrine system (unlike most of our fabrics) "with filters in the designers heads, rather than in pipes and ducts." [6] They designed a line of fabric that can be used as compost when its useful life is over. If only the idea of the milk carton and the fabric would carry through to the way we make most of our products and materials. Imagine if everything we created contributed to the birth of something else. If we do not create problems to begin with, we do not need to clean up or monitor them.

Unfortunately, much of what our society creates is actually harmful to the overall cycle of life, creating dead-zones rather than places of life. An inventory of typical building materials found in our homes and offices will find an incredibly long list of materials that contain chemicals that are in many ways unsafe for human contact—either at the time of installation (making it unsafe for construction workers), for a period of time after construction (that new car/new home smell that is actually not a good thing) and, in a few cases, throughout the material's life. In all cases these chemicals eventually find their way into a landfill or groundwater and end up inside us or some other living thing.

Over the years we have been slowly pulling out the most toxic of substances from our environment, or at least those such as asbestos and lead that could be conclusively linked to direct human suffering. But many more toxic materials remain, in large part because without a direct link to cancer, industry has fought against any changes in the way materials are made. Like the tobacco industry, many material manufacturers deny for as long as possible substantial evidence that material sub-ingredients can cause cancer, bio-accumulate or create birth defects. The environmental movement for a long time fought the wood preservative industry over the use of arsenic in pressure-treated wood. Was it safe to use a material that contained such a powerful chemical in children's play structures, picnic tables or decks? The industry claimed it was perfectly safe. Finally, in 2002 the EPA banned the use of Copper Chromate Arsenic (CCA) treated wood for sale to the public for most building related uses after it was conclusively proven that the arsenic leaches out of the wood after just a few years. Currently, the materials that are in the most heated debate include Polyvinyl Chloride (PVC), fiberglass and mercury. PVC is found in an incredibly wide array of both consumer and building products and has proven remarkably useful in everything from hospital equipment to plumbing pipe. However, the manufacture of PVC is known to create dioxin, a deadly chemical that has been linked to a wide range of health problems. The PVC industry argues that once in place the material is inert and poses no risk to people or the environment. Recently, a documentary entitled "Blue Vinyl" was released to the public and it exposes the dangers present in the material at various stages of its life cycle-from production, to fire, to ultimate disposal. The documentary has become an instant cult favorite among environmentalists. The information on PVC continues to pile on both sides of the argument, and so the debate continues.

For many people fiberglass is considered the next asbestos, and there is fear that like the material that is known to cause asbestosis, a painful and fatal lung disease, fiberglass also lodges in the lungs. Like PVC, the issue is tricky because of the usefulness of the product to the industry and even its role in reducing environmental impact. The debate around mercury is much more clear as there is no arguing the deadly effects caused by this element. It is amazing that we still use the substance in thermometers when it can be so toxic. While mercury is still used in florescent lights because it is the only substance that has the right mix of chemical properties, the industry's current approach is to develop ways to use smaller and smaller amounts of the substance to do the same job. Low-mercury florescent tubes are now very common.

While these are currently the materials in hot debate, the truth is that there are many more that cause severe harm to people and the environment. Most things in the interior of a building contain chemicals that are harmful to people at some dosage. Furniture, paints, stains, carpets and wall coverings all emit harmful Volatile Organic Compounds (VOC). Many times when fires occur in buildings, it is the chemicals released in the materials that kill people before the fire itself. To the chagrin of some industries, sustainable design focuses on eliminating from use chemicals and materials that are known to be toxic. The movement also focuses on eliminating materials such as the urea formaldehydes found in materials like particleboards, even if the link to health problems is not 100 percent proven. It is much better to focus on materials that we know are safe, instead of using each other and the planet as trial subjects.

The philosophy of Respect for the Cycle of Life also stresses the idea that all of our built artifacts must be safe "to all people, for all time" [7] and that just because a material is inert in one phase does not make it okay to use in all phases. Even if PVC is one hundred percent inert while in place as is claimed, do we want to risk the lives of those making the chemical and its products? Often times, these workers are the uneducated, the poor and the illiterate who do not always know or understand the consequences of the chemicals they are dealing with. McHarg convincingly discusses this point.

While great efforts are made to ensure that you do not break an ankle, there are few deterrents to arrest the dumping of poisons into the sources of public water supply or their injection into groundwater resources. You are clearly protected from assault by fist, knife or gun, but not from the equally dangerous threats of hydrocarbons, lead, nitrous oxides, ozone or carbon monoxide in the atmosphere. [7]

And if Rachael Carson, mother of the environmental movement, taught us anything, it is that the chemicals we create do not always stay in the places we expect them. Once we create something that is harmful to the cycle of life, there is a good chance that it will find a way to harm it. Pollution does not respect boundaries, and chemicals do not know that they are supposed to stay put in safe places. The hole in the ozone layer over the south pole is now the size of the United States. This hole is caused in large part by Chlorofluorocarbons (CFC) escaping from air conditioning systems and from some other commercial uses and ending up in the upper atmosphere where it is reacting to destroy the ozone that protects all of us from the deadly effects of the sun's ultraviolet radiation. Recently, the growing ozone hole extended for the first time over land in southern Argentina that is inhabited by people, putting thousands at serious risk. Our world is now riddled with toxins. They are in our blood, fatty tissues and organs. Allergies, asthma, cancers and many other environmental diseases, which are a direct result of these assaults to our immune system and health, are on the rise. Unlike fifty or sixty years ago chemicals like DDT are now found in people's bloodstreams.

This problem of pollution is not only related to the physical things we create, but also to our urban infrastructure. The industrial methods used to handle our own nutrient effluent are particularly troublesome. As a species, we consume an enormous portion of the earth's biological output, and yet our output—our feces and urine are not returned to the earth for use. We defecate in our water supply, creating enormous environmental and economic problems in our communities and then use amazing amounts of energy and chemicals to render this nutrient-laden, polluted water sterile. Respecting the Cycle of Life means understanding that our waste, just like any organism, is valuable food for something else. Through the use of composting toilets, these nutrients can be returned to use. We throw our food scraps away in plastic bags alongside metal cans and plastic jugs and bury them deep in the ground rather than separating the organics for compost and the metals and plastics for recycling to continue their useful life.

But perhaps the most insidious example is how we generate our energy in many communities. After World War II, the world ushered in a nuclear age where people lived in fear of the ever-present threat of a nuclear war between Russia and the United States. At the same time people were told that nuclear power was a great new technology that would give us all the energy we needed, safely, quietly and cleanly. The juxtaposition in messages could not be more confusing. At first, nuclear power did, in fact, seem like an ideal solution. The production of energy through nuclear fission produced no air pollution and seemed like a futurist technology. With nuclear power we would be ushered into the ideal future where none of us would have to work as hard, and energy would be nearly free. The risks that were involved seemed minor when compared to the optimism and faith that people had in the ability of science and technology to solve any problems. Surely, if we could split the atom we could handle its wastes. Each nuclear power plant construction created many new jobs for the region and, because of the advanced technology involved, nuclear power could be commercially exported to other countries for great profit. Like a lot of things, nuclear plant construction made a few people very, very rich. The nuclear industry was born. Nuclear plants were soon sold all over the world to countries like India, Pakistan and China, all of whom soon thereafter developed nuclear weapons as well.

The full promise of nuclear power was never delivered. Nuclear power never became as cheap as people fantasized. In fact the opposite was true. High plant maintenance, problems with safety and the cost of production kept the price up and rising. Communities began to be saddled with a waste problem that was far greater than what was ever imagined. Protection from and storage of the waste was also very expensive. In parts of the world, including in the United States at Three Mile Island and the Hanford Nuclear Reactor, accidents happened. The popular support of nuclear technology began to fade quickly. The huge disaster at Chernobyl, which claimed dozens of lives and subjected thousands to unhealthy levels of radioactivity, sealed the deal for many. People began to realize that even if the technology was perfect (which it wasn't) people were not. Mistakes happen, and with nuclear we cannot afford to have mistakes happen. When the British government tried to privatize its nuclear plants in the nineties, it could not find a single buyer. Nobody wanted them. They were too expensive, too risky, and too dangerous. The people of Britain, just like the people of dozens of countries around the world, were stuck with the technology and the legacy that will persist and require constant vigilance for the next one thousand years. After September 11, 2001 many people began to realize that nuclear power plants were also a threat to our safety as a target for terrorism.

As an industrial society, we need to begin the arduous process of identifying and systematically eliminating the things that are toxic to the cycle of life. Architects, engineers and interior designers are not chemists and physicians and they should not be responsible for determining which materials are safe for life and which are not safe. This quandary is why it is necessary for governments to work with industry to label and find replacements for problematic materials. Severely toxic materials should be banned from production. Respecting the Cycle of Life means turning our backs on all nuclear and ozone-depleting technologies. Over the next decade we will see the voluntary replacement of current products with more benign ones due to the rise in awareness and pressure from the public. Industry can take heart that there are non-toxic alternatives out there in nature as described in the biomimicry principle by Janine Benyus.

> Nature can't put its factory on the edge of town; it has to live where it works. As a result, nature's first trick of the trade is that nature manufactures its materials under life-friendly conditions—in water, at room temperature, without harsh chemicals or high pressures… The inner shell of a sea creature called an abalone is twice as tough as our high-tech ceramics. Spider silk, ounce for ounce is five times stronger than steel. Mussel adhesive works underwater and sticks to anything, even without a primer. Rhino horn manages to repair itself, though it contains no living cells. Bone, wood, skin, tusks, antlers, and heart muscle—miracle materials all—are made to live out their useful life and then to fade back, to be reabsorbed by another kind of life through the grand cycle of death and renewal.[9]

When industry does find healthy replacements for toxic products these companies will find themselves quickly rewarded by the rapidly growing sustainable design industry which will buy their products. Respecting the Cycle of Life involves eliminating things wherever possible that are toxic to people and the environment. With our current system of production this is not always possible, so the sustainable designer does his or her best to minimize or eliminate problematic materials wherever feasible and to support appropriate alternatives. Respecting the Cycle of Life honors the idea that we are responsible for the things that we create and that through careful, informed design it is possible to create solutions that are safe and responsible. The choices we make today will have consequences for people and animals yet to be born. It should no longer be about choosing between the lesser of two evils, but rather about choosing the right solution. For, as Rachel Carson has put it, "the human race is challenged more than ever before to demonstrate our mastery—not over nature—but of ourselves." [10]

The Principles of Sustainable Design

Respect for Energy and Natural Resources
The Conservation and Renewable Resources Principle

"If we keep going the way we are going, we are going to end up where we are headed."

—Groucho Marx

Respect for Energy and Natural Resources —The Conservation and Renewable Resources Principle

If there is one fact that should be most apparent to us, it is that our society has little respect for the energy and natural resources we have available on this planet. Surely no society that had respect for what it takes to harness energy or what nature does to provide us with material goods would use nature's resources so wantonly, so carelessly, and throw so much away. Based on the best knowledge available today, it appears that we are alone in the solar system in inhabiting a planet that has such an abundance of natural resources—indeed the only one capable of sustaining life. And yet we use our resources as if we have access to multiple planets for sustenance. Of all the principles, The Respect for Energy and Natural Resources covers the most ground and is most directly at the heart of the environmental problems we face today. Simply put, we live in a finite world but treat our resources like they are infinite.

First, let's look at energy. In some way or another, almost all the energy that is available on the earth comes from the sun, or came from the sun at one time. The warm temperature that sustains all life on the earth comes from the sun in the form of electromagnetic radiation. Our atmosphere has been designed beautifully to keep enough of this heat on the earth's surface rather than scattering it back out into the universe as it does in all the other planets and moons in our solar system. At the same time, the atmosphere lets out enough heat that the planet does not bake and dry up, a remarkable feat to say the least. Plants harness the sun's rays using a phenomenal chemical process that is found in a substance called chlorophyll—their efficiency the envy to the makers of the photovoltaic industry. Higher order species derive their energy in turn by ingesting this stored solar energy into their bodies—from the sun's rays to calories on your plate. The fossil fuels we enjoy that fill our cars, heat our homes and cool our beer comes from the same source and converts stored potential energy in decomposing organic matter into kinetic energy. Even wind and tidal power has solar roots. Our currents are owed to the unequal heating of the planet's oceans and the tides to the uneven pull of the sun on our oceans. The only energy sources that are not directly attributable to the sun is that of harnessing nuclear energy from earthen elements and geothermal heat which comes from the earth's core.

The actual amount of energy that is provided by the sun is staggering.

Enough solar energy falls on the earth in a single day to provide the whole planet with its electricity needs for the next twenty-seven years![1] However, this energy is not so easily harnessed. For thousands of years the only source of energy that was available to us was from the food we ingested, and of that food, our bodies are able to convert only eighteen percent of it to useable energy, the rest is wasted as heat. When we learned to domesticate large animals we were able to dramatically improve the amount of energy we had access to, even though an animal like a horse can convert only about ten percent of the food it eats into mechanical energy.

Of course, we benefit in many direct ways from the inefficiency of trying to capture energy from most materials. Burning wood to produce electricity, for example, is terribly inefficient—we derive much more use from the heat that is given off. The transition from wood to peat and coal as a fuel for our heating and energy needs occurred for much of the world in the eighteenth century. However, many third world countries still depend heavily on firewood for their heating and cooking needs, severely impacting our world's forests and increasing desertification. The addition of petroleum-based products as energy sources occurred at the beginning of this century and, as we have already discussed, this transition has resulted in severe consequences to the environment as we moved from utilizing current solar income (food ingested by us or our animals) to old solar capital. It took millions of years for organic matter to turn into petroleum. We run our cars off the remains of pterodactyls and tyrannosaurus rexs. It is amazing to think that we might have used up millions of years of stored potential energy within one hundred and fifty years. Our appetites would have impressed the dinosaurs!

Electricity was first harnessed in the nineteenth century and did not receive widespread usage until early in the twentieth century. Nuclear power was not harnessed as an energy source until the latter half of the century—and we are only just now acknowledging the damaging potential of this technology. It was between the eighteenth and twentieth centuries that our disregard for the preciousness of energy took form. For the first time in human history energy was easy to come by. All people had to do was dig a well in the right place and they could heat millions of homes and fuel the fires of industrial engines all over the world. Energy no longer seemed precious, so why worry about how much was used! Compared to the benefits we were inheriting (or so we thought), even questioning our use of it was folly. In hindsight we know how naive that viewpoint was.

The ultra-conveniences of current energy acquisition and what energy provides for us has blinded us to its consequences. As a society we have totally accepted the idea that it is acceptable to get our energy from old solar capital despite huge repercussions, even when ample renewable energy is available for all our energy needs. Lester Brown shows us that it is possible to get all of our energy needs in this country from the wind available in just three states; Texas, North Dakota and Kansas.[2] We are the only species on the planet that uses combustion as its primary energy source for locomotion—every other species does it through chemical or electrochemical reactions using current solar income.[3] What do they know that we do not? If combustion was such an improvement over biochemical processes that would be one thing, but it is a woefully inefficient way to get energy. A primitive way one might say. We set things on fire, waste the majority of the energy as heat and pollute our water, soil and air in the process. Some great human advancement!

Our beloved automobiles with their internal combustion engines are primary examples of the inefficiency of the combustion process. The authors of Natural Capitalism illustrate this point nicely, showing how the internal combustion engine, as part of our automobile's overall design, is ridiculously inefficient.[4]

> The contemporary automobile, after a century of engineering is embarrassingly inefficient: Of the energy in the fuel it consumes, at least 80 percent is lost, mainly in the engine's heat and exhaust, so that at most only 20 percent is actually used to turn the wheels...of the resulting force, 95 percent moves the car, while only 5 percent moves the driver...Five percent of 20 percent is one percent![5]

Even more frustrating is that despite this embarrassing level of performance we, and the American automobile industry in particular, have resisted the introduction of any innovations that would drastically improve the performance of the technology. The reasons are motivated by greed, ostensibly because it would mean selling less oil to the public, making a few people less rich (often the same people making the cars). Designs for automobiles have been available for twenty years that would yield vehicles that are just as high performing and just as safe as those of today and yet get close to one hundred miles per gallon compared to our present day abysmal fleet average of 20.9 miles per gallon.[6] Thankfully, the fuel cell engine is not far away and will, within the next twenty years, make the internal combustion engine obsolete, powering our cars and buildings while emitting only warm water as a byproduct (and maybe even supplying hot cappuccino from the dashboard of the vehicle!).[7]

Even when we do manage to harness energy from our inefficient and outdated technologies, we are terribly wasteful with how we use it. Most North Americans would be appalled if they learned how much money was thrown away each year and how much pollution could have been avoided by the wasteful practices of our industrial society. Our economy is less than ten percent efficient, and wastes approximately three hundred billion each year with how we use our energy. An average American uses twice as much fossil fuel as the average resident of Great Britain and two and one half times as much as the average Japanese. In fact, the amount of energy we waste in our power plants is roughly equal to the amount of energy that the whole country of Japan actually uses![8] As it is, the United States imports about a third of its energy from abroad, and almost sixty percent of its petroleum.

Let's take a snapshot look at how energy is used and wasted in our country. The United States uses approximately ninety-nine quads of electricity per year.[9] Of that, approximately a third comes from our building power usage.[10] When we turn on our lights or stock our fridge with beer and chicken, we enjoy the benefits of the electricity from these power plants. But behind the scenes there is another story. The electricity we enjoy was created by power plants, usually coal driven but sometimes produced by natural gas turbines or nuclear power plants.[11] The power plants themselves, as we have learned before, are also not very efficient, typically burning coal, mined hundreds of miles away (brought in by rail) and releasing hundreds of thousands of tons of air pollutants including toxic mercury into the atmosphere.[12] Approximately sixteen percent of the energy being generated is wasted during its production into electricity. The remaining energy is brought to our houses by power-lines, stretching dozens of miles from the power plant making stops along the way at stations and substations. During this travel we throw more energy away due to friction in the wires and subject people who live near these power-lines to potentially cancer-causing electromagnetic fields. Once we do get the electricity we wanted (while wasting most of the energy to get it to us) we continue to waste a good deal of the remaining energy through the use of our inefficient refrigerators, lighting and other electrical equipment. For example, a typical incandescent light-bulb found in most homes converts only ten percent of the electricity that it needs to provide light. The rest is wasted as heat. The result is that our grand system of harnessing power is less than one percent efficient from point of generation to end-use. The ultimate example of this wastefulness is the parasitic loads found in almost all of our appliances. Added together, a typical household will throw away ten to twenty percent of its energy in parasitic loads.[13] These are loads that serve almost no purpose, but cost us money and create pollution.

The transportation sector uses about a quarter of our nation's energy. Filling up our automobiles that we now know are only one percent efficient on average is equally telling. The petroleum we use was likely imported from the Middle East, thousands of miles away, in ships so big that it takes two miles for them to come to a stop. It is not surprising that they occasionally break open and do irreparable damage to local ecosystems! At the same time we send several hundred thousand of our finest young people off to risk their lives guarding supplies that are not necessary in the first place.[14] And do not be fooled by the conservatives in Washington and the oil companies that back them. In five to ten years our nation could cut its energy demand by thirty to fifty percent and eliminate the need for all foreign sources of energy without having to drill in the arctic wildlife refuge. We have the technology available today to cut the average building's energy usage in half with only small incremental costs but with paybacks that would make any investor happy. We have the technologies available today to triple the mileage of our cars and trucks without sacrificing performance. If we were really interested in national security and charting our own destiny as a nation and we had the political will to do it, we would get there. The result would 100-200 billion more dollars per year that could be available for critical things like educating our children or universal health care that would actually improve our lives.[15] In fact, the savings would be even more dramatic if we factored in the lives lost and the money spent funding our huge military machine to protect our oil supplies. Our dependence on foreign energy derives from policy, driven by powerful, vested interests trying to maintain the status quo while making financial profit at the expense of the economy, people's lives and the health of the environment.

The Principle of Respect for Energy and Natural Resources states that energy is a critically valuable resource and that the use of energy always comes with great responsibility. We have a responsibility to use as little energy as technologically possible within any design, while striving to maximize the quality of the built environment. We need to head to a future where combustion as a primary mode of deriving energy has been replaced with only renewable sources of fuel. We need to head to a future where all our energy should come directly from the sun, the wind and the tides and from chemical processes within a hydrogen economy.

We must start by recognizing the true costs of energy supply systems in order to level the playing field. Presently, we have a perverse economic framework where it does not pay to conserve because the true costs of polluting have been so cleverly externalized on the public and the environment. If we had to truly account for the true costs of our petroleum, coal and nuclear addictions and recognize their true efficiencies we would be astounded. Suddenly, a solar panel that converts twelve percent of its incident energy to electricity with no operating costs sounds pretty good.

Resources

"No businessman would calculate his net gain without first taking into account the depreciation of his machinery, and the depletion of his stock of raw materials. Why then do Western governments continue to worship the temple of Gross National Product? Is it not time we paid heed to resource exhaustion, to environmental degradation, to the social costs of overcrowding, to the extent of solid waste disposal?"

—Pierre Trudeau

The Conservation and Renewable Resource Principle extends beyond energy to all natural resources we use in the design of the built environment. Our appetite for material or other natural resources in many ways eclipses our appetite for energy. For the most part energy use is a means to an end, whereas the natural resources we consume are typically the end. The Principle of Respecting Energy and Natural Resources extends to how we manage and use the natural resources that we have come to depend on such as water, wood products, metals, and plastics.

The United States is proud to be the biggest and the best at many things, but one thing that we should not be proud of is the fact that the United States holds all the records for resource consumption and wastefulness in the world. Since 1940 Americans alone have used up as large a share of the Earth's mineral resources as all previous generations put together.[16] Due to our voracious appetite for consuming and expanding over the last two hundred years the United States has lost fifty percent of its wetlands, ninety percent of its northwestern old-growth forests and ninety-nine percent of its tall grass prairies.[17] Indeed, the moniker of consumer to describe the typical American is a fitting one. Just a few decades ago people referred to themselves as citizens during an age when the accumulation of material goods was not in and of itself a recreational pursuit. But somewhere in the seventies and eighties the term citizen (which implied responsibility to something greater than an individual) lost favor to the word consumer, appropriately describing our almost cancer-like consumption of the resources around us.[18] In many ways we could be described as resource bulimics, gorging on natural resources without valuing their beauty and function and regurgitating them before their useful life is even over.

Our unhealthy relationship to natural resources is exemplified by the sheer quantity of buildings we erect and demolish in our communities each year. However much we take them for granted, buildings are where Americans spend almost all of their time, as we are an outdoor society no longer. The amount of infrastructure we have in this country is staggering. According to statistics compiled by Environmental Building News, we have approximately 4.6 million commercial buildings in the United States, and we build nearly one hundred and seventy thousand more each year. At the same time, we demolish forty-four thousand commercial buildings each year and send most of the materials to the landfill – many of these buildings are less than thirty years old. On the residential side, there are 101.5 million housing units in the nation, and 63.8 percent are single-family homes. We build nearly two million more homes each year while tearing down a quarter million old ones. The new houses we build to replace the old also tend to be much bigger and carry with it much larger embodied environmental impact. In the forties and fifties the average house size was one thousand one hundred square feet and the average family had five to seven people in it. By 1999 the average new home was two thousand two hundred and fifty square feet with an average of less than four people. While we have made some strides in the efficiency of our homes, at the same time we now have to heat and cool twice as much square footage— an overall drop in environmental performance with nearly a quadrupling of embodied energy per person!

Have we changed so much that we really need three to four times the space for ourselves in just fifty years? The obvious answer is that we now need all of this space to store all of the stuff that we buy each year. While people have not gotten any bigger (well, maybe a little fatter) their possessions sure have. As a consequence, the construction of our buildings consumes about one-fourth of all wood harvested. In fact, according to the Rocky Mountain Institute, three billion tons of raw materials are used annually to construct buildings worldwide.[19] Although we have just five percent of the world's population, we consume a hugely disproportionate share of natural resources such as twenty-seven percent of the aluminum and nineteen percent of the copper. To further illustrate our addiction to the consumption of natural resources, we will look at how we use water, perhaps the most precious natural resource used (and abused) in our buildings.

"Of all our natural resources, water has become the most precious... In an age when man has forgotten his origins and is blind even to his most essential needs for survival, water along with other natural resources has become the victim of his indifference."[20]

As most people know, we need water each day for our very survival. And yet, for a resource that is so fundamental, we do little to protect its quality or to ensure that ample supplies will always be there for future generations. We place little value on the natural resource because we are currently able to get it so cheap. People who sell bottled water understand better its true value. Flying over Phoenix and seeing swimming pool after swimming pool next to lawns and golf courses is a sobering example of how we misuse this precious resource-pumping water from a near depleted aquifer for outdoor uses that result in the water's quick evaporation under the searing desert heat.

An important note to acknowledge is that we are in little danger of running out of water on the planet. The problem is not the amount of water available, but the quality and distribution of that water. The planet earth is comprised of 70.8 percent water. Of this, ninety-seven percent of it is saltwater. Of the remaining three percent, ninety percent is locked up in glaciers, leaving only 0.0001 percent of the fresh water for all our uses and all other terrestrial species on the planet. Of this tiny fraction an almost unfair amount can be found in just three countries—Canada, the United States and Russia, a fact that makes our wastefulness even more irresponsible. While others live with only the barest minimum of water to survive, we throw our water away by the bucketful...or to be more correct, we flush it away. One flush of a standard American toilet requires more water than most individuals around the world get for all their water needs in an entire day.[21]

The United States uses one hundred-twenty-four trillion gallons of water each year. The large majority of that water goes to our food and energy production systems, but approximately thirteen percent is consumed through domestic water use.[22] Breaking this down further, we see that a typical American single-family home uses about 146 000 gallons of water per year (roughly seventy gallons/person/day—forty-two percent indoors and fifty-eight percent outdoors.[23] What is so frustrating is that this amount of water use is extravagant and unnecessary. With the utilization of just a few key technologies and sustainable design strategies we could cut our water use in buildings by up to eighty percent.[24] Composting toilets and xeriscaping alone could reduce our potable water usage by two-thirds.[25] Of this remaining water, a large portion could come from rainwater harvested from rooftops, depending on the climate. A significant portion could also be returned as grey water to be used again, further lowering our water consumption.

The good news is that since the early eighties the overall efficiency of water use in the United States and Canada has been improving. Thirty years ago a typical toilet used five to seven gallons per flush and a typical showerhead spouted two and one half gallons per minute. Today, a toilet uses just over one and a half gallons per flush and a showerhead around one and a half gallons per flush per minute—all without a drop in performance and quality. Thanks to water saving technologies, we may soon be on the path to responsible water use. Waterless urinals are now becoming popular in the market, and hopefully composting toilets and grey water systems are not far behind.

Of course, water is just one case in point. A multitude of further examples abound regarding how we place little respect on the natural resources that sustain us, from our mining practices that give us metals, to our laboratories that turn petrochemicals into plastics and the timber industry that gives us the multitude of wood products. As long as we take the view that what nature provides is without value, indeed that value is only added once industry has transformed it into something new, we will disrespect our natural resources. The Respect for Energy and Natural Resources is a principle that starts out by recognizing that all of our natural resources have intrinsic value and foundational economic value in their natural state.

It is a principle that recognizes that our whole industrial economy is but a mere subset of the natural economy. The more we degrade the natural environment, the more we deplete our natural resource base and the more we erase the base of support for our own economic health.

As with energy, the Principle of Respect for Energy and Natural Resources states that we have a responsibility to use as little of any resource as is necessary for a given job without sacrificing the project's quality and the long-term availability of that resource. Indeed, any natural resource

Life cycle analysis considers a material's impact through all stages of its life from resource extraction through construction, use and disposal.

needs to be chosen based on its appropriateness and environmental impact throughout its entire life cycle. A material that has a low embodied energy or environmental impact in one phase of its life, might in fact have very high impacts in another. Only by studying something from this holistic perspective can we really be certain that the right decisions have been made. Thankfully, a growing field called Life Cycle Analysis (LCA) is beginning to appear that is helping designers make more educated decisions about the overall environmental impact of materials.[26] The diagram shown on the previous page describes the LCA process which investigates the impact of a given material or system at all stages of its life from the extraction of raw materials, to its primary and secondary manufacturing stages, on to installation, use and disposal or reuse.

The final point, is that Respect for Energy and Natural Resources demands that we put strong focus on renewable resources that are harvested and extracted in a way that ensures that they remain renewable. With water, this would mean utilizing water amounts in balance with annual rainfall rather than pumping groundwater. For wood products it would mean cutting trees within a given forest's sustainable yields or using rapidly renewable resources to replace lumber. Countless other examples exist.

Oberlin College by Bill McDonough.

A Brief Survey of Green Buildings

One of the most exciting aspects of the green building movement today is the large diversity of exemplary projects emerging. The photos shown here clearly illustrate the idea that sustainable design is a philosophical approach and not a stylistic endeavor appropriate only in some circumstances with a predetermined aesthetic.

Each project, designed by individuals and firms with a passion for the environment, showcases something different, depending on their location, building type and size. The common thread is the invisible strand that comprises *The Philosophy of Sustainable Design.*

REI Seattle by Mithun Architects.

Island Wood Nature Center in Seattle by Mithun.

The Bateson Building – an early example of green design by Van Der Ryn Architects in Sacremento.

Photo courtesy of JD Peterson.

Photo of Camp Arroyo in California by Siegel & Strain Architects.

Photo courtesy of RMI and Cameron Burns.

Rocky Mountain Institute Headquarters in Colorado.

Photo courtesy of DeWees Island.

DeWees Island aerial photo showing a small green community.

Photo courtesy of Paul Bardagjy.

Headquarters of the Center for Maximum Potential Building Systems (CMPBS) in Austin Texas by Pliny Fisk and Gail Vittori.

Photo courtesy of Matsusaki, Wright.

The CK Choi Building in Vancouver, Canada by Matsuzaki Wright Architects.

Photo courtesy of McDonough + Partners.

The Herman Miller Headquarters Building by Bill Mcdonough.

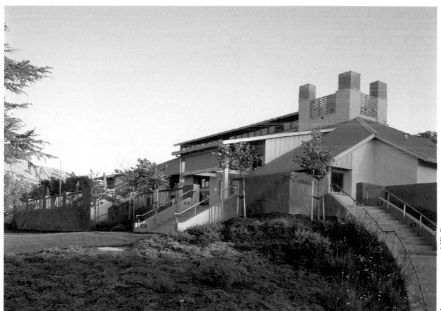

Photo courtesy of JD Peterson.

Camp Arroyo in California by Siegel & Strain Architects.

The Deramus Education Pavilion in Kansas City by BNIM Architects.

The University of Texas Health Science Center School of Nursing and Student Community Center in Houston, TX by BNIM Architects and Lake Flato.

The Deramus Education Pavilion in Kansas City by BNIM Architects.

The Edificio Malecon in Buenos Aires, Argentina by HOK Architects.

The Green Dirt Sheep Barn in Weston, Missouri by Jason McLennan & Chris DeVolder.

Photo courtesy of McLennan.

The San Mateo County Sheriff's Forensic Laboratory and Coroner's Office in San Mateo, CA by HOK Architects.

Photo courtesy of HOK Architects.

The LadyBird Johnson Wildflower Center in Austin, Texas by Overland Architects.

Photo courtesy of Timothy Hursley.

The LadyBird Johnson Wildflower Center in Austin, Texas by Overland Architects.

Photo courtesy of Timothy Hursley.

The Cusano Environmental Education Center in Philadelphia, PA by Susan Maxman and Partners

Photo Courtesy of Barry Halkin.

The Cusano Environmental Education Center in Philadelphia, PA by Susan Maxman and Partners

Photo Courtesy of Barry Halkin.

Courtesy of ZGF.

The Donald Bren School of Environmental Science & Management in Santa Barbara by Zimmer Gunsel Fransca Architects.

Photo courtesy of Lake Flato Architects.

The Shrack residence in Virginia by Lake Flato Architects.

CHAPTER EIGHT

Photo Courtesy of BNIM Architects

The Principles of Sustainable Design

Respect for Process
The Holistic Thinking Principle

> *"Most people are more comfortable with old problems than with new solutions."*
>
> —Charles Browe

Respect for Process—The Holistic Thinking Principle

The final principle of sustainable design is Respect for Process. In some ways it is the least tangible of the principles because it deals not so much with what things are done, but the ways in which they are done. It is also the most simple of the principles in that its major message can be summed up by a single sentence; **if we want to change a result, we must first change the process that led to the result.**

As a society, we are famous for doing things the same old way, and yet being surprised when the result is not different. We continue to under-invest in education, and wonder why our children are not being educated properly. We continue to celebrate the gun culture, and make handguns available to just about anyone, and then wonder why there are so many gun-related deaths. In the Middle East, we counter aggression with aggression, and wonder why there is no peace.

Respect for Process requires an unyielding recognition that we must change the way we think and the way we act if we want a different result from the past. With sustainable design this is imperative. It is not possible to build sustainably with the same design and construction processes that have created the environmental burdens in the first place. In the design world, change can sometimes be incredibly difficult, not because people do not see the need to change, or are not willing to try out new materials or technologies, but because people often do not see the connection between how they do something and the result. They focus instead on individual components, and making small scale changes to the tangible parts of the project. Rarely do they revisit the framework upon which the need for components is identified. They do not question their decision-making process and underlying assumptions. Indeed, for many in the building profession, their design, engineering or construction process is sacred. For architects and designers it is often a process that was ingrained in school because the studio culture[1] influenced how they approached a new design assignment. Many designers still look back fondly to the time when they learned to design and feel uncomfortable with anything that forces them to reconsider the process by which they make decisions. Until very recently few design schools in North America focused on the broader impacts and responsibilities of design that the sustainable design movement has brought to the forefront. Successful designs were judged within a narrow band of criterion, often with a focus on aesthetics at the cost of other issues such as constructability, cost and environmental impact. Some of the best minds in the business were sent out to practice armed with incomplete information and an incomplete understanding of the interconnections between decisions and the resulting impacts.

For engineers the process was different, but no less limiting. For many engineers, their education consisted of learning formulas and rules of thumb solutions with an almost religious focus on mechanical, and often energy and resource intensive solutions. The notion of first looking to nature for innovations or for comfort would not only have been foreign, but would have been ridiculed. Serious engineers learned the one right way of solving problems. If it was not in the textbook or did not fit on the chart it would not work. Many engineering schools discouraged innovation and rewarded a more conservative approach to problem solving, which explains the slow rate of acceptance for green ideas within this sector of the building industry. With many engineers that which "cannot be weighed, measured or counted does not exist."[2]

The construction profession shared similar characteristics with engineering, albeit with a much less academic basis focused on experience, or how things have always been done. Builders learned how to build from other builders and the process of thinking about how buildings should be built was passed on through generations. For many, there is definitely a right and wrong way of building; the right way being the way that they learned, or the way that is the most simple and cost effective for them. Construction solutions that differed from the norm would often meet with extreme skepticism and sometimes ridicule. It is no surprise that we are building houses in almost the exact same way we built them one hundred years ago, with the construction industry being one of the least innovative fields in our economy. In fact, quality workmanship has also gone down over the same time period. A quick comparison to the health care industry in the last one hundred years provides a meaningful comparison to the amount of change that has occurred in other fields. The hospital has changed greatly in one hundred years. The house on the other hand, is not much different, except that its size and cost has risen while qualities of workmanship have declined. In most ways it has remained the same. What is interesting, however, is that the green building movement is creating more change to the building industry in the last twenty years than any other factor.

Once someone's design process has been ingrained within an individual, he or she views all future interactions with the built environment and the natural environment through this filter. The Respect for Process principle clearly states that to truly achieve sustainability, people must change the way they think, change the way they interact with other individuals in the profession and change the process to design and construction. The biggest single change that could be made in the building profession is not the invention of a new technology but a change in the mindset of all the designers and engineers who select technologies to begin with. Bill McDonough has eloquently stated this idea by saying "we need to take the filters from our pipes and put them in our designers' heads."[3] It is far more powerful to design a process that does not require energy than one that has been optimized to use as little energy as possible. The goals might have been the same, but the process resulted in a big difference in performance. So how does someone follow this last sustainable design principle? The answer is to be found through adopting all of the sub-principles explained below.

The Sub-Principles of the Respect for Process

1. A Commitment to Collaboration and Interdisciplinary Communication
2. A Commitment to Holistic Thinking
3. A Commitment to Life-long Learning and Continual Improvement
4. A Commitment to Challenging Rules of Thumb
5. A Commitment to Allowing for Time to Make Good Decisions
6. A Commitment to Rewarding Innovation

1. A Commitment to Collaboration and Interdisciplinary Communication

Sustainable design requires a commitment to breaking down the barriers that often exist between the disciplines. Architects, engineers, builders and developers must learn to find ways to increase communication and increase integration between the disciplines. Too often people hide behind their particular field of experience and do not try to venture outside that which is familiar to them. To build sustainably, design teams must embrace the knowledge that can be found in all professions. In many cases, the circle of those who contribute to a project should be widened. It is rare that one individual has the capacity to create design solutions that are robust enough to meet all the requirements for a project to be sustainable.

The idea of the lone creative genius as found in Ayn Rand's *Fountainhead* must be replaced with a circle of creative genius spanning a diverse array of experiences and expertise.

This sub-principle recognizes that the current focus on specialization often weakens our potential to come up with innovative solutions to critical problems. John Ralston Saul has strongly stated that: "There is absolutely no need …. to turn out 21 year old specialists equipped with no memory of their civilization's experience, no ethical context, no sense of the larger shape of their society"[4] "…But what could be cruder than a human being, who is limited to a narrow area of knowledge and practice and has the naiveté of a child in most other areas?"[5]

The truth is that we do, in fact, need people who intimately understand the workings of very specific subjects, but they need to be taught a different process of thinking. This process is inclusive and respectful of other disciplines, and incorporates ideas brought forth by individuals even when they are not experts in the particular field in question. Sometimes the people who know the most about the field overlook the simple questions and solutions to problems. Specialists need to be instilled with an understanding of how their field must rely on and contribute to other fields and have a humbleness to know that specialization by its nature means limited knowledge of other areas. In addition to specialists, project teams also need integrators, generalists who have enough specific information in a variety of topics to understand how to make connections between people, their ideas and their solutions.

Bob Berkebile tells a story of when he was once a member of a seven-person team picked by the National Science Foundation to travel to Antarctic. The team was sent to help investigate how research scientists stationed at the North Pole could continue their research while minimizing their impact on the fragile ecosystem that they were trying to protect. A year earlier the scientists underwent a change that saw computer labs in each department or field of expertise get combined into one larger computer lab to save on costs. At the time this was a widely unpopular decision as each department thought that their research would be weakened by having to share resources with individuals who were studying completely different issues in different disciplines. A year later, when Berkebile arrived, the "experiment" was showing some very different results. Twelve months after the shift to a combined lab it was shown that almost every major breakthrough in the year's research had occurred in that computer lab. Problems would be solved as scientists shared their problems with scientists in other disciplines sitting next to them. Sometimes it was the simple questions asked by other scientists that led to the breakthrough. At other times an answer was found in the other person's research that was originally thought to be unrelated. This finding proved to be a powerful lesson in the strength of collaboration and interdisciplinary communication.

2. A Commitment to Holistic Thinking

Albert Einstein once said, "No problem can be solved by the same manner of thinking that created it."[6] Respect for Process requires challenging conventional thinking to broaden the issues that are considered with any problem. Done right, this is called holistic thinking. Holistic thinking is the mode of thinking that is required for any project to truly be sustainable in performance. This sub-principle is so important that a whole chapter of this book is devoted to it. See Chapter Fourteen—Holistic Thinking–The Sustainable Design Process.

To provide one example of how we are taught to think within a very rigid framework we turn to author Benjamin Hoff. In his book the *TE of Piglet*, he tells a convincing story of the type of education we receive that teaches us a narrowly defined way of thinking:

"This sort of thing, we're told, will help us once we graduate—help us apply our learning to everyday matters and, ideally, help us discern the true from the false...

There are three hundred cows in a field. The gate has been left open, and two cows pass through it every minute. How many cows are left in the field after an hour and a half?"[7]

Hoff goes on to point out, "If you have ever herded cattle, you know that cows do not pass through an open gate at the rate of two per minute. They either go through all at once, or not at all"[8] Holistic thinking always looks, to the greatest extent possible, beyond how issues are narrowly defined.

3. A Commitment to Life-long Learning and Continual Improvement

"The problem is not to teach skills in a galloping technology, but to teach students to think and to give them the tools of thought so that they can react to the myriad of changes, including technological, that will inevitably face them over the next decades."[9]

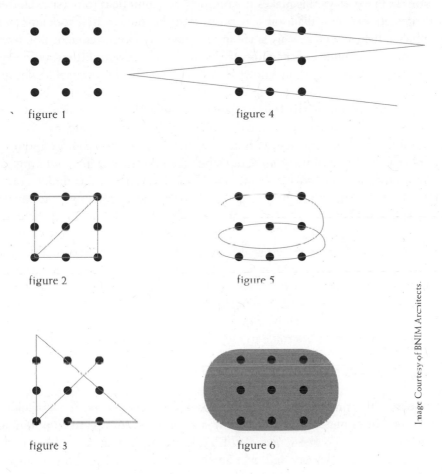

figure 1   figure 4

figure 2   figure 5

figure 3   figure 6

Image Courtesy of BNIM Architects.

The diagram above illustrates the principle of Holistic Thinking. Six dots are drawn (figure. 1) and a person is asked to connect the dots in as few lines as possible. Conventional thinking would result in several lines shown in order to connect the dots as in figure 2. However, the instructions never said you had to 'stay within the box'. Someone thinking more holistically might connect the dots in four lines as in figure 3 or three lines as in figure 4. And yet, the instructions also did not say anything about the lines having to be straight. Figure 5 shows the dots being connected with one curvy line! Figure 6 shows another holistic approach – this time achieved by using a very fat pen. Holistic thinking requires thinking outside conventional processes and realizing that most barriers are perceptual rather than real.

The issues that surround sustainable design are complex and challenging. In many ways this makes it a highly rewarding field to pursue. Under conventional specialization it is possible to become quite proficient at a chosen field and make only small improvements to knowledge or skill over many years. Since other fields are deemed less relevant, little time needs to be wasted expanding knowledge outwards. With sustainable design comes an understanding that all knowledge is connected, and therefore, very little is not worth learning about. As Francis Bacon once said, "all knowledge must be you're providence." Pushing the boundaries of environmental performance without sacrificing cost and comfort requires more knowledge of the connections between disciplines. It is not enough to study things in isolation, one must look for synergies as underscored by E.O Wilson, when he notes that "a balanced perspective cannot be acquired by studying disciplines in pieces but through pursuit of the consileince among them."[10] The only true barriers stem from our own limitations. With sustainable design it is impossible in any one person's lifetime to become an expert in all aspects of the field. Therefore, the practice of sustainable design requires a commitment to life-long learning and continual improvement. Since the field is rapidly expanding, and technologies and systems being developed, one must continue to pursue active self-education. We need to continue to raise the bar in our own standards.

4. A Commitment to Challenging Rules of Thumb

Most of the time environmental problems are created not by malicious intent, but rather by a system that was set up without regard to potential environmental consequences. Without changing the underlying system, mistakes get made over and over again, despite often-good intentions. In the building industry, an example of this phenomena are the millions of "rules of thumb" decisions that get made by architects, engineers, builders and developers. For the architect it is often standard specifications or standard details that get implemented on dozens of projects. For the engineers, it is rule of thumb sizing of mechanical or structural systems. For the builder, it is the process of building itself, and for the developer it may be standard payback rules or tenant requirements. Regardless of the exact form, when rules of thumb exist, they open up the possibility of systematizing mistakes or imposing high impact environmental burdens.

While it is inefficient to reinvent something for each project it is certainly appropriate to revisit and question standard assumptions or rules of thumb to see if they still apply for a given situation (climate, building type, etc.) or whether the issue in question could be improved in any way, including its environmental performance. The principle of Respect for Process requires that individuals routinely revisit standard process, looking for ways to improve all aspects of its use. It also requires that individuals routinely compare rules of thumb with reality, by measuring and monitoring real, built examples of the issue in question. Is it really working as planned? Does a better way become apparent? It is amazing how few people in the design professions revisit old projects with a skeptical eye to learn what things could have been done better. Similarly, few engineers ever measure how their building is actually behaving. Is the building using as much energy as was planned? Does the delivery system really provide comfort? Without a reality check, mistakes get repeated and repeated, when often a simple visit would have caught the error.

5. A Commitment to Allowing for Time to Make Good Decisions

Often in the building industry clients or developers are in a desperate hurry to get construction underway as time costs a lot of money. The longer a project is in construction the greater the financial implication related to the project's financing, the length of time until rents can be collected or staff begin working. While the desire to wait until the last moment and then to build quickly is understandable, it rarely makes long-term financial or operational success. The rushed process often is the cause of many mistakes that could easily have been avoided. Bob Berkebile describes it as "ready, fire, aim", which is unfortunately the paradigm in the majority of the projects built each year. Scrimping on the planning process might seem to save money, but invariably costs an organization a great deal more money year in and year out. While no amount of planning can eliminate all potential problems, allowing for adequate time to thoroughly plan and think things through can pay off significantly in the future. It is essential to recognize and respect the added time needed for effective collaboration among disciplines. A lack of respect for the time it takes to do a project is not just the domain of traditional developers. Many individuals in the green movement also seem to fall trap to this paradigm. These individuals will set high performance goals and lofty standards, but will then squeeze the project schedule as tight as possible, not recognizing that through their actions they have effectively killed the potential to actually meet their goals.

This is not to say that building green will always take more time. The time factor depends on a lot of variables such as the experience of the team, type of project and level of performance targeted but one should not assume that it will take the same time or less than normal if high levels of performance are desired. Extra time is not intended to make it easier for the design team or to build in slack, as the pace of the project should be just as fast as with a normal project. The added time is necessary to allow for additional things to happen that are important such as more design meetings, material and systems research, and modeling. At the beginning of a project the whole team should make a concerted effort to estimate how much time is really needed to do a project well and then to fight to see that this time is kept in the process. The final point is that sometimes allowing for the right time to make good decisions is not about adding overall time to the design process, but redistributing how that time is spent. Spending more time in the early stages of a project, including the programming and schematic design phase, often does the most to make sure that the big mistakes at least are avoided.

The responsibility of the Respect for Process principle extends to the development community as well as the design community. This principle states that good design takes time in order to allow for greater collaboration and communication among all members of the design team. It requires a recognition that economic decisions must be made within a larger framework and it discourages the approach of cheapest solution at all costs and advocates one that looks at the overall costs of a construction project.

6. A Commitment to Rewarding Innovation

Our society, for all its advances, has a funny way of rewarding mediocrity and the status quo rather than institutionalizing a way of continual improvement and excellence. Our history has taught us that rewarding people for their ideas, innovations and inventions makes for a better society. But people fear that somehow new things will make changes for the worse, because sometimes they do. Those at the top, who often set the rules, fear that with too much change or innovation their own position might change.

In most sectors of the economy, great ideas happen in spite of the system rather than because of it. As a society we are extremely fearful of change, even while mouthing the words that "change is good." We stunt our growth and potential every day with the decisions that we make. Many times our lack of commitment to rewarding innovation is demonstrated by how we describe things. For example,

"Growth, as we currently understand it, classifies education as a cost, thus a liability. A golf ball, on the other hand, is an asset and the sale of it a measurable factor of growth. A face-lift is an element of economic activity while a heart bypass is a liability, which the economy must finance. Holidays are among the pearls of the service industry, while childcare is a cost."[11]

The sub-principle of rewarding innovation requires that individuals accept a certain amount of risk. Being too risk averse leads to mediocrity. Sometimes it seems amazing that buildings get built at all with how risk averse the industry has become. It is essential to find ways to support emerging territories of technologies and approaches. If we are to be successful at safeguarding the environment for future generations and maintaining the quality of life we now enjoy, we will need to find the fortitude to try vastly different things than we currently embrace. We must also find ways to recognize and reward individuals who take these steps and in so doing help us all move closer to environmental stewardship. We must reward engineers for the efficiency of their designs, not just their sufficiency. We must reward designers of all types for productivity improvements and environmental performance and not just for aesthetic qualities.

CHAPTER NINE

Photo courtesy of McDonough + Partners Gap Headquarters

The Technologies and Components of Sustainable Design

"the only way to make change, is to make that which you hope to change obsolete"

—Buckminster Fuller

The Technologies and Components of Sustainable Design

Sustainable design is much more than a shopping list of technologies and strategies that can be found in any particular building. It is a philosophical approach to the design process with clear objectives regarding environmental performance and the impact to human health and well-being. The presence of any particular technology or strategy does not necessarily mean that the project is green, and so evaluation solely on a list of features should be avoided. And yet, certain technologies and strategies seem to reoccur with frequency and when people describe a green building they invariably begin to list its features. It is the intent of this chapter to introduce the technologies and strategies that are most commonly utilized in green buildings. The chapter is a mere starting point for an understanding of a few of the key technologies and issues involved in sustainable design and so people are encouraged to look at the resource list for further information.

This chapter highlights the topics that receive the most attention in the green building industry today or have the most potential to contribute to the reduction of environmental impact in the near future. For the sake of clarity, each topic will be addressed in the following manner:

- What is the technology or strategy in question?
- What is its potential to reduce environmental impact?
- What are the barriers (if any) of increased use of the technology or strategy?
- Where can people go to learn more about the subject? (Building your own green library could be a good by-product of this chapter!)

The topics listed are organized loosely around a few key categories:

1. Water and Waste
2. Energy Generation
3. Green Comfort Systems
4. Alternative Construction
5. Materials
6. Envelope Systems

Water and Waste

Water resource issues will likely become one of the most important problems facing people in the decades ahead. The scarcity of clean, potable water will likely fuel conflicts between nations and lead to suffering for millions. Even in the United States and Canada, where much of the world's fresh water can be found, water scarcity and water quality problems are becoming a growing issue. While many technologies and strategies exist to help conserve or protect water resources, not enough are in common use. For instance, only in the last few years have we seen the adoption of low-flow fixtures for showers, sinks and toilets to reduce the amount of water used and motion sensors that turn water on only when it is needed. Even more scarce is a water conservation ethic. Many people use water wantonly, further exacerbating the problem. As a result, green buildings often focus on ways to reduce the amount of water used and to protect water quality. A few key technologies and strategies receive the most attention from green designers in relation to water and waste.

Living Machines and Biological Waste Water Treatment Centers

In the eighties John Todd, a biologist in Vermont, invented a technology that he called a living machine to treat building effluent in a way that mimicked nature's ability to purify water in swamps and marshes. A Living Machine is actually the trademark name for a new class of waste treatment (ecological waste treatment) that utilizes microorganisms, plants, oxygen and sunlight to neutralize waste. Todd realized that if he could create a system that maximized nature's ability to do its job it could become an effective way of reducing the amount of chemicals and energy needed to purify waste. The discovery was an elegant alternative to the conventional rancid waste treatment plant that people hate to drive by. In its place is a system so beautiful and elegant that many of the high profile green buildings have living machines featured prominently in the design. Imagine a waste treatment plant that people would actually want to visit! A living machine is often designed in the most prominent part of the building such as a lobby or other gathering area, encouraging many visitors to see the system and begin to connect what happens to the environment with each flush. The living machine in many ways became the poster child for green design in the nineties. Many people believe that it was hard to get much

Waste treatment tank as part of a 'Living Machine' system in Burlington, Vermont.

greener when toilet water was being scrubbed in a large greenhouse filled with tropical foliage.

Living machines operate with the help of sunlight, oxygen and a large array of microorganisms, plants, snails and fish that break down and digest organic pollutants. The water can then be used again in the building for toilet flushing or irrigation or released, as it would in typical treatment plants. While living machines are custom designed for each application and range in size from just a few square feet to several hundred, specific components remain constant. The effluent flows from the building into an anaerobic reactor (without oxygen) where bio-solids are digested. The effluent is then transported to a closed, aerated aerobic reactor that removes odor and continues the purification process. From there the waste travels through a series of open aerobic reactors, each functioning as a mini-eco-system, with toilet waste serving as the system's food. A clarifier allows any solids to settle and the resulting fluids are further filtered in specialized ecosystems in combination with a UV disinfection process. Solids from the clarifier are then fed back into the system and the cycle continues.

While popular and effective, the systems have their problems, most notably the cost. The budget for most buildings does not include funds for their own waste treatment facility, which requires substantial initial first-cost premiums and also requires ongoing maintenance and operation expenses. As a living system, the technology must be kept alive, even when building occupants are away for periods of time (dog food turned out to be a good substitute for human waste!) In other words, the system requires that knowledgeable operators be on hand to make sure that the system stays on-line. From an environmental standpoint, it is also not clear if the living machine automatically results in reduced environmental impact. The construction of living machines (tanks, pumps, filters, etc.) carry a certain amount of embodied energy that can be offset with certain economies of scale, but perhaps cannot be justified on the basis of every building having a living machine. More reasonable is the idea of living machines on a neighborhood or building complex scale, where the operational impacts can offset the embodied ones and the financial premium can be shared among building owners, just like conventional utilities. It is also important to point out that living machines do not actually reduce the amount of water used and for real advantage should be combined with water conservation strategies such as low flush toilets and fixtures. Living machines will continue to have a small, albeit highly visible role in the green buildings of the next decade.

For more information on Living Machines and Waste Treatment Centers see the following books and websites:

From Eco-Cities to Living Machines: Principles of Ecological Design
John Todd and Nancy Jack Todd 1994

Living Machines Inc.
http://www.livingmachines.com

Living Technologies
http://www.ltluk.com

Composting Toilets

In the seventies, Sym Van Der Ryn wrote a great little book called *The Toilet Papers* that reminded us that we should not be defecating in our water sup-

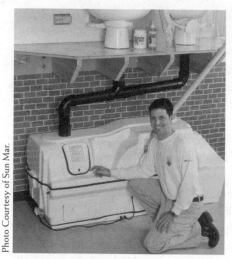

A Centrex 3000 composting toilet from Sun Mar Corporation.

ply and preached the virtues of the composting toilet. Since that time, composting toilets have seen only limited use around the country, mostly in remote camping situations. In fact, in many jurisdictions around the country, it is against code to install a composting toilet as a replacement for conventional flush systems. For many individuals, composting toilets conjure up bad memories of stinky outhouses and uncomfortable camping experiences. Composting toilets are hard for many to adopt, even among sustainable design supporters because this type of toilet, unlike the living machine, requires a behavioral change and a perceptual shift in thinking. Many people are attached to the habit of the flush. With a whoosh of water our wastes are carried away, out of sight, out of mind. We have become a culture embarrassed by our bodily functions! There is also a collective cultural memory of health problems caused by sewage before the invention of the toilet by Thomas Crapper in the nineteenth century. For most people, anything other than the flush toilet somehow seems less sanitary. And yet, this is no longer true.

To be clear, composting toilets are not outhouses. The good ones are odour free and work well. Typically, waste is dropped down a small hole in the bottom of the vessel, and any odors are kept in check by a small downdraft fan and an aerobic composting process in the receiving tank that eliminates smells. Some of the newer models even look like normal toilets and come with a flushing feature that emits a small amount of a soap solution, instantly conjuring up images of cleanliness.

Today, in the United States, flush toilets account for close to half of the water used in a typical household. Each year we waste five billion gallons of potable water by flushing toilets.[1] Almost as important as this water waste is the disruption to the Cycle of Life through the destruction of valuable nutrients contained in our bodily waste. In nature, nutrients in food that is consumed by other animals is always returned to the soil to provide nutrients to other plants and animals. Nothing is wasted. Unfortunately, on the human side, much is wasted. A large portion of the earth's productive land is now used to provide nutrients for human consumption but the nutrients in human excrement are lost to the Cycle of Life by the flush and chemical treatment process. Composting toilets could help restore some balance by providing safe, useable compost with almost no negative environmental impact.

In the coming decades composting toilets will slowly gain acceptance as the appropriate replacement for flush toilets in low-rise buildings.[2] Some of the acceptance will be generational based - as those not old enough to remember the era of outhouses will have less bias against composting toilets. More widespread acceptance will take time however, until perceptual and legal barriers to the technology break down.

For good bathroom reading, try the following websites and resources:

The Toilet Papers: Designs to Recycle Human Waste and Water,
by Sim Van Der Ryn and Wendell Berry, 1978

Clivus Multrum
http://www.clivus.com

Sun Mar Composting Toilets
http://sun-mar.com

Waterless Urinals

Why do we need water to transport water? The answer is that we do not. Waterless urinals which are designed to drain urine without the need for flushing have now hit the market. A small liquid chemical trap is usually incorporated into the design that allows urine to drain quickly, but prevents odors from rising through it. In almost every other way, waterless urinals are similar to conventional urinals. They look, function, cost and require about the same maintenance as conventional urinals yet they save thousands of gallons of water per year. Waterless urinals are quickly catching on around the country, and unlike the composting toilet, will see widespread mainstream use within the decade.

No books exist yet on the waterless urinal. Visit these websites for more information:

Falcon WaterFree Technologies
http://www.falconwaterfree.com

WaterLess Company
http://www.waterless.com

Xeriscaping

Americans love their lawns almost as much as their cars. The two go hand-in-hand in creating environmental problems but in different areas; one with air pollution, the other with water. The way most homeowners and businesses landscape requires huge amounts of water and chemical fertilizers. The typical culprit is the selection of grass and plants that were never designed or evolved to be in areas that have dry periods. For example, the plants used in landscaping in Phoenix, Arizona should be very different than the plants used in Atlanta, Georgia. Unfortunately,

Photo courtesy of 2020 Engineers.

A green roof on a building in Seattle.

we have developed an aesthetic fondness for the perfect lawn that requires chemicals to control weeds (defined as any plant other than the grass) and frequent mowing with gas-eating mowers that are extremely polluting.

The appropriate environmental response is called Xeriscape or natural landscape. Xeriscape is not so much a technology as it is the landscape equivalent of the sustainable design philosophy. The term refers to the use of indigenous plantings (or at least plants from a similar climate) that require no use of water or chemical inputs to keep them healthy or alive.

The only water that is typically used in addition to rainfall is for propagation, and sometimes to weather unusually harsh periods of drought. In these instances, stored rainwater is preferred. Planting species that evolved in the same region helps to maintain genetic diversity against an onslaught of foreign, invasive species. This type of planting can also be a way of helping local biodiversity because some native plants are endangered, as are the insects and birds that feed on them. The result of xeriscaping helps enrich the cultural heritage of a place.

In many cases xeriscaping also saves money because of reduced maintenance and water costs. While it is not clear when the love affair with the lawn or exotic plant species will diminish, rising pressures on water resources and large potential cost savings will eventually help xeriscaping gain mainstream acceptance. As it becomes more mainstream, aesthetic sensibilities will change, further hastening the switch. Hopefully, in a few decades Kentucky bluegrass (which is not even from Kentucky) will only be found in climates that can truly support it!

There are many great resources on the topic of xeriscaping. Try these two to learn more:

Xeriscape Handbook: A How—To Guide to Natural, Resource Wise Gardening
Gayle Weinstein 2003

Xeriscape Plant Guide: 100 Water-Wise Plants for Gardens and Landscapes
Denver Water, Rob Proctor 1999

Rainwater Collection and Grey-water Systems

The last major pieces to the water conservation and water quality puzzle is that of rooftop rainwater collection and grey-water systems. Of the two, rainwater collection systems are the most straightforward and can be as simple as having the roof downspouts drain to a small barrel. More sophisticated is a series of above or below ground tanks properly sized to ensure that water is available year-round through periods of little rain. The complexity of rainwater systems changes depending on the use for the water. If used for irrigation, the system can be quite simple. If used to flush toilets, or for other internal building uses, rainwater systems can become

Photo courtesy of HOK and Steve Hall, Hedrich-Blessing.

Rooftop rain collection cisterns shown on the Nidus Center for Scientific Enterprise in St. Louis, Missouri by HOK Architects.

more complex and become a part of a grey-water system for the house.

The term grey-water acknowledges the fact that water has various levels of quality, many of which are very suitable for a variety of things we currently use only potable water for—like flushing toilets. Why do we need drinking quality water to flush toilets? Instead of the black and white division of water that we currently have, grey-water systems differentiate between black-water (which potentially contains harmful pathogens) and grey-water, which is not suitable for ingestion, but could be useful for certain functions, and potable water which is fit for human consumption. Since grey-water systems allow for water to be useful more than once in a building, they have the potential to save large amounts of water.

However, grey-water systems are used very infrequently in North America. As with composting toilets, there is a collective cultural memory of unsanitary water causing severe health problems, and so in many jurisdictions it is actually against code to install a true grey-water system, although the areas where it is approved is growing. Grey-water systems also add significant first costs to a project by requiring double plumbing to keep the water separate, and tanks or cisterns to store it. In parts of the country, where water costs are high, it makes long-term economic sense to install a grey-water system, but in most places the payback is extremely long. Grey-water systems will continue to be rare over the next decade, with the exception of rooftop rainwater collection for irrigation which will see increased usage. As water problems intensify over the next twenty to thirty years, full grey-water systems will become an important part of our building future.

For more information on Rain Water Systems and Grey Water look to the following:

Texas Guide to Rainwater Harvesting
The Center for Maximum Potential Building Systems, 1997

Create an Oasis With Greywater: Your Complete Guide to Choosing, Building and Using Greywater Systems
Art Ludwig, 1997

Energy Generation

In terms of iconic technologies of the green building movement, nothing has been as powerful as that of a solar panel or wind turbine next to a building. Generating energy cleanly through the sun and wind represents the holy grail of sustainable living. And yet, the paradox is that these technologies are still rarely used in most green buildings, and where used, they are often used in token amounts to raise awareness or make a statement or proclamation of sustainability rather than to really lower impact. The holy trinity of sustainable energy generation could be identified as photovoltaics, wind turbines and fuel cells (although other promising technologies exist such as micro-turbines and sterling engines). These three alternatives are discussed here.

Photovoltaics

Photovoltaics (PV), otherwise known as solar panels, are wonderful technologies that generate electricity from sunlight while creating no pollution. Simply put, the technology works because particles in the panel get excited in the presence of sunlight and emit electricity. The more intense the solar radiation is, the more energy is generated. Solar panels typically come as rigid, single or mono-crystalline cells[3] arranged in a small panel, or as flexible strips called amorphous silicon.[4] Crystalline solar panels are typically mounted on rooftop stand-alone structures but can also be integrated into glazing units or skylights. Small panels can be grouped into larger arrays that can generate significant amounts of power for a building

Photo Courtesy of BNIM Architects.

Photovoltaic Cells integrated into a greenhouse at the Missouri Department of Conservation Headquarters in Kansas City, Missouri by BNIM Architects.

or industrial application. Amorphous silicon panels can be more closely integrated into building products such as metal roofing or shingles and can be made to conform to many shapes. From a designer's standpoint, the most exciting development in the PV industry has been the development of a range of building-integrated photovoltaics (BIPV) that can be used as an integral part of an architectural design. With BIPV products, solar panels are not applied to a roof or wall surface, but instead are the roof or wall-weathering surface. Unlike a granite or metal panel the product performs an aesthetic and weatherproofing function and saves money through reduced energy costs. Photovoltaic panels should not be confused with solar thermal panels that use the sun to heat water or that use a chemical solution in a panel for water heating purposes. Solar thermal panels are also an important technology in the green building movement.

Obviously, photovoltaics cannot generate electricity at night and so the energy must be stored to be useful when the sun goes down, or configured as part of the utility grid that shares and takes energy when needed. Storing energy requires the use of batteries, which are the weakest link in the PV technology toolkit. The batteries typically have high-embodied environmental impacts, a short to moderate lifespan, and are expensive (not to mention a toxic disposal hazard). More compelling is the notion of a grid-interactive system that does away with the need for batteries and gives and sells power to a local utility. In summer months, a building might generate more power than it needs and ideally be able to sell excess power back to the grid, usually at peak usage times for the utility—the hot summer. Then, in the winter when not enough energy is generated, the building can purchase additional power from the grid. This process is called net metering. In some states, local utilities are required to purchase excess power from a building but in most jurisdictions this is not the case.

Photovoltaics panels are most effective when perpendicular to the sun's rays on the south side of a building. The farther away from the ideal orientation, the less effective the panels are. In general, for a fixed array, the ideal overall orientation is for a panel to be oriented due south at the same angle as the site's latitude. As one goes north the angle increases, and south to the equator it flattens out. To maximize summer harvest a panel is laid more horizontal; to maximize winter, more vertical. Expensive tracking systems have been developed that move with the sun to maximize output. However, due to the expense and maintenance issues, fixed position solar panels are more common.

At the moment solar panels continue to be a very expensive technology with fairly long paybacks that most decision makers find difficult to justify. This is the single most influential reason why photovoltaics are not used more commonly. The technology is no longer an experimental technology, and very few technical reasons exist to avoid it. Prices continue to come down, albeit slowly, and at some point in the near future, likely within the next fifteen years, the price will become competitive with other forms of electricity generation.[5] Due to the low cost of energy, there has been little incentive for people to invest in photovoltaics and so mass production that would bring the costs down significantly has not materialized. Most of the companies that are now producing photovoltaics are also owned by petrochemical corporations (which seem to be hedging their bets) that have little incentive to lower costs and begin to compete with their more profitable business of changing climate through oil.[6]

The next barrier to photovoltaic panels is the amount of aperture that is needed to generate the kinds of energy that most buildings use. It is relatively easy, with ample money, to take a house off the grid because the amount of aperture compared with the square footage of the building is high. In a large building, the amount of rooftop surface is typically small compared to the number of floors and square footage below it. As efficiencies in our buildings and the panels rise, smaller apertures will be needed to produce the same energy. While the future for PV is very bright, we will likely see a slow growth in PV use over the next ten to fifteen years with the pace picking up substantially in the next twenty years.

There are some great resources on Photovotaics and building integrated PV. To begin your journey look to the following resources:

American Solar Energy Society
http://www.ases.org

The National Center for Photovoltaics
http://www.nrel.gov/ncpv/

The National Renewable Energy Lab
http://www.nrel.gov/

The Solar Electric House,
by Steven J. Strong

Wind Power

Wind power has outstanding promise to help us in our efforts to transform to a sustainable society. The technology has made huge leaps and bounds over the last decade in terms of cost, efficiency and reliability. In some parts of the country, wind power is now competitive with any other electricity sources and substantive wind-farms are popping up all over parts of the world. Indeed, wind power is the fastest growing energy source in the country. Over the next decade we will see a plethora of new wind-farms in certain regions of the country and despite current political policies, wind will begin to play a major role in our country's energy future. A major obstacle appears to be a growing dislike by some segments of the population regarding how wind turbines look, creating a small "not in my backyard"

Courtesy of American Wind Energy Association.

Wind Turbines.

(NIMBY) backlash. The principle of wind power is simple. The wind blows. It turns a turbine and electricity is generated. The more the wind blows the more energy is generated. Simple, elegant and pollution-free. Better yet is the fact that the land below a wind turbine is still perfectly useful for other applications. Many farmers are now integrating windmills into their property to generate much needed additional income, while being able to farm underneath the windmill canopy.

Increasingly, our buildings will get all of their power from wind-farms rather than from nuclear or coal sources, but little of this power will be generated on site at the building level. Windmills are typically not appropriate in urban settings because ideal harvesting can only be achieved without obstructions to wind. Therefore, except in rural locations, the resulting impact on architectural forms will likely be minimal.

For more information on wind, try the following resources:

Eco-Economy: Building an Economy for the Earth
Lester Brown, 2001

American Wind Energy Association
http://www.awea.org/default.htm

Home Power Magazine
http://www.homepower.com/

National Wind Technology Center
http://www.nrel.gov/wind/

Fuel Cells

Perhaps no technology will transform society in the next twenty years as much as that of the fuel cell. Fuel cells are the future of energy generation for applications as wide ranging as automobiles, buildings, computers and cell phones. In no uncertain terms, the fuel cell will soon make the internal combustion engine obsolete. At the moment, fuel cells play almost no role in green buildings, with only a handful of structures using fuel cells in any significant way. Currently, there is only one type of fuel cell on the market for buildings, manufactured by ONSI, an American company.[7] But in the next few years a host of fuel cells will appear—many of which will be under the hoods of automobiles. Honda, perennially a leader in efficient technologies, has just unveiled the first commercial fuel cell vehicle for 2004 available in Japan. Even General Motors, perhaps the most conservative of the big automakers has gone on record as saying that the fuel cell will completely replace the internal combustion engine within a decade.

Fuel cells work very much like a battery, providing consistent, clean and reliable power, provided that a fuel source is continually supplied to it.

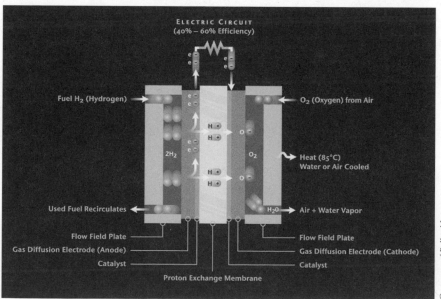

Courtesy of Ballard Inc.

Diagram shows how a Proton Exchange Membrane (PEM) Fuel Cell works.

Unlike the internal combustion engine, fuel cells generate their electricity through an electrochemical reaction instead of through combustion. Hydrogen, the fuel of choice, is fed through a semi-porous membrane (on the molecular level), which has the effect of briefly separating the hydrogen's protons and electrons, causing an electric charge. The process is considerably more efficient than combustion, and it is potentially pollution free depending on the fuel source. As a by-product, fuel cells generate hot water, which forms as the hydrogen combines with oxygen in the atmosphere to create water. Under certain conditions the fuel cell can then supply hot water to a building, further increasing the efficiency of the technology.

Fuel cells are scalable, so a wide variety of applications become possible, with small units capable of powering a piece of equipment, and large units capable of powering a neighborhood. The current barrier to fuel cell proliferation continues to be the cost of production, which is dropping steadily but still not to a level that is currently viable for most projects. This will change as the mass-production automobile industry starts churning out fuel cells. The other problem is that of the fuel itself. Hydrogen is naturally abundant, but not in its pure form, and it requires some sort of transformation to be useful. With current ONSI fuel cells (that are of a type called phosphoric acid—the more promising technology is known as proton exchange membrane PEM technology) a built-in reformer splits hydrogen from natural gas. Using fossil fuels as the source of hydrogen is certainly one option, but more interesting and ecologically sound would be to use water as the source.

An electrolyzer has the ability to crack water into hydrogen and oxygen. It is compelling to think of a future where all we need is a water hose and a solar panel to create our own fuel. Imagine if our homes and cars were powered by water collected from rainfall and sunshine! Of course, using fuel cells does not guarantee such a compelling future. It all depends on how the hydrogen is provided. Electrolyzers powered by coal plants or nuclear plants could have the opposite effect to that which is desired. The most appropriate synergy is likely with wind power, as wind farms are usually ideally located in areas that are sparsely populated. Using the wind to generate a fuel that can be transported to a more populated area is an effective use of both of the technologies.

To learn more about the exciting future of fuel cells, look to the following resources:

Tomorrow's Energy: Hydrogen, Fuel Cells, and the Prospects for a Cleaner Planet
Peter Hoffmann, 2002

Ballard Fuel Cells
http://www.ballard.com/

National Fuel Cell Research Center
http://www.nrcrc.uci.edu/

UTC Fuel Cells
http://www.utcfuelcells.com/index.htm

Green Comfort Systems

The green mechanical engineer has a large array of technologies at his or her disposal to provide comfort to building occupants with minimal to zero energy use. Of course the term *mechanical* engineer implies a built-in bias that should not exist. In many cases it is possible to achieve comfort in a building without the use of mechanical solutions. The profession should be renamed **Comfort Engineering**. What is a sustainable mechanical or comfort system? As with the master definition, sustainable design engineering follows the same philosophy as that of sustainable design itself—that is, to provide solutions that maximize the quality of the built environment while minimizing or eliminating negative environmental impact. For the comfort engineer, the definition is quite literal as the perceived quality of the built environment is very much dependent on how well temperature, humidity and air quality are regulated. Also, few other sectors of the building profession, if any, have as much direct environmental impact as that of the comfort engineer. In most cases it should be stressed that there is no such thing as one perfect green solution or technology. Improperly used, any technology can become an energy hog or environmental drain. This is particularly true of mechanical systems. Any mechanical comfort technology needs to be evaluated as appropriate on a building-by-building, climate-by-climate basis for a solution that is efficient. For brevity sake in this section, many great technologies such as radiant heating systems and heat pumps, both of which often form a key part of many green buildings, have been omitted.

The list of technologies and strategies is much too long and complex to provide in this summary. Instead, this section briefly discusses some of the technologies that are consistently mentioned in the green design arena. The technologies and strategies that are mentioned were chosen because they are either emerging in the field or are misunderstood or improperly applied.

Raised Access Flooring with Under Floor Air Distribution

Photos courtesy of KEEN Engineering

Photos show raised floor construction at KEEN Engineering Headquarters in Vancouver, Canada.

Raised floor systems with under floor air distribution are quickly becoming a staple in the comfort engineer's toolkit, quickly turning a system that was only recently introduced to the American market into one that is now enjoying widespread use and discussion. Under floor air systems dramatically change the way air is distributed in a space. In conventional HVAC systems, air is distributed through a series of ducts in the ceiling of a room that blow hot or cold air downward to the occupants. Spaces are typically grouped into one or more zones depending on the size of the space and the loads required. With a raised floor system the tempered air is delivered in the floor of the room through a pressurized plenum. Cool air does not have to be forced through the hottest zone of the room (the ceiling) and air can be delivered at warmer temperatures thus potentially saving energy.

The main reason for the success of raised floor systems has less to do with reducing environmental impact than for productivity and economic benefits that arise. While significantly more expensive than traditional air delivery systems on a first-cost basis, the system allows building owners to reconfigure furniture layouts and office organization with much less disruption. Because essential services are located in the floor rather than the ceiling, it takes considerably less time to rewire and reconfigure office operations. Known as "churn", this change can be incredibly expensive because of the cost of employee downtime, and thus for organizations that go through regular shifting, raised floors have been a real bonus. Another significant benefit of the raised floor system has been its potential improvement to the physical and psychological well-being of building occupants. Unlike an overhead system, it is very easy to give considerable user control of comfort to individuals (overhead systems can also have good user control, but with more difficulty). Floor diffusers can be located throughout a raised floor space and relocated easily. Rather than being locked into one or two temperature zones that may be too hot or too cold, building occupants can simply reach down and adjust the amount of air that is being delivered directly in their workspace. The psychological benefits of this user control alone are thought to be huge.

It is important to point out that raised floor systems have the *potential* to lower energy use, but they do not automatically do so. A few raised floor systems have been tested and shown to use more energy than conventional systems as a result of poor engineering. Raised floor systems are only one part (the air delivery mechanism) of a total mechanical system and not the complete story. Diligence in selecting efficient pumps, fans, cooling towers and chillers still needs to occur for this to be considered a green technology.

The best information on raised floor systems can still be found with the manufacturers, here are two:

Tate Access Floors
http://www.tateaccessfloors.com/main.html

Jindao Floors
http://www.jindaofloors.com/underfloor/index.html

Commissioning

Commissioning is quickly becoming an important process in the sustainable design umbrella. Commissioning is not a technology, but rather a procedure that is performed either by the comfort engineer on the project, or by an outside commissioning agent whose sole job is to perform the service. Commissioning is simple in theory. The intent is to ensure that mechanical and electrical systems on the project are installed in a building in a way that conforms to the construction documents and that systems are operated as effectively and efficiently as intended. Simple commissioning, which usually consisted of a very basic quality control review, has been common in the industry for years. With the advent of LEED, the focus on commissioning has increased significantly, with much greater emphasis placed on ensuring that all systems are operating as efficiently as possible. Many comfort engineers around the country are now adding commissioning to their basic practice as a service they can provide. The most effective time to bring a commissioning agent on to a project is before design development. When brought in early a commissioning agent can become intimately familiar with the design intent and is able to be much more effective in the field. Commissioning has been shown to be an incredibly cost-effective service and without it some surprising and wasteful things have happened on project—everything from fans installed backwards, to temperature sensors that tell mechanical systems to add air conditioning when heat is really needed. Commissioning is an essential part of green design to ensure that environmental performance predicted on a job is actually achieved.

For more information on the important subject of commissioning, look to the following resources:

Building Commissioning Handbook, Second Edition. Author: John A. Heinz and Rick Casault, 2003

The Building Commissioning Association
http://www.bcxa.org/

The Department of Energy Building Technologies Program:
Building Commissioning
http://www.eere.energy.gov/buildings/operate/buildingcommiss
ioning.cfm

Natural Ventilation

Natural ventilation is starting to become popular again as a method of
delivering comfort to building occupants in a large variety of building
types around the country. For years the standard practice has been to
hermetically seal off buildings and allow no option of simply opening
up a window for cooling or fresh air purposes. If given the choice, most
building occupants would prefer to be in a space with operable windows.
For some the loss of control and disconnect from outside conditions has
been distressing.

Unfortunately, most engineers actively shy away from natural ventilation as much as possible, and try to design buildings with no operable
windows. While this approach is perhaps the wrong attitude, it comes
from a very rational and sometimes environmental concern standpoint.
The use of natural venti-
lation usually takes away
the engineers' ability to
actively control comfort
conditions and thus in-
creases the possibility
of comfort-related com-
plaints. Improperly done,
a naturally ventilated
building also has the po-
tential to use more energy
than one with no natural
ventilation. At the same
time, if properly done, a

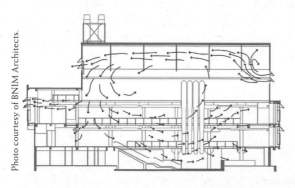

Photo courtesy of BNIM Architects.

Diagram of natural ventilation airflow at the Montana
State University EpiCenter project by BNIM
Architects.

naturally ventilated building can be more comfortable and use signifi-cantly less energy than its mechanically conditioned counterpart. Like any system, a naturally ventilated system needs to be evaluated based on all its implications. These implications could include the healthiness of outside air (is it polluted air?), the building type (lab buildings are not usually good candidates due to the need to strictly control temperature and humidity and to prevent drafts near fume hoods), the building's orientation or site, or the type of occupants in the building.

The first step in natural ventilation design requires an accurate under-standing of the climate and building type. Certain climates are conducive to natural ventilation, while others present more difficulties. Climates with high summer temperature and humidity levels make natural ventilation less feasible. Areas with high levels of air pollution could make indoor condi-tions less healthy than ones with good filtration. If people open windows when outside conditions are not favorable, they either make their space more uncomfortable or increase their air conditioning loads substantially. This sounds intuitive, but in many cases people open their windows at precisely the wrong times or forget to shut windows that they have previ-ously opened. The trick with natural ventilation is to open a building to the elements when the outside conditions are within the right temperature and humidity range to provide comfort—and then to shut it when con-ditions are not favorable. This range needs to be clearly communicated to building owners and occupants or the system to control the openings needs to be handled mechanically. A successful naturally ventilated build-ing requires cooperation from building occupants. For some building types this is simple, such as in a house where the occupants are few in number. But in other building types it is more problematic as people do not feel ownership over windows in their space and they can not be counted on to open and shut windows as needed.

Natural ventilation usually requires that a building has been designed from the beginning to be cooled naturally. Simply putting windows in a building design does little to provide comfort. Naturally ventilated build-ings typically have shallow depths to allow breezes to flush hot air out of the space effectively. The buildings are usually oriented according to prevailing breezes and have large amounts of thermal mass to temper the effects of temperature gains and to store nighttime coolth. Sometimes naturally ventilated buildings are designed with cooling towers or atrium that allow the stack effect to occur as warm air is sucked out of a tall space.

Photo by Jason F. McLennan.

Photo of Gerhlinger Hall in Eugene, Oregon shows a sunspace that partially suffers from a lack of thermal mass and sun control.

Naturally ventilated buildings require a strong commitment to climate responsive design and, properly done, can improve human health, productivity and energy use.

To learn more about Natural Ventilation look to the following:

Mechanical and Electrical Equipment for Buildings, 9th Edition
Ben Stein and John S. Reynold 1999

Passive Low Energy Cooling of Buildings
Baruch Givoni, 1994

Sun, Wind, And Light
G.Z. Brown and V. Cartwright 1985

Passive Solar Design

Like natural ventilation, passive solar design requires a shift in how build-ings are designed and if properly done can greatly improve the environ-mental performance of a building. For the most part the building industry does not adequately harness the ability of the sun to provide free heat. The principles behind passive solar design are simple.

1. Allow heat through solar radiation to enter a building when it is need-ed in the heating season, and block this heat through shading devices when the heat is not desired in the cooling season.
2. Use thermal mass to capture the heat gain and even out indoor temperatures.

Adhering to these simple principles requires an attention to orientation and building form. A building that is elongated in the east-west direction provides ideal orientation and configuration, as south-facing sunlight can be more easily controlled than east or west-facing sunlight that is always at a lower angle. Passive solar design is more appropriate in externally load dominated buildings (usually small to medium sized buildings) as internally load dominated buildings typically require year round cooling. A building need not be heated solely by solar to be effective. The principle of solar tempering is to use heat from the sun to provide warmth for as much of the year as possible, but still rely on a back-up heating system to provide additional heat through especially cold patches of overcast weather.

To Get the Scoop on Passive Solar Design try the following.

The Passive Solar House
by James Kachadorian 1997

The Solar House: Passive Heating and Cooling
by Daniel D., Ph.D. Chira, 2002

Sustainable Building Industry Council
http://www.sbicouncil.org/home/index.html

Alternative Construction

The rise of sustainable design from the seventies to the nineties saw a resurgence of alternative building materials that take their roots from vernacular construction processes. Some that fall into this category include straw-bale, rammed earth, cob and cordwood construction. For the most part, these types of construction have occurred in residential buildings only where fire and structural construction concerns have been low. The alternative construction movement is decidedly a grassroots movement occurring with builders, homeowners, and designers eschewing the typical ways things are done. Many alternative construction homes have been built by the homeowners themselves, using their own labor in the process to offset costs. Due to the grassroots nature of the people involved, the quality and appropriateness of the structures and their attributes varies greatly. In some cases the structures can only be described as experimental. In others the quality is as high or higher than anything on the market. With this group blanket statements rarely apply. As with the quality of the buildings, the information about many of the construction types varies in quality as well, particularly when it comes to issues of cost and all claims should be viewed with caution. Many word-of-mouth claims have arisen over just how inexpensive many of these materials are to build with, yet the fact remains that in almost all cases the materials in question are more labor intensive than most conventional materials by a significant factor. With an army of volunteer laborers willing to chip in to "experience the alternative" the costs indeed sometimes come in much cheaper, but for most projects increased labor equals increased costs. In this section straw-bale construction and rammed earth are explained in more detail, as these will likely continue to be the most common of the alternative construction techniques.

For more information about Alternative Construction in general, look to the following resources:

Alternative Construction: Contemporary Natural Building Methods
Lynne Elizabeth (Editor) and Cassandra Adams, 2000

Art of Natural Building
Joseph F. Kennedy, Michael Smith and Catherine Wanek, 2002

Photo courtesy of Seigal and Strain Architects.

Strawbale Construction at Camp Arroyo in Livermore, California by Seigal & Strain Architects.

Natural Home Magazine
http://www.naturalhomemagazine.com/

Straw-bale Construction

About one hundred years ago farmers in the sand hills of Nebraska decided to try building homes out of the one material they had an abundance of …straw. With timber scarce, the only alternative was the sod house. To what must have been their delight the straw-bale homes were quite comfortable and some of these early homes persist today, testament to the appropriateness and potential longevity of the structures. In the eighties the material was rediscovered by a few individuals looking to find more environmentally friendly alternatives to conventional home construction. Soon thereafter the use of the material among individuals looking for alternatives found advocates all over the country.

A straw-bale building is quite literally built out of straw, but unlike the home popularized by the three little pigs, it can be engineered to be durable and practical. Straw-bale homes utilize straw-bales pinned together using rebar and some form of top plate. After the walls are erected, expanded metal lathe is applied to the inside and outside of the walls, which is then, in turn, covered with stucco on the exterior and plaster on the interior. Most straw-bale homes use the bale walls as infill and rely on a structural frame (usually wood post and beam) to bear the weight of the roof. A few homes have been built with the straw-bale as a load-bearing wall. Unfortunately, settlement issues present significant problems in terms of cracking stucco and the plaster and exerting of pressure on doors and windows.

Issues of fire have proven to be a non-issue in straw-bale homes as bales of straw tend to smolder rather than catch fire, and once impregnated between stucco and plaster are essentially fire-proof. Issues of water and water vapor are other challenges. A significant amount of debate exists about the appropriateness of straw bales in hot humid climates and the long-term durability in such conditions. The jury is still out on whether this will in fact be a problem in well-detailed homes. It has proven to be essential to protect the bales during the construction process to ensure that they do not become wet before being sealed within stucco. All straw-bale structures are designed to have a "good hat and a good pair of boots" to protect against water (which translates into a roof with a wide overhang and a high foundation to keep the straw-bale wall off the ground).

One of the most compelling features of a straw-bale building is the unique feeling of being in one. Few construction practices produce the wonderful intangible qualities of a thick straw-bale wall with built-in window seats and nooks. There is an overall feeling of warmth and security that seems to come with the construction of a straw-bale home that is not found in any other. Few visitors to a straw-bale building at first know that the building is built with something so unconventional. It has become custom to create a "truth" window in every straw-bale building to let visitors know that the house is indeed built out of straw.

To learn more about strawbale building try the following resources:

The Beauty of Straw Bale Homes
by Athena Swentzell Steen, Bill Steen, 2001

The New Straw Bale Home
by Catherine Wane, 2003

Serious Straw Bale: A Home Construction Guide for All Climates
by Paul Lacinski, 2000

The Last Straw Journal
http://www.azstarnet.com/~dcat/tls.htm

Rammed Earth

The material that shares the most in common with straw-bale construction is that of rammed earth. Like straw-bale, the recent resurgence of the material has been primarily a grass-roots one. Also like straw-bale, it is an older building practice that only recently has been rediscovered and used in North America. Unlike straw-bale, rammed earth has a history that spans centuries rather than just one hundred years. Rammed earth should not be confused with adobe, which is not nearly as strong and consists of small clay bricks stacked together. Rammed earth structures can be found throughout the world with many that have been standing for hundreds of years. The distribution of the material is widespread. Some in North Africa have been built up to seven stories in height and perhaps could be considered the first high-rise buildings! Even the Great Wall of China is made up of rammed earth in part. In southern France whole villages are made of rammed earth, where there the technology is known as Pisé.

Rammed earth walls are built using a specific mix of soils to produce a desired consistency, strength and workability, which is then compacted (or rammed) between form-work using either manual tampers or pneumatic ones. Unlike straw-bale which is relatively easy, the rammed earth process can be complex and incredibly laborious, a factor which will always limit its appeal when labor costs are high. In more modern applications a small bit of Portland cement is sometimes added to the mix to increase strength and to account for soil mixes that are not always ideal. A few pioneers in southern California have invented a process of horizontally ramming earth against a one sided form-work using gunite, a swimming pool technology that blasts the earth mixture against the form-work at high speeds.

As with straw-bale the results with rammed earth can be very beautiful with buildings that seem to grow out of the very earth surrounding the building (although it is rare that the exact soil mix can be found on one site). Both share the need for a good hat and a good pair of boots. While limited in ultimate use, rammed earth buildings will continue to be built on a small basis in warm, dry climates around the world.

To learn more about playing with earth try the following:

Adobe and Rammed Earth Buildings: Design and Construction
Paul Graham McHenry, 1989

Buildings of Earth and Straw: Structural Design for Rammed Earth and Straw Bale Architecture
Bruce King, 1997

The Rammed Earth House (Real Goods Independent Living Book)
David Easton, Cynthia Wright, 1996

Materials

Since the nineties a growing list of green materials has flooded the market. The materials tend to fall into four major categories: new materials that have some sort of environmental feature, old materials that now highlight the environmental feature that always existed, and old or new materials that falsely boast environmental performance. The challenge lies in being able to tell which is which. Is a green material really green or is it greenwash? Thankfully, a few guidebooks have emerged that analyze materials using predetermined criteria. The best are published by *Environmental Building News*. Look to this resource for help in telling the difference between true green and false green materials. For materials that are not listed, it is good to do investigation into the claims presented. In general, materials are marketed as green because they contain one of the following characteristics:

- Recycled content
- Salvaged material content
- Materials made from the waste stream
- Healthy characteristics
- Contributes to energy efficiency
- Is free of ozone-depleting chemicals
- Does not contribute to global warming

- Is from a renewable resource
- Is natural
- Is non-toxic
- Has low-embodied energy
- Can be recycled

In general, most materials that make claims to one or more of the features listed above do, in fact, have that benefit, but sometimes the material has poor performance in another area. An example would be an insulation product with recycled content that is free of ozone-depleting chemicals. If the material had poor thermal performance it might do more harm than good to use it. Not all claims are equal either. It is important to be wary of claims that a material is natural, non-toxic and can be recycled. Claims like these are ambiguous and have little meaning. The claim that something can be recycled is particularly vexing. Just because some material can be recycled does not mean it will be recycled.

In this following section a few green materials that are typically misunderstood are briefly described.

To get smarter about Green Material Selection in general take a look at the following resources:

Athena Sustainable Materials Institute
http://www.athenasmi.ca/smi_info/about/athena_smi.htm

BEES (Building for Environmental and Economic Sustainability)
http://www.ofee.gov/sb/nistbs.htm

The Green Spec Directory & Environmental Building News
http://www.buildinggreen.com/

Low VOC Paints and Finishes

Low Volatile Organic Compound (VOC) paints and finishes have made a large entry into the building market. Almost every major paint manufacturer now produces a low VOC formula paint. Regular paint and finish compounds are comprised of chemicals that have been tested to be irritants and contribute to poor and unhealthy indoor air quality. A low VOC paint is one that has been tested to contain less VOCs than a typical paint and therefore should have less negative impact on the quality of indoor air. Some low VOC paints are of high quality and can be substituted directly in place of typical paints and finishes. Most of these paints have considerably less odor than conventional paints. The problem with low VOC paints and finishes is that the quality in the products is not universal. Some of the paints require additional coatings to have the same level of coverage thus increasing the total number of VOCs released. Many of the paints are not available in darker colors and achieve their low VOC ratings by containing less pigment. However, the biggest problem is that not all of the VOCs found in paints and finishes are monitored by law. A paint product may be called low VOC and yet still have other harmful additives that will negatively impact air quality. In fact, some low VOC paints have different curing times and while they may off-gas less at any given time, some off-gas for longer periods of time than their traditional counterparts, sometimes resulting in greater overall exposure.

Over time most of these negative aspects will improve. In the meantime designers should be encouraged to find a quality brand that meets the conventional performance requirements and use low VOC paints.

To get the scoop on low VOC Paints try the following resources:

City of Austin, Green Builder Program
http://www.ci.austin.tx.us/greenbuilder/fs_paint.htm

US Green Building Council
http://www.usgbc.org

Certified Wood Products

Most wood products come from forests that are managed in ways that are inherently unsustainable for a variety of reasons. Most of these reasons have been discussed already, but in summary include damage to biological systems, soil erosion, impact to salmon or riparian habitat, biodiversity loss and the replacement of functioning ecosystems with tree farms that contain trees of one species planted in neat rows for future harvesting. In

Courtesy of the Forest Stewardship Council.

A piece of lumber showing the FSC label.

many cases the lumber companies are abusing their land so much that a renewable resource is being turned into a non-renewable one.

In reaction to this situation, many green designers are now specifying certified, sustainably-harvested wood. Certified wood products are an essential part of the sustainable design philosophy. This certified wood comes from forests that have been identified as being well managed by independent auditors such as Smart Wood, FSC and Scientific Certification Systems (SCS). These auditors look to see if forests are being managed to minimize erosion and to ensure that a functioning ecosystem is being kept intact. As well as a host of other indicators of sustainability, clear cuts are not allowed within the certification system. Forests that have been managed in this way are able to consistently harvest lumber in perpetuity, keeping the quality of the products high while lowering environmental impact. Initially these products were substantially more expensive than conventional lumber and they were less available. While still slightly more expensive, the prices are coming down considerably and certified wood can be found in almost any species and size desired. Furniture makers are also starting to offer standard products built with sustainably-harvested wood.

To learn more about the important subject of Certified wood try these websites:

Forest Stewardship Council
http://www.fscus.org

Scientific Certification Systems
http://www.scscertified.com/

Smart Wood
http://www.smartwood.org/

Fly-ash Concrete

It is more and more common to find concrete mixes that contain high percentages of fly-ash in lieu of Portland cement in green buildings. The manufacturing of Portland cement requires a huge amount of energy to create and therefore contributes a great deal to pollution and global warming through the energy used. Some estimates point to Portland cement contributing almost eight percent of the world's global warming gases.[8] In contrast fly-ash is a waste product of the coal industry and has unique chemical properties that allow it to be used as a binder in the same way that Portland cement is used. The environmental impact of concrete is reduced for every bit of Portland cement that is replaced with fly-ash. The fact is that fly-ash has shown up in concrete mixes for quite sometime because using it has the benefit of reducing the cost of the concrete mix. Typically, the amount of substitution was small, from five to fifteen percent. Green buildings tend to use a higher percentage of fly-ash with ranges between twenty and sixty percent depending on what the structural engineer specifies. Unfortunately, not all fly-ash is the same and this reality poses challenges for its use. The quality of fly-ash varies greatly from source to source depending on the type of coal that was used and the pollution controls in the coal plant.

To use fly-ash as a partial replacement for Portland cement requires a good understanding of the source of the fly-ash. At the present, testing is being done on a piecemeal basis with little co-ordinated national sharing of information. Many structural engineers are wary of using too much fly-ash for fear of weakening the structural mix that they are working with. In the next decade it is likely that a national database of information will be compiled so that designers will know what amount of fly-ash from each source is acceptable for particular uses. Fly-ash has different working properties than Portland cement. Set times, workability and strength changes as the percentage of fly-ash changes and therefore a sound knowledge of the material is essential for construction purposes. Fly-ash will continue to play a prominent role in green buildings in the next few decades but ultimately it is a material without a future. When coal goes the way of the dinosaur so will fly-ash.

To understand more about Fly-Ash Concrete contact the following:

The Sustainable Building Source Book
http://www.greenbuilder.com/sourcebook/Flyash.html

Environmental Building News
http://www.buildinggreen.com/

Lighting Design

About a third of the electricity used in buildings in the United States is used for lighting and thus offers a large area for efficiency improvement. Many technologies exist that can contribute to lowering the cost and environmental impact of providing light. Some of these technologies include high efficiency florescent light-bulbs with dimming or on/off controls that work if enough daylight is available. Florescent lights typically convert close to seventy percent of the energy supplied to them as light with thirty percent given off as heat. In contrast, the standard incandescent bulbs only convert ten percent of the incoming energy to light with ninety percent wasted as heat, thus making them heaters that happen to give off light rather than lights that give off heat. Occupancy sensors can be combined with efficient lighting to turn on only when people enter a space, further reducing energy. Sensors can also be integrated with a building's daylight availability—sensing light levels and continuously dimming to ensure even luminescence. Lighting design is complex and requires more than a quick summary for meaningful understanding.

Courtesy of HOK and Steve Hall, Hedrich-Blessing.

Efficient lighting design integrated with daylight at the Nidus Center for Scientific Enterprise in St. Louis, Missouri by HOK Architects.

To learn more about Efficient Lighting Design look to:

California Title 24 Guidelines
http://www.energy.ca.gov/title24/

Illuminating Engineering Society of North America
Advanced Lighting Guidelines: 2003 Edition
http://www.iesna.org/

Daylighting

Providing light to a space does not always have to require the use of electric lighting, at least during daylight hours. In fact, diffuse daylight (no sunbeam) produces the most amount of light to the least amount of heat of any light source, so using daylight to replace electric lighting saves a great deal of energy and environmental impact. Bringing daylight into a space brings pleasing psychological benefits as well, and most green buildings rely heavily on daylight for ambient lighting needs.

Radience daylight simulation performed by Elements shows available light levels in a space from rooftop light monitors.

Image courtesy of BNIM Architects.

As with electric lighting, daylighting design is incredibly complex and cannot adequately be summarized here. It involves much more than placing a window in a room and can be considered both an art and a science. The amount and type of natural light that is available varies widely from season to season, by orientation and even by time of day and therefore requires careful consideration if it is to replace electric lights as the primary light source. In addition, daylight design requires careful attention to orientation and to the form and shape of the building. It requires attention to the types of glazing chosen, the color and reflectance of materials in a space and the balance of light and heat gain. A whole field of daylight specialists has emerged to address the complexity and importance of the strategy.

To hear more about how to effectively daylight your building try the following resources:

Daylighting Performance and Design
Gregg D. Ander, 2003

Daylighting for Sustainable Design
Mary Guzowski, 1999

Tips for Daylighting With Windows – online publication
http://eetd.lbl.gov/btp/pub/designguide/

Light Shelves

Light shelves have become an important iconic component in many green commercial buildings. The technology, which is almost always a custom fabricated solution, is an important tool in the daylighting designer's toolkit. Light shelves are typically constructed of metal, painted wood or gyp-board and are located on the south walls of buildings separating a lower "vision-glass" from an upper "daylight glass". Light shelves are almost always white for reflectivity, but some have mirrored tops.

The purpose of the light shelf is three-fold. The first purpose is to bounce sunlight deeper into the space without causing glare to occupants. It performs this function by intercepting the sun's rays and reflecting the light up at the ceiling. The second function is to diminish glare by reducing the difference in light levels at the front of the room with the light

Exterior Light Shelves on Edificio Malecon building in Buenos Aires, Argentina by HOK Architects.

Photo courtesy of HOK and Daniela Mac Adden.

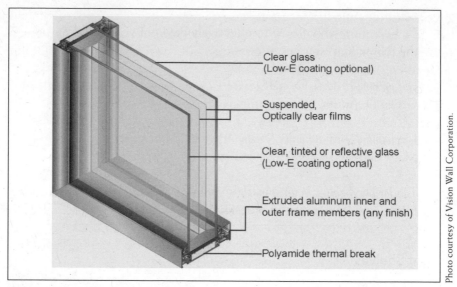

Photo courtesy of Vision Wall Corporation.

Diagram showing high performance glazing unit with three airspaces by Vision Wall.

levels found deeper in the room. The third function is to block heat gain from entering the main vision window during the cooling season on the external portion of the light shelf.

To learn more specifically about Light shelves look for:

Tips for Daylighting With Windows – online publication
http://eetd.lbl.gov/btp/pub/designguide/

Super Glazing

Only a few decades ago glazing came with one option—clear single pane. The last twenty years have seen the emergence of a large array of glazing options that can be used to improve the environmental performance and comfort of buildings. We ask much of glazing. We require it to be waterproof and easy to maintain, to let in light and keep out heat in the summer and let in solar gain in the winter without losing too much heat through the material. It provides us with views and connection to the external world while inside. Designers can now select glazing that is tuned to perform a variety of functions and satisfy a variety of needs. The green designer often selects very different glazing even on the same building depending on the orientation and the amount of glass required.

Super glazings now exist that are especially good at letting in light, which we usually want, while blocking out heat, which we usually do not want in most buildings. These glazings are called spectrally selective glazing because they block only a portion of the light spectrum, the infrared. Super windows now exist that perform nearly as well as a wall in terms of blocking the flow of heat through the material. Most of these glazings are part of an overall assembly that increases energy efficiency through a variety of steps including a thermally broken frame, multiple layers of glass, suspended films, coatings on the glass and gas filled interiors. Super glazings are currently being tested and manufactured in small quantities that go even further. In the next decade we will see the emergence of electrochromic glazing that can allow a user to adjust the properties of the glass using a small control device. The windows can switch from clear to tinted for privacy or to block heat as needed. Other advanced glazings on the market include the integration of transparent photovoltaics that allow for the window to generate electricity while letting light in.

To learn more specifically about glazing, try the following:

AIA Glazing Design Handbook
Greg Franta and Gregg D. Ander, 1997

The Dumb Architect's Guide to Glazing Selection
Jason F. McLennan, 2004

CHAPTER TEN

Photo courtesy of the Forest Stewardship Council

Shades of Green–The Levels of Sustainability

Never doubt that a small group of thoughtful committed citizens
can change the world. Indeed, it's the only thing that ever has.
—Margaret Mead

A Question of Green

Until recently, it has been very difficult to judge how environmentally friendly or green a given project was. In many cases projects were called green because of the marketing spin of the project or the reputation of the designer, not from any real scientific basis for how the building performed. For the most part, this standard was arbitrarily given, based on the presence of certain green technologies or features that most likely achieved some environmental impact reduction, but did not always guarantee great performance. If a project looked green to many people it was. As we will discuss in Chapter Fifteen—**The Aesthetics of Sustainable Design**, this approach has actually hurt the acceleration of the green building movement because it isolated the number of designers willing to go green from those who were uncomfortable with this perceived style (remembering, of course, that sustainable design is emphatically not a style).

Also common was the belief that a project was green simply because of how much energy the building was predicted to use in energy models. This approach, although potentially an improvement, was also deeply flawed for two reasons. The first is that energy, although extremely important, is only a portion of the overall sustainability umbrella and therefore energy assessment is an incomplete assessment of the overall impact. The second is that predicted energy use does not always match up with actual energy use and many so- called energy efficient buildings may, in fact, be using much more energy than anticipated. To properly gauge energy use, monitoring and measuring of the actual building during operation is required.

In the early nineties the push to make the process more scientific and inclusive of all the issues related to sustainable design began in the United States with the creation of programs at various levels of government, from city to federal. In the late eighties, the Department of Energy created its Energy Star program to help improve the efficiency of buildings and equipment. This voluntary program set guidelines for energy use based on good practice. Individual building, workplace and household products were rated based on their efficiency.

In the early nineties the City of Austin, through incredibly progressive leadership from the city and local professionals (including Pliny Fisk and Gail Vittori) launched its Green Builder Program[1], a program aimed at improving the environmental performance of residential projects in the city. The Austin program was designed with four levels of performance depending on how many green strategies were employed on the project. This program, the first to attempt a more inclusive approach to sustainable design covering energy, materials, water and indoor air, was widely successful, garnering the program a Commendation at the Rio Earth Summit and spawning countless other programs around the country in cities like Denver, San Diego and Kansas City. The Austin program rates the greenness of buildings on a scale of one to five stars depending on how a given project does in five categories including energy efficiency, water efficiency, materials efficiency, health and safety and community.

In addition to Green Building programs, many states began adopting green building guidelines to help accelerate the adoption of sustainable techniques in the marketplace. These guidelines usually did not contain a ranking system or levels of sustainability, but instead provided information on how to make a project green by offering strategies, details and sometimes specifications that were meant to be swapped out in place of the traditional way of building.

One of the things that all of these Green Builder programs had in common was that they were voluntary in nature and provided rewards or recognition as incentive. None of the programs made it mandatory. For the most part, the residential market was the first to receive guidance in how to build a green building and, in general, how to rate how green a given project was. On both the residential and commercial side, the American Institute of Architects Committee on the Environment started an annual awards recognition program coinciding with Earth Day to recognize building designs that balanced environmental performance with good aesthetic design. Each year this program picks the nation's Ten Best sustainable design projects through a small private jury that meets in Washington D.C.[2] This program started out as a purely subjective exercise but has evolved into one that now looks at performance targets (also called metrics) alongside thoughtful design. In many ways the role of the AIA Committee on the Environment is to reward and recognize thoughtful architectural articulation of strategies that touch lightly on the land. The emphasis is placed on the broader definition of what constitutes good design.

In general, each of these programs attempted to ask several important questions such as: How do we determine how green a given project really is? At what point does a project stop being ordinary and become green? What are the criteria and standards by which to judge and compare projects that may be very different? Is a project green only when its negative environmental impact has been reduced to zero or is a project green because it does less harm or is less bad than a conventional building? How should we reward or recognize people when they go out of their way to make building design decisions that lower environmental impact?

Answering these challenging questions takes quite a balancing act. And within the sustainable design world it begs for the creation of a program that can do several things simultaneously. A sustainable design rating system should, as a starting point, encompass all of the issues described in the previous chapter of the book, (energy, water, resources, indoor air quality, etc.) but also find a way to assign a weighting to them, because not all of the issues have the same impact on either the environment or their importance to people. A sustainable design rating system should take into account the differences in climate and place that may result in very different environmental priorities. For example, in the southwest water issues are highly critical, whereas in Minnesota water is less of an issue (although still important). A good rating system should have a way of accounting for these differences. Equally important is an accounting for the differences in building types. A laboratory, for example, has a very different environmental impact than does a house. A good environmental rating system should take into account these differences. Another important point is that a good rating system should not only reward and recognize environmental performance but also should identify a way to drive and change the marketplace so that more people will become actively involved in sustainability efforts. The final requirement for a sustainable design rating system is simplicity and clarity; a system that can help designers with their process but without adding a huge burden of time and resources. Unfortunately, the multiple challenges of creating a meaningful design rating system that addresses all of the above issues is what has kept its creation back for so long.

The US Green Building Council and LEED

As described in Chapter Two, in 1993 David Gottfried and Mike Italiano, two businessmen with a keen interest in green building, gathered together a small group of the leading practitioners and thinkers in sustainability to form the US Green Building Council (USGBC), a non-profit organization based in Washington D.C. The main goal of the US Green Building Council was to foster market acceptance of sustainable design issues, materials and technologies and thereby transform what was a fringe movement into a mainstream one. Within a short time, the US Green Building Council grew from a small organization with a handful of members to a nationally prominent organization with diverse membership consisting of architects, engineers, developers, builders, product manufacturers, universities, non-profits and public institutions. In the Council's own words its membership is comprised of the "nation's foremost coalition of leaders from across the building industry working to promote buildings that are environmentally responsible, profitable, and healthy places to live and work."

The US Green Building Council is run by a small, knowledgeable, voluntary board that consists of representatives from many different industries. Only a small paid staff operationalizes board policy. Its programs, such as Leadership in Energy and Environmental Design (LEED) and the LEED Designer Accreditation program, have been developed by an incredible collection of technical leaders in all areas of the sustainability umbrella who have volunteered time to work out the details of the program.

Perhaps no other organization in the United States has done as much to create positive change in the sustainable design world as the US Green Building Council. Indeed, the success of the Council is due in large part to the overwhelming support and co-operation of countless individuals who have created an outstanding system for market transformation and designer/consumer education. In many ways, the US Green Building Council came along at just the right time, when consumer interest in sustainable building was growing, but clear direction as to what constituted green building was absent. From now on, in the United States at least, the authoritative source for this information will likely be the US Green Building Council, providing that it continues its collaborative, member-driven approach.[3] In fact, the US Green Building Council has grown beyond all initial expectations to the point that the rate of growth and interest in its programs are currently its biggest challenge.

Shortly after its formation the Council began work on several programs, most notably its LEED rating system, which was designed to rate the greenness of commercial office buildings. The Council also created an accreditation program for designers who had a proficient knowledge of sustainable design issues and were able to pass a two-hour exam on the subject. With its LEED rating system, the USGBC attempted to recognize that there were different levels of sustainability, or perhaps more accurately, that there were stages on the way to the goal of sustainability.

Development of the LEED rating system began with the pilot version of the program (version 1.0) released in 1998. The first version of the program contained only a handful of projects intended to test how well the tool worked as a rating system and checklist for sustainability. Projects with a wide variety in building types and size (even though the program was to debut as a commercial office building tool) were selected from a broad geographic area. Most notable of the first pilot projects was the only building to reach the Platinum Level (the highest rating achievable in the system), the Chesapeake Bay Foundation Building in Annapolis, Maryland. Because of its success with the LEED system, the Foundation has received an incredible amount of publicity and marketing support and instantly became a green building icon in the country. Based on the success and overwhelming attention given to the pilot program, the Council refined the program and in March of 2000, with much anticipation and support, released version 2.0 to the public. At the time of publication of this book over four hundred buildings all across the United States have been registered with the USGBC for certification, with perhaps several thousand more using LEED as a checklist in the design process.

Even though the LEED rating system was defined for commercial office buildings, the demand has been so great for a tool that certifies the greenness of buildings that certified projects have sprung up in almost every building type including retail, manufacturing, schools, libraries, laboratories and firehouses. This demand continues despite the fact that the tool does not always do a good job of representing the particular issues affecting each of these building types. Because of this great demand, the US Green Building Council is active in creating different versions of LEED that more comprehensively meet the needs of the different building types. In 2002 the Council released its program for existing buildings and will be launching a version for residences and interior projects in the next few years.

The US Green Building Council was not alone in trying to determine the level of sustainability for a given project on a national level. In Canada, the Green Building Challenge[4] was created as a competition between projects in multiple countries based on a complex rating system that looked at all aspects of sustainability. Every two years countries select their best green building projects to be assessed and presented at an international conference held at a different location (similar to an Olympics for green buildings). Previous conferences have been held in Vancouver, Canada, and

Maastricht, the Netherlands. The best projects from the United States continue to compete in this program sponsored by the Department of Energy.

Other programs such as the BRE Environmental Assessment Method (BREEAM), which was founded in the UK in 1990 had been around in Europe prior to the creation of LEED. BREEAM also attempted to gauge how green a project really is from a holistic perspective. The BREEAM[5] system analyzes a building's operating impacts on the environment and the building receives a score on a proprietary performance index. Certain scores give buildings overall ratings such as "good" and "very good."

While the tool is completely voluntary, a growing number of jurisdictions have adopted LEED as a standard for all new buildings. The first to do so was the City of Seattle, which has mandated that all new city projects achieve a LEED silver level or higher. The General Services Administration (GSA) of the federal government has also called for a similar mandate. All new federal buildings over two million dollars must also achieve a LEED silver rating. A growing list is following this leadership.

A Brief Introduction to the LEED Rating System[6]

The LEED rating system is divided into four general levels of certification or shades of green: Certified, Silver, Gold, and Platinum.

Initially, a few individuals criticized or joked with the Council for naming the system after precious metals that are responsible for a great deal of environmental damage, instead of trees or something living. However, in defense of the selection, the Olympics rather than precious metals, seems to be the metaphor intended. Indeed, like an Olympic competition, the various levels of the rating system have spawned an intense competition among building owners and developers committed to sustainability, with the LEED rating serving as bragging rights. How green a business or organization is viewed is now often being based on the level the building achieved in the LEED rating. Overall, the LEED system has a total of sixty-nine points available. The point totals and levels break out in the following way:

LEED Certified 26-32 points:
The LEED certified level is fairly easy to achieve and for most projects requires only a few changes to the design process and usually little additional cost to achieve. This is a good baseline for all new buildings constructed today, although most would not even reach this standard.

LEED Silver 33-38 points:
The LEED Silver level is probably where the threshold between typical good construction and green design resides. Projects that achieve a silver rating are beginning to do things that are not typically done and this level starts to require changes to the design process including the potential of some first-cost increases. In short, it requires much more attention to sustainable design. At the same time, a silver level is very achievable by most projects in the country. Most LEED projects end up with a silver rating.

LEED Gold Level 39-51 points:
The LEED Gold level is really an achievement and requires a firm commitment to all aspects of sustainable design. Few projects reach this level of performance because it requires an integrated design approach to achieve.

LEED Platinum 52 + points:
The LEED Platinum level is extremely difficult to attain. In fact, in the first version of LEED, (which is slightly easier than the second) only one project achieved a platinum rating – the Chesapeake Bay Foundation Headquarters. Projects that achieve this level of sustainability are reaching high point totals in each of the overall categories.

Buildings achieve their LEED rating based on the number of points that a project receives in various categories that relate to the overall sustainability umbrella. The categories include:

- Energy and Atmosphere
- Water Efficiency
- Materials and Resources
- Indoor Environmental Quality
- Sustainable Sites
- Innovation

Energy and Atmosphere credits deal with how much energy is used compared to standard buildings as well as how that energy was generated (is it from a renewable source?). Similarly, the Water Efficiency credits deal with how much water is used compared to a standard project, how it is treated, and if the water is re-used. The Materials and Resources category involves understanding where materials have come from, how they were harvested (in the case of trees or rapidly renewable fibers) or how much recycled or salvaged content is contained in a project.

The Indoor Environmental Quality category deals with a host of issues as they relate to overall human comfort and health including access to daylight and views, indoor air quality, thermal comfort and ventilation. This category is perhaps the most complicated in the system. The Sustainable Sites category is more straightforward and awards points based on where a building is located, in terms of adjacencies to public transportation or urban infrastructure, or conversely where it is not located, such as in prime farmland or floodplains. The category also deals with how the site is developed.

The Innovation category deals with the design process, and awards a point if a project has a LEED accredited designer which theoretically ensures that someone on the team is asking the right questions (often not the case) but as it turns out it is probably a clever way to get people to seek accreditation and pay the USGBC dues! More importantly, this category offers a series of innovation points that allow applicants to submit customized requests for additional points based on innovative approaches to environmental health not currently in the program. These credits are perhaps the most exciting part of the rating system because the credits encourage designers to think outside the typical box for solutions or to find ways to get rewarded for issues that are particularly important for their region or their building type.

The point distribution is set up in such a way that to achieve good ratings projects must address some of the issues in each environmental category. A building that only addressed energy issues, for example, might make the certified designation, but would not reach the higher levels. The rationale for this weighting is to drive home the point that to be sustainable all of the issues need to be addressed. The LEED system is not intended to be an overtly weighted system that scientifically assigns value to certain environmental issues over others, but it has a de facto weighting due to the distribution of points. Energy, for example, appropriately has the largest share of points. 17 points are awarded in energy, 5 in water, 14 in sustainable sites, 15 in indoor environmental quality and 13 in materials and resources. The Innovation category awards up to 5 points. For more specific information on the credits and prerequisites of the LEED rating system see the USGBC website.

In addition to the points awarded in each category, LEED also has a series of project pre-requisites that must be met in order to participate in the program and to establish a base-line for things that are easy to do and fundamental to the principles of the movement. An example of this requirement is a prerequisite that all chillers must be Chlorofluorocarbons (CFC) free – something that is mandatory for new buildings, except those being serviced at a central plant. CFCs are largely responsible for the degradation of stratospheric ozone that shields our planet from harmful ultraviolet radiation.

It is important to mention, however, that aside from the prerequisites, the program is completely performance based rather than prescriptive—both in the points that can be chosen, and how they are achieved. A LEED rating can be achieved with any combination of points—it is up to the design team to determine which points are the most appropriate for a given project. The US Green Building Council did not want to get into the business of warranting certain technologies or approaches. Instead, the Council wanted to leave design teams with the responsibility of reaching certain target levels of performance such as on the energy side where points are awarded based on how much better a building will perform than the Ashrae (American Society of Heating, Refrigeration, Air Conditioning Engineers) code standards. For example, two points are awarded for exceeding the code by ten percent, four points for twenty percent, six points for thirty percent and so on to ten points. Prescriptive programs (programs that tell you exactly what to do) have some purpose in that they leave no room for misinterpretation but for the most part they hamper innovation and creativity in the design team.

The Council has also shied away from establishing its own standards and, for the most part, has chosen to rely on industry-accepted benchmarks for performance in recognizing projects that outperform or meet these standards. This idea was particularly astute on the Council's part because it selected standards that were already part of common practice or, at least, had been tested in some jurisdiction for a period of time with workable precedents and supporting information.

Getting a LEED rating can be a challenging exercise. The development of any rating system is always a balancing act between ease of use and the rigor and thoroughness required to really ensure that targets are being met. The USGBC chose the route with the most integrity—creating a cutting edge system that contains a great deal of rigor and thoroughness and holds up to close scrutiny. The green building movement is intense in ferreting out green-wash and programs that have no teeth. But the rigor and thoroughness has come at the expense of ease of use and cost because design professionals are not inexpensive.

As good as LEED is, it is also important to remember that by its very nature no national standard can begin to address all of the issues that exist from a bioclimatic standpoint and from variations in building types. It must be remembered that LEED is, after all, only a tool that helps drive the market place and hopefully gets designers to think of certain issues throughout the design process. It is not the be-all and end-all of sustainability. A LEED rating is not needed to have a green building and a LEED rating does not mean that a building is necessarily all that green. In fact, if we recall the definition of sustainable design, none of the levels, including platinum are, in fact, truly sustainable…merely a lot less bad!

Applying for a LEED rating is simple enough. Project managers simply fill out a one-page registration form and pay a very modest fee. But after that, the paperwork and the additional time to document the process and co-ordinate among consultants on a project adds significant time and money. Most design firms with some experience with LEED are now charging a fee between forty and sixty thousand dollars just to handle the management of the program. This is not a lot of money for a three hundred thousand square foot office building, but it is quite significant for a thirty thousand square foot building. The time to document LEED does not go down with building size. Because of this, many designers are using LEED as a design checklist instead of registering their projects, an unfortunate side effect for the Council, but one that presents an opportunity as well as a challenge. Once a project is complete, the design team hands over the documentation for review by the Council in the hopes of being awarded a good rating for the project. The Council is currently studying how to make the certification process less onerous without watering down its message.

An interesting development that perhaps reveals much about human nature is that most design teams, at the urging of their clients, shoot for the credits that are the cheapest and easiest to achieve rather than the points that may, in real terms, make the most environmental impact. Like shopping for a car, people try to get all the features they can for as little money as possible. As such, the LEED rating system is an imperfect judge of the true levels of sustainability. Indeed, perhaps the most frustrating thing about the LEED rating system is that it does not go quite far enough. People who think that Platinum is the final level of sustainability are grossly mistaken – indeed, the Platinum rating is not yet even a truly sustainable building! In actuality, if we kept on constructing buildings at the platinum level we might substantially slow the impact on environmental degradation but never actually eliminate it. The LEED rating system understandably starts at a point that is slightly better than conventional construction but stops at a point (platinum) that *most* projects can realistically achieve. But more is possible, and more is needed, and that is why the system needs to set its sights higher. As an industry, we cannot be complacent with merely doing less damage. We must start by truly believing that we can turn the corner and set our sights as high as possible. But what does this mean?

The Living Building – The Truly Sustainable Building

Any movement, if it is to succeed, must have at its core a solid vision of where it must head, or steering would be impossible. For sustainable design this vision must center on what a truly sustainable building must be like—not one that is merely less intrusive.

As part of this need, Bob Berkebile and the author defined what a truly sustainable building must do to deserve the designation in an article called *The Living Building* in the October 1998 issue of the *World* and *I* magazine. This article built on a previous vision statement crafted by McLennan for the national ACEEE conference in 1997 (American Society for an Energy Efficient Economy). This definition of the Living Building came out of a four-year research and design project called the EpiCenter, at Montana State University (MSU) in Bozeman, Montana, which was substantially funded by the National Institute of Standards and Technology (NIST). The purpose of the awarded grant was to design the most environmentally friendly building on the planet - in this case a laboratory—and to identify and fund technologies and strategies that could help take the project in this direction.

From the beginning, MSU's EpiCenter project was an attempt to define and make possible a new vision for the future of architecture. The goals, technologies and methodologies pursued in the NIST grant were all small steps toward a future where human efforts to provide shelter and comfort have no more impact than if nature itself was the designer. This vision of discovery relied on the wisdom inherent in living systems and rejected the notion that humans had to invent everything. The "Living Building" concept was the culmination of a large team of experts' efforts to achieve an incredible list of sustainable design goals in a simple metaphor, a paradigm shift in the way we approach architecture. Its power lies in the rejection of the "machine as metaphor" so prevalent in the mythology of architecture and technology in western culture. This mythology has been the driver behind humankind's use of nature simply as fuel in the machines that give us comfort, allow us to travel long distances, or provide us with food and entertainment. In its place the Living Building concept inserts the simple flower as a new metaphor for the buildings of the future.

Flowers are marvels of adaptation, growing in various shapes, sizes, and forms. Some lie dormant through the harshest of winters only to emerge each spring once the ground has thawed. Others stay rooted all year round, opening and closing as necessary to respond to changing conditions in the environment such as the availability of sunlight. Like buildings, flowers are literally and figuratively rooted to place, able to draw resources only from the square inches of earth and sky that they inhabit. The flower must receive all of its energy from the sun, all of its water needs from the sky, and all of its nutrients from the soil. Flowers are also ecosystems, supporting and sheltering microorganisms and insects just as our buildings support and shelter us. Equally important, flowers are beautiful and can provide the inspiration needed for architecture to truly be successful.

With this as a background, we can define what a living building, a sustainable building must do. Living Buildings will:

- Harvest all their own water and energy needs on site or in their immediate environment without creating pollution
- Be adapted specifically to their site and their climate while evolving as conditions change
- Operate pollution-free and generate no wastes that are not useful for some other process in the building or immediate environment
- Promote the health and well-being of all inhabitants—consistent with being an ecosystem
- Be comprised of integrated systems that maximize efficiency and comfort
- Improve the health and diversity of the local ecosystem rather than degrade it—move beyond sustainability to restoration
- Be beautiful and inspire us to dream

In essence, the true power of the living building lies within its ability to not only take care of its own wastes and impacts, but to begin to account for the transgressions of others—in other words to be a restorative building or project. Can our buildings of the future be restorative? Can they generate cleanly more energy than they need to help other buildings eliminate their energy footprint? Because of the magnitude of issues addressed in sustainability, it is possible to create an infinite number of sustainable design levels. The US Green Building Council has perhaps done the best job within just a few levels, although it too has much room for improvement. In the end a building is either truly sustainable or it is not. There are different shades of green. But they all point to the simplicity and beauty of a flower.

CHAPTER ELEVEN

Photo courtesy of McDonough + Partners

Productivity and Well-Being

"While an upgrade that cuts energy use in half can save one dollar per square foot in annual energy costs, it can generate more than ten dollars per square foot in new profits every year if it boosts productivity even five percent!" [1]

—Joseph Romm
Cool Companies

Introduction to Productivity

In the early years of energy conserving design human health issues were not at the foreground as they are today. The link between human health and the built environment had not been studied extensively, and the role that material selection and energy conservation itself would play had not yet been shown. Indeed, as some designers with very good intentions were to learn, the tightening of the building envelope, while saving energy, sometimes caused considerable indoor air quality problems as people were exposed to elevated carbon dioxide levels and trapped pollutants off-gassing from materials. Even less well understood was the psychological impact that our buildings had on our productivity and well-being. Home and office environments featured greater separation between the inside, daylight, and the outdoors. Along with this separation was an increased loss of personal control over comfort conditions, as people gave up operable windows and the ability to control heating and air conditioning.

For many Americans today the daily work experience is a drab one that consists of spending several hours behind a desk, within a cube devoid of daylight, architectural character or much personal control over thermal comfort or ventilation. Many of these offices are in large, ubiquitous glass boxes designed to maximize the number of work cubes that can be placed on a single floor. Further distinguishing characteristics of this work environment are uniform lighting and thermal conditions, minimal connections to the outside and often poor indoor air quality caused by toxic cleaning practices, unhealthy material off-gassing and poor ventilation. Little differentiation is also made between the type of work being performed and the work environment that supports it—a one size fits all mentality that denies the uniqueness of people and process. Considering how much time we spend at work, what kind of effect does this environment have on our health, on our well-being and even on our productivity and profitability? If this is our habitat, what kind of people and what kind of work does it support?

Human health and productivity are greatly affected by the buildings we inhabit. Our physical health and well-being are linked closely to the quality of the environments where we spend our time. Today, many Americans spend close to ninety percent of their lives indoors and, not surprisingly, if these indoor environments are unhealthy, they adversely affect individual health and productivity. Most of us have experienced less than optimal work conditions and we have been aware, to some degree, of how this can affect the quality of the work that we do, the speed at which we do it, and in many cases, our willingness to stick around to do it. In extreme cases, such as buildings that suffer from sick building syndrome, the negative environment is enough to send people home for extended periods of time with immune systems unable to fend off the repeated assaults by unhealthy indoor air. For most buildings the effects are not so dramatic, but still significant when looked at in whole. How much does our work suffer when there are distractions in the environment? How much does our work suffer when we are too cold? Too hot? When there is glare on our computer screens? Over the course of a typical day, hundreds of environmental barriers stand in the way of creating comfortable and safe environments for people and profitability for companies.

The typical American home, where most of us spend the rest of our time, is often little better as a habitat for human use, designed as catch basins for dust, dirt and allergens and sometimes as places of extreme mold growth. At other times, there is sometimes an improper separation between automobile exhaust in the garage and the home, subjecting people to potentially fatal carbon monoxide. According to the American Lung Association, the average home suffers from air quality significantly worse than can be found outside, even in industrial cities. It is a perverse outcome when our homes, which should be refuges, make us sick.

In recent years, one of the most compelling side benefits of the sustainable design movement is that building occupants in green buildings consistently report less environment-related problems than those in conventional buildings. Numerous studies in the United States, Canada and Europe have shown, as people moved from conventional buildings to green buildings, sick days and absenteeism declined and people reported less problems with thermal comfort. While this result was perhaps not surprising to some, it caught many people unaware, especially some of the most ardent of green supporters. In their passion to produce better buildings for the environment, many overlooked the fact that this would have a positive effect on individuals as well.

Many of the things that lower energy use or environmental impact help improve our well-being at the same time. For example, indoor air quality problems are sometimes caused by mold growth that occurs through improperly detailed walls that have become wet due to leaks or condensation. These wet walls often lose their ability to insulate as most insulation products degrade when moist. Paying close attention to protecting the energy efficiency of the wall over time has the dual benefit of safeguarding the air quality in the building and vice versa. It has been too easy to think of us as separate from the environment and we forget that environmental health is good for all organisms, including ourselves. Creating better places for people is crucial to business from a variety of standpoints. But the most compelling is the economic reason.

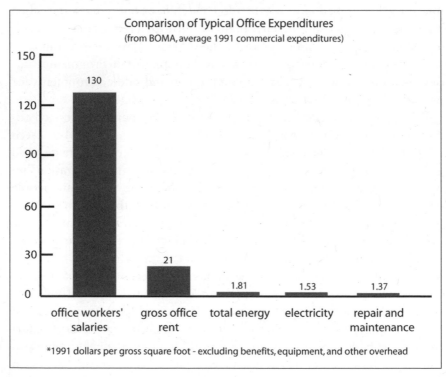

Diagram shows how salaries are by far the largest expenditure in a typical company– greatly out shadowing expenditures in energy and rent. Image created by BNIM Architects based on Statistics from BOMA.

The chart above from the Building Operators and Managers Association (BOMA) shows that the single largest expense of any business is the cost of people's salaries, which is significantly higher than all the other categories combined, including rent and energy. While the environmental movement spends a great deal of time trying to lower the energy bar by thirty to sixty percent, a much more compelling shift is to begin to affect the cost of people. A small improvement in productivity goes a long way towards the bottom line. Successful companies in the future will be those that realize that their people are their most valuable and expensive resource and will be willing to spend money to protect that large investment. The smartest businesses will track the quality of their work environments like they track the stock market or product quality, understanding that the best return on investment lies in maximizing what they have already spent. A compelling example of this is illustrated in the following example.

What if we could improve the productivity of a typical one hundred thousand square foot office with one hundred employees by five percent through improvements to lighting, air quality and thermal control at a price of two hundred thousand dollars? What would that be worth to this hypothetical company on an annual basis? What would it be worth over a ten-year time frame? What would be the amount of time required to pay back the electrical and mechanical investment with energy savings only? If we assumed an average salary of thirty-five thousand dollars per year per person, with a combined payroll of three and a half million dollars per year, this would equate to one hundred and seventy-five thousand dollars per year in productivity savings. Combined with the energy savings this equals almost a one hundred percent return on investment (ROI). The financial investment looks even more sound if we realize that once we have paid off the initial upgrades to building design or retrofit the rest goes straight to the bottom line. After ten years this same company would have saved the equivalent of one and three-quarter million dollars. Another twist on this example would be to imagine that this same company manufactures widgets, with a twenty percent profit margin on each widget sold. This company would need to sell two and one half million dollars worth of widgets each year to generate the same amount of profit to equal the one hundred and seventy-five thousand dollars through enhanced productivity—quite an incentive for the owners of the company to invest in a quality environment for their employees.

A five percent increase in profitability is entirely reasonable according to numerous studies done on productivity and the work environment in *Green Buildings*. In fact, ten to fifteen percent improvements are not unrealistic according to the Rocky Mountain Institute which documents that green buildings show "consistent gains in labor productivity of around 6-16 percent when workers feel more comfortable thermally, when they can see what they're doing, and when they can hear themselves think." (See

Greening the Building and the Bottom Line).[2] Joseph Romm, in *Cool Companies*, also says that:

"Productivity-enhancing design requires a shift in your corporate thinking. Companies under-invest in their workplaces in part because they tend to see efficiency improvements as simple cost-cutting, which rarely motivates much management attention or capital spending."[3]

Even more important than the idea that people are expensive is the realization that people are *valuable*. At the heart of every company are its people. Without the ideas and creativity of the people within an organization, growth and productivity would be eliminated. What companies get out of their employees is much more than the sum of their salaries. Most individuals feel a sense of pride when it is obvious that their company has spent money on their office and workspace. How many more winning ideas are created in great work environments versus typical ones? How many more great employees are lured and retained by companies that create positive work environments? When people are not healthy, happy or comfortable, the value of the company suffers with it. What kind of messages do businesses send when they do not give their employees access to a window with daylight, or do not provide good air quality and thermal conditions to a space? Perhaps those employees and their work are not that important! In the last few decades, it has been rare for companies or institutions to first ask the question "what does it take to make our workforce comfortable, productive and proud of their office?" and then design or retrofit their work environment based on the answers. For the last thirty years, most corporations and institutions have assumed that the built environment does not matter and the typical office of today is a manifestation of that philosophy. Fortunately, this is a trend that is starting to be challenged by progressive groups that see the value in investing in quality work environments. To the extent that a growing number of Americans are aligning themselves with environmental values, it provides additional reason for companies and institutions to support these issues, because people want to work in companies that consistently express these values in practice.

One of the earliest and most dramatic studies of the link between environmental performance and productivity has been of the ING (now NMB) Bank outside of Amsterdam designed by Ton Alberts. In 1978 the bank decided that it needed to make a move to a new facility for growth reasons, but also to help create a new image for the bank. Alberts, a believer in sustainability, and also in a philosophy known as "anthroposy", which supports the use of curves and rounded forms rather than rectilinear forms typical in the industry, encouraged the bank to consider a very untraditional building form. As reported in *Greening The Building and the Bottom Line*, a groundbreaking report by the Rocky Mountain Institute, the bank wanted a building that was "organic, which integrated art, natural materials, sunlight, plants, energy conservation, low noise, and water." [4] The design featured an undulating floor plan that was organized around a series of atriums designed to bring in daylight and bring life to the interior of the building. All workers in the building had access to natural daylight through the atriums and windows to the exterior.

The building's environmental performance was impressive. The new building consumed less than ten percent of the energy of the old facility and only a fifth of its neighbors being built at the same time. The incremental costs to improve the efficiency of the building from a standard facility was only seven hundred thousand dollars while its annual energy savings (due to the high European costs of energy) was estimated at a little over two and a half million dollars per year—a staggering three month payback. The most impressive story, however, was the result on human health and productivity. Absenteeism dropped and has remained at fifteen percent lower than in their old facility, with huge implications to the bottom line. Today, the building has become so popular that there is a one-year waiting list to even tour the building. That kind of marketing cannot be purchased at any price.

Since the late nineties, many other studies have made significant linkages between green buildings and increased productivity, including several in the United States. In Reno, simple improvements to the lighting and acoustics at the Main Post Office improved the working conditions so much (while lowering energy use) that the post office became the most productive of all the sorting stations in the Western Region of the United States with a six percent improvement in the amount of mail sorted per person. The $300,000 renovation was responsible for an economic productivity improvement of $400,000 - $500,000 annually! [5] At Boeing, improvements to lighting were done as part of the EPA's voluntary "Green Lights" program with a traditional return on investment of fifty-three percent, just a two-year payback due to improved energy efficiency. But much more importantly, safety in the plant was greatly increased as employees could better see the work they were performing. According to the company the ability to detect imperfections in work had improved by twenty percent. Simple improvements to environmental performance resulted in huge implications to airline passengers all over the country.[6]

Several schools around the country have been tracking changes in attendance, grade scores and even dental records of students who have moved from a conventional school to a school that used daylighting as the primary ambient light source. Students in a North Carolina school were shown to improve grade scores dramatically-up to fifteen percent as they were relocated to their new daylight school, with attendance and dental records also improving dramatically.[7] Our ability to learn is greatly affected by environmental conditions, the ability to see our work, minimization of auditory distractions and access to fresh air to keep us alert and healthy. Dental health relies on our ability to metabolize vitamin E, which is only possible in the presence of UV found in daylight. With so many children spending almost all of their time indoors, dental health as well as the connection to nature is suffering.

Similar studies have found the same results in schools in California and in Canada. Indeed, productivity studies in a variety of building types around the country have shown the same results with a rise in productivity of between five and fifteen percent which is very powerful. As Joseph Romm points out,

"While an upgrade that cuts energy use in half can save one dollar per square foot in annual energy costs, it can generate more than ten dollars per square foot in new profits every year if it boosts productivity even five percent!"[8]

In many ways, productivity issues may soon become the major driver behind the adoption of many green strategies. While a few people are willing to make changes based on environmental considerations alone, almost everyone is concerned with health and money—the two major things tied to productivity and well-being in occupants. More and more businesses are beginning to see the link between the environments they provide for their employees and the economic well-being of their company. But if the link to productivity and economics has been so strong, why has it not caught on even faster? The reason is that many people believe that productivity studies are a very soft science and subject to huge potential errors because of the variability of human behavior. To an extent their criticism is justified. Human productivity depends on an enormous array of factors, and it has been very difficult to measure and correlate improvements in the built environment to improvements in productivity.

Productivity can be greatly affected by many factors such as people's moods, their personal relationships, work relationships, and what they had for lunch. How much is truly linked to the work environment? To make it more complicated, it is even harder to determine what specific improvements make the most or no difference. How important is daylight compared to air quality? Is thermal comfort more important than having control over your lighting? At what point does it make sense to stop improving air quality? Lighting? These are all questions that need to be better answered, although it is unlikely that we will ever see definitive answers, but rather we should expect ranges with high degrees of correlation. The other problem with productivity studies is that there is as yet no consistent basis for performing them—no hard protocols accepted as industry standards. So even among the productivity studies that exist, the quality of the studies varies dramatically. However, even though it is difficult to measure productivity, we must continue to try because, as we have seen, the benefits can be so dramatic. And, more importantly, just because we have not figured out how much productivity is tied specifically to our physical environments does not mean the answer is zero.

Productivity studies tend to fall into two categories; studies that monitor things that can be empirically tracked and studies that rely on subjective information. Not surprisingly, the empirical studies have consistently carried more weight. These types of studies look at data that is typically available in most organizations such as absenteeism and sick days, or number of complaints. In manufacturing facilities the number of widgets being processed per person per day can be tracked before and after improvements have been made. While it is sometimes difficult to apportion the productivity enhancements between several building improvements, the overall results are clear. Subjective productivity studies rely on focus groups and surveys to determine how people are responding to their work environment before and after a new facility is built or a retrofit or remodel occurs. These studies demonstrate employee satisfaction, morale and describe productivity improvements. The results from these studies are more tenuous but, if reliable, are even more powerful than the empirical studies.

One individual who is trying to make what has been viewed as a soft science into a hard one is Judy Heerwagen. Heerwagen is an environmental psychologist who specializes in studying the link between productivity, well-being and green architecture. She has done numerous studies for corporate and institutional clients such as Sun Microsystems, Boeing and the GSA and her results also back up this link. She attempts, through non-obtrusive behavioral studies, focus groups, surveys and interviews to ascertain more closely which factors have the most effect on behavior and performance. Heerwagen believes that "buildings have far reaching impacts on human well-being and on organizational effectiveness" and that "we need to shift our focus from thinking of buildings as real estate costs to thinking of buildings as an employee benefit—one that contributes significantly to health, well-being, organizational attachment."[9]

The future for these studies could lie in establishing a link between subjective data and empirical data, such as making a link between the number of "cold" or "hot" complaints and the locations of air supply diffusers or the locations of windows as compared to where the majority of the complaints occur. Given the extreme importance of our architecture on our well-being and productivity, what factors have been shown to be the most important? In general, it can be said that there are two main categories of factors that affect well-being and productivity—physical factors and psychological factors.

Physical Comfort Factors

Physical comfort factors are easier to measure and include the following, which will be summarized briefly:

Ergonomics–Ergonomics is the study of physical human movement needs. Ergonomics is of vital importance to workplace comfort and productivity and includes a wide range of physical issues from the comfort of chairs and workstations, to the height and adjustability of keyboards. Good ergonomic design focuses on the ability to change and adjust the position of work-related tools to properly fit the needs of different people. Poor ergonomic design can greatly inhibit comfort and can lead to repetitive stress injuries, physical cramping and more. For the most part, this aspect of comfort has had significant focus in the office environment in the last two decades and the quality of our work environments in this area has improved as a result. The average office chair of today is significantly improved from just over a decade ago, although significant differences do exist between office equipment on the market. The workplace of the future will continue to improve on the ergonomic qualities of office furniture and systems to promote comfort and productivity. In general, ergonomics has little direct connection to environmental performance.

Acoustic comfort–Noise in the office environment is often a major factor in determining productivity, as distractions of this sort break concentration and waste time. Overly loud environments can make it hard to do work at all. Repeated distractions can significantly disrupt cognitive work tasks that require large chunks of uninterrupted thinking time. The trend towards open office plans has in some cases produced greater collaboration, but also seriously hurt productivity in others. The balance is to match the type of work being performed with a space that supports this activity, or to provide employees the opportunity to seek out quiet areas for specific tasks. As with a lot of things, one size does not fit all. Acoustic comfort also has little direct impact on environmental performance with a few exceptions. The traditional work environment, designed to be fully enclosed for privacy often eliminates the potential for daylighting and natural ventilation and increases the amount of energy required to heat and cool the space. Some sources of noise can also be a sign of energy inefficiency. Poorly designed mechanical systems with undersized ducts can create loud "whooshing" sounds in the office, the result of a great deal of friction in the ducts (called pressure drop) that requires fans to work harder and expend more energy to push the air. As mechanical guru Peter Rumsey points out "if you can hear air dancing, that's a bad sign."[10]

Thermal comfort–Thermal comfort is a problem that plagues almost every office in some form. It is a little known fact that every mechanical system designed is *based* on the assumption that a certain percentage of people will be uncomfortable thermally at any given time! The acceptable rate is usually around eighty percent of occupants satisfied, accounting for the fact that some people will always be too hot or too cold. This means that twenty percent are always uncomfortable! And this is at the start of the mechanical system life. Over time, as systems degrade and if maintenance is not kept up, or building managers are not adequately trained, the percentage of unsatisfied occupants grows even larger. It is not uncommon for thirty to forty percent of individuals to be uncomfortable thermally in a typical office (usually women who tend to wear lighter clothing or have exposed legs).

Thermal comfort is based on a variety of factors including temperature, humidity, air speed and the mean radiant temperature of surrounding surfaces (why we may be cold if we sit next to a big window in the winter). Things that also affect comfort include how we dress, which is called the *clo* rate and how active we are, called the *met* rate. For the most part, engineers ignore these last factors, and leave the temperature at one constant point year round (seventy-two degrees) with only slight variations, forgetting that people tend to dress differently in the summer and in the winter. This practice leads to a lot of discomfort and a great deal of wasted energy. Each degree that we set the temperatures below seventy-two in the winter and above in the summer represents a significant amount of energy saved. How many of us have come into our offices from outside in the heat of the summer and had to put a jacket on to stay warm because the office was over air conditioned? The temperature was probably within the comfort range, but *felt* cold because we were dressed for summer weather and because our bodies had acclimated to a certain degree to the outside temperatures. The converse is true in the winter. The differences in metabolic rates of people are also ignored as everyone, regardless of job description or physical size, is subjected to the same standard of comfort. Productivity is enhanced when comfort can be tailored more to individuals such as with the use of raised floor systems and thermofusers that allow users more control over air speed and delivery. Environmental impact can be greatly increased by poor thermal comfort, because individuals will do just about anything to stay comfortable. It is not uncommon in offices that are over air conditioned for people to bring in personal electric heaters that consume a great deal of energy; or in offices where people are too hot for people to open windows even when it does nothing but make the problem worse as outside air temperatures are hotter than inside.

Visual comfort–Visual comfort is a complex issue with a lot of variables, but in its simplest form deals with how well an individual can see his or her task during the workday. Visual comfort generally is dependent on having enough light on the visual task (but not too much) and as little contrast between this task and the field of view, which otherwise causes glare and eyestrain. The typical office environment of today is over lit, especially considering computer use, which demands lower light levels than in the past and more attention to lighting fixture position and type to avoid reflections and hot spots on computer screens. Like the uniformity problem encountered in thermal comfort, lighting design is typically done to ensure that most occupants can see properly. This approach does not account for the fact that people of different ages require different amounts of light or that we require different amounts of light for different tasks. As people get older more light is needed to do the same work. Too often lighting is done purely through the process of setting foot-candle targets—targets that are often outdated. A uniform fifty foot-candles has become a hidden standard in many people's minds, when this standard alone is no longer even endorsed by the Illuminating Engineers Society (IES).

"Lighting should be designed for people, not foot-candles,"[11] says Nancy Clanton of Clanton and Associates, one of the nation's top lighting designers. She reminds us that just as there should be seasonal temperature variation in thermal comfort, there should be some difference in the lighting environment from day to night and between different tasks. Good visual comfort is dependent on the type of light source as well. Direct lighting tends to create more shadows and contrast and is more harsh than indirect lighting. An office environment with light colored walls and ceilings and indirect lighting can improve visual comfort with only thirty-five foot-candles as compared to the traditional targets. The environmental impact is clear; the higher the light level, the more energy consumed. The workplace of the future will balance energy efficiency while giving more individual control over lighting conditions. The trick is to give people control over their own visual needs by providing task lights that people can turn on if they need more light.

Daylight is also a major part of visual comfort that is often improperly handled. Most work environments either have no effective daylight or do not properly control the daylight that enters their spaces resulting in glare and reduced comfort. Most of us have been in office environments where the blinds were always closed to block the harsh west sun; windows are of little use when the blinds are pulled! The access to windows is also important for another physiological reason. Concentrating on an object close at hand, such as a computer screen, for a long period of time can cause eyestrain and headaches. In order to rest the eye individuals need to be able to have opportunities to change the field of view or focal length of what they are seeing in order to reduce eyestrain. Being able to look out a window provides this visual relief. Good daylighting design will be the hallmark of the workplace of the future.

Indoor Air Quality–Indoor air quality is perhaps the most important part of the workplace of the future because it relates to personal health and productivity. As the American Lung Association says, "When you can't breathe, nothing else matters."[12] All buildings, regardless of the type, should have healthy indoor air quality to protect the well-being of occupants. Considering how fundamental good air quality is to health and productivity, it is amazing how little attention is paid to it in most environments, especially when it is the largest contributor to sick days and absenteeism among employees. Since 1995, thirty percent of new and remodeled buildings have been subject to excessive complaints about indoor air quality (EPA)[13]. Indoor pollutant levels can be two to five times, and on occasion up to one hundred times worse than outdoors according to the EPA. Sick Building Syndrome awoke many people to the importance of good air quality, but buildings with slightly less bad air often go undetected or unreported. Many people suffer from poor indoor air without ever knowing or complaining.

Air quality problems in buildings can be from a variety of sources such as from the off-gassing of building materials, molds, dust, dirt, combustion appliances and from the quality of the air brought in from outside. Good maintenance practices, along with filtration and ventilation, are essential to keeping air quality positive. However, it is important to note that many times the cleaning practices themselves are a major cause of unhealthy air in a space because of the toxicity of the cleaning agents themselves or due to new irritants created by the reaction between the cleaners and other gases in the air.

The typical mechanical system is designed to deliver a certain *quantity* of air, which is supposed to result in good air quality, but the office of the future will actively measure air *quality* in order to inform about the appropriate amount of air needed at any given time. Where possible, ventilation rates should be slightly higher than presently typical. This rate increase does not have to hurt energy efficiency. Carbon dioxide sensors can be used to monitor air quality and increase or decrease the amount of air delivered by the mechanical system as the number of occupants fluctuates.

While the focus in this section has been primarily on the office, the stakes are often higher in the home where indoor air quality can wreak havoc on our health and the health of our children. Allergies, asthma and chronic sinusitis are on the rise, in part due to the unhealthy air found in the place that should be a refuge for us.

Psychological Comfort Factors

Psychological comfort factors are harder to quantify and study than physical comfort factors, but they are no less real in terms of their impact on productivity. Once again, it is important to recognize that just because it is hard to quantify some of these factors does not mean that they do not have an impact on health and productivity. Psychological comfort factors include the following:

User Control–One of the most important psychological factors related to productivity is the ability to alter the work environment. In many cases the perception of control is often more important than anything else. People need to be able to have some sort of control over their environment and personal comfort. The ability to open a window, turn on a task light, adjust a thermostat or adjust the height of chairs are examples of user control options. In many cases, people do not often exercise these options. What appears important is that they can if they want to. Newer technologies such as raised floor systems are allowing people to have more user control of their thermal environment just as new chair designs like Herman Miller's aeron chair allows for maximum control over sitting posture and support on an individual basis. Giving people control over their environment can, in some cases, lower environmental impact.

Connection to the Outdoors and Daylight–Some of the strongest links to productivity have to do with the access to daylight. Emerging evidence is showing that people need to maintain some sort of connection to the outside and have access to quality, glare free daylighting in the work environment. This daylighting, if properly designed, can provide the majority of the ambient lighting in the office, supplemented with electric lighting that is dimmed or brightened depending on the amount of daylight available (which also saves energy). The office of the future will banish the windowless office and allow people to work in closer connection to the natural world.

Boundaries and Personalization–One factor that is universally important to people is the ability, at some meaningful level, to personalize their workspace. Backward thinking organizations are those that take the approach that everyone's work environment should be exactly the same with no ability to customize, hang pictures and celebrate the uniqueness of the individual. This sameness philosophy denies the uniqueness of individuals and at some level suppresses creativity and innovation. The workplace of the future will allow for customization and the creation of boundaries. People need to make claims to territory; "I am here, I exist!"

Beauty–Perhaps the hardest thing to measure is the effect that beauty and good design plays on our ability to work effectively. Although on the surface the idea of beauty and good design may appear trivial, beautiful environments are often the root of inspiration and creativity and the same is no less true in the work environment. While some individuals may be more sensitive to the quality of the aesthetic environment than others, there is no doubt that a dingy, ugly office environment does little to motivate or to send messages about the quality of the work that should be produced on a daily basis. If a company does not care enough to create a beautiful, quality work environment, then why should an individual be bothered to create quality work either? If an individual had a choice between an office that paid no attention to aesthetics and one that had beautiful furnishings and artwork, which one is the most likely choice? Which would any person be more proud of showing to family and friends? Human beings are greatly affected by the subtle messages found all around them, including messages about how important they are relative to the perceived investment in their work environment. Progressive companies of the future are those that realize that it pays to invest in quality architecture, art and design in order to motivate employees.

In addition to the psychological factors outlined above, one more such factor remains.

Biophilia—An Emerging Concept

> We forget that there is more wisdom in the voices of wind and water than can be found in any talk show, self help tome, or politician: that there is as much spiritual sustenance in a night sky or a misty morning as an ornate cathedral or charismatic sermon: and that there is more life purpose in growing a garden than in many careers, and more education in exploring a marsh, pond, or prairie than can be gained from months in a classroom.[14]

The Healing Earth by Philip Sutton Chard

In 1984 two-time Pulitzer Prize winner E.O. Wilson coined the term *Biophilia* to describe the innate tendency of people to "focus on life and lifelike processes." A growing group of designers are realizing that the discontent and negative reactions many of us have to our built environments is due to the fact that we have denied this innate tendency. It took a biologist to remind us that we, too, are biological creatures. Surrounding ourselves on a continual basis with inanimate, lifeless surroundings has a draining effect on our well-being and morale. We have an industrial economy that rewards only sameness, and this has bled too far into the fabric of the built environment. We spend hours surrounded only by concrete, steel and sheet rock. As author Philip Chard describes, "Most of our children live as bubble babies, and grow up to be prisoners of technology and materialism."[15] Many individuals feel trapped and depressed in clinical surroundings—a symptom that could be called the "biophilia effect."

As the use of technology has exploded, we have felt compelled to create physical habitats that appear to change along with it, and yet the basic human needs for our buildings and shelter have changed little, if at all, on a fundamental level over the past few thousand years. We still have the same basic needs of safety and comfort; it is only that our definitions and standards for what this means have changed. Technology should be used to assist in meeting our needs, not drive us away from what we need. This philosophy is based on the phenomenon that people, just like all living things, are attracted to life and life-like features and if given a chance, will go out of their way to bring these things to their home or office if they have not been made available in sufficient quantities. People fill their spaces with plants and greenery, with running water in fountains, and many of us, mostly subconsciously, seek out these places whenever we can. The concrete jungle is no replacement for the real one. "Technology may leap forward and as it does the economy may undergo spasms of change, but we are foolhardy if we base the nature of our communities on the latest technological and economic innovations while blinding ourselves to innate human needs.[16]"

It is a sad commentary on the design professions that many designers have an intellectual aversion to creating places that are filled with life and natural energy. It is as if the professions, still in the throes of the modernist doctrine, feel an uncontrollable need to remove the unpredictable spirit of nature at every turn and embrace the certainty and boldness of the machine. At the same time, these designers express surprise when the layman, who is uneducated in the rhetoric and jargon of modern design does not openly embrace the same aesthetic. Indeed, there is a running joke that architectural projects that win awards are often those that turn out to be least loved by the general public—suggesting either that the general public is ignorant and incapable of knowing what is good for them, or the architectural community is out of touch with what people want or need and is too arrogant to want to know or care. The truth, like many things, is probably somewhere in the middle. A classic example of this is the Pruitt Igoe housing development in St. Louis that was once awarded many design awards in the sixties as a shining example of modernism. It proved to be a horrible place to live, made worse by the economic conditions, and was torn down within twenty years of being built. How unsustainable is that!

When people outside the design professions are asked what they like, they usually ask for curves, for warm materials, for lots of light and for water, and reject the orthogonal, Cartesian forms built with concrete and steel. The reaction from the design community is usually disdain—"they do not know better" the designer proclaims. And while this is true in some ways (most people cannot articulate or create the places of beauty that design professionals can), it is not true in all ways, and perhaps not in the most fundamental way. The layman, although not always able to articulate why certain places and spaces are positive, is in some ways more in touch, if only subconsciously, with an innate need for life and life-like processes. For all its good, education can sometimes separate us from our intrinsic needs.

Truly great architecture, modern or traditional, does appeal to a lot of people, but not because the architect designed exactly what the public said it wanted. Instead, the architect found a way to respect the underlying emotional needs of people, incorporating these needs within the overall design of the building—a goal that resonates from the six principles of sustainable design. Good design respects the idea of biophilia, and finds a way to interject life and life-like processes throughout the design. All of us, on some level must feel that our basic needs are met by the buildings that enclose us—the need for shelter, warmth and beauty, and perhaps surprise and whimsy. Architecture fails when designers turn their backs on these needs and feelings. The biophilia effect ties heavily into the principle of respecting the cycle of life, for it is this connection that helps make us human. When we disconnect ourselves from nature it has adverse psychological effects. The idea of biophilia does not imply that all architecture must be organic and overrun with ferns and philodendrons. Indeed, there is something in us that seems to require a balance, a degree of separation from wildness, that allows us to feel somewhat removed, to be human.

Designing with biophilia in mind implies balance. When nature feels oppressive and overwhelming, as in the desert, people need a refuge that is more clinical, cool and austere. In a dense urban environment, where people are surrounded only by concrete and bricks, designers must do everything they can to introduce life throughout the design. A brutalist office building needs to have gardens that offer a green refuge from the hard concrete. More than most designers, the designer of a brutalist structure, (defined typically by extensive use of concrete and no ornamentation) requires an even greater understanding of the concept of biophilia to be successful. The designer must convey life in other ways than through the structure of the building, such as through a heightened sense of contrast, to the role daylight plays out on the interior of the building, or perhaps how the building itself relates to the site and views beyond.[17] In contrast, a forest camp should have a few places where nature is kept at bay, a place that carries the unmistakable hand of the man-made, indeed of our tools and machines—a place that offers refuge, not from the clinical, but from too much wildness.

The balance is different for different people to be sure. The major lesson that this chapter on productivity should teach is that people and their needs are diverse and like the natural environment, the built environment must allow for a diversity of experiences for us to be healthy, comfortable and productive.

Prospect and Refuge

The Pritzker Prize winning architect, Glenn Murcutt, integrates this balance successfully into all his work, embracing the idea of prospect and refuge that allows people access to something greater beyond, something natural and wild, while protected and sheltered in a place of our own making. There are many who believe that this balance is part of our genetic history, from a time when being too exposed to the elements and to nature was a risky proposition, and being too enclosed and sheltered, without a view to what was beyond (presumably sneaking up on us) was equally dangerous. Our genetic make-up perhaps compels us to seek a balance of prospect and refuge.

The Architecture of the Future—The Living Habitat

Over the next few generations we will continue to understand ways in which to create environments more closely tuned to the varying needs of the people within them. We will draw from nature to give us clues and insights into the effects our work and home environments have on our health, our well-being and even our productivity and profitability. The living habitat of the future will spell the end to boiler-plate solutions to comfort and design and will be characterized by flexibility and adaptability, perhaps even encompassing virtual environments that will help people adapt their surroundings based on the changing demands of the day.

Architects, builders and developers of the future will be charged with the job of redesigning work habitats in which to encourage the type of work necessary within, through the appropriate balance of physical and psychological factors. Like examples drawn from nature, our future habitat will have no net negative environmental impact[18] and will serve as an eco-tone, if not for other organisms then at least metaphorically as a place to cultivate a diversity of ideas.

The buildings of the future will provide people with more possibilities for connecting to external environments. As well, tomorrow's work place will be designed for people, not cubes, and tailored to the type of work being performed, with sound investments in healthy and beautiful interiors. Access to quality daylight and good air will also become hallmarks of the workplace of the future. The workplace of the future will be designed to more closely maximize the substantial investment in the people that it supports. Many companies that thought that they could not afford to invest in quality work environments will realize that they must do so. Progressive companies will be willing to spend more money upfront for buildings and systems to promote the well-being of their workforce and to cultivate the atmosphere of innovation and quality. As a consequence, these buildings will use more durable materials and be much more healthier, environmentally friendly places, with significantly reduced energy and resource consumption. In addition, technologies that reduce energy use, while improving comfort and user control, will prevail in the buildings of the future.

The Building Habitat of the future will:

a. Allow for seasonal and day/night variations in lighting and thermal conditions
b. Reconnect people to the external environment through views and daylight
c. Give control back to people for thermal comfort, ventilation, and lighting
d. Use daylight as the primary ambient light source when available
e. Use healthy, durable materials that require little maintenance

f. Use passive strategies such as natural ventilation and passive solar for thermal comfort where possible
g. Invest in art and design to create beautiful environments
h. Focus on acoustical comfort tied to tasks being performed
i. Allow for views and access to a range of visual experiences
j. Require regular maintenance to keep the building performing well
k. Closely monitor and regulate indoor air quality
l. Allow for personalization of spaces
m. Emphasize good ergonomics
n. Reduce environmental impact and waste
o. Be designed around the notion of biophilia and allow access to life and life-like processes throughout the interaction with the building.

CHAPTER TWELVE

Photo courtesy of BNIM Architects.

Greening Your Organization

"Whatever you can do or dream you can, begin it.
Boldness has genius, power and magic in it."

—Goethe

Greening Your Organization

Let's face it. Change is hard. On an individual level it is a difficult task to break old habits, unlearn old processes and learn new things. We were good at it when we were young, but not so good now. Given that this is the case, making change on an organizational level is an extremely difficult and daunting task. And yet, in organizations and design firms around the country, many have begun the journey of making change to green their organization. Many more are now seeking to begin the journey, and looking for some sort of road map or direction on how to do so. Organizational change of this nature seldom occurs on predetermined paths, as usually it involves a certain amount of kicking and screaming as people shed entrenched old habits. Organizational change from a conventional company to a green company or institution requires changing the mindsets and patterns of numerous people, all at different points in their overall journey and at different levels of interest in sustainable design.

Change usually starts with a few individuals who push within the organization, and it occurs in "fits and starts" rather than in a continuous, streamlined process. Rarely do whole groups agree on the priorities in sustainable design, even in so-called progressive institutions. It takes time to build knowledge and to build consensus and, as we shall see, the most time is spent on eliminating barriers. The key lesson to internalize is that change takes time. But this does not mean that one should not try to move quickly and move boldly to shake up an organization. Urgency is needed and as Goethe said, "there is genius in boldness."[1] But one should realistically be ready for change to happen much slower than what may be desired or imagined, and to source victories wherever they can be taken.

John Knott, CEO of DeWees Island and a pioneer in the green building movement reminds us that "a pace that may seem slow and painful to the change-agent, may in fact feel like incredibly fast-paced change to the rest of the people in the organization."[2] It is essential to put ourselves in the shoes of others, before we ask them to move in the direction we want them to go. So how does one make organizational change?

Step One—Establish Measurable Benchmarks

The first step in greening an organization must always begin with understanding how green the organization is to begin with by establishing a series of measurable benchmarks. Change cannot begin without an understanding of what needs to be changed and this can only be accurately gauged through some form of measurement. In general, organizations can be divided into four general phases related to how green they are.

The Four Green Phases of Firms
The four phases of sustainable design knowledge are as follows:

Phase One – The Brown-Green Phase

Phase One organizations are defined simply as those organizations that have zero to little interest in or knowledge of sustainable design. Needless to say, most petrochemical and automotive companies would fit in this category. Unfortunately, the same could also be said for most organizations involved in the building industry, although this is changing at a phenomenal rate. Just a few years ago, most architecture firms fell into the Phase One category alongside their counterparts in engineering and construction. However, most architecture and design firms have now moved beyond this phase, leaving engineering and construction firms behind. Many Phase One firms exist, not because they are against environmental stewardship per se, but rather, until recently, they did not understand the connection between their work and its impact on environmental health. The Phase One organizations can be summed up by describing them as being "green" about "green."

Phase Two – The Light Green Phase

Phase Two organizations are those with a mild interest and beginner's knowledge in sustainable design. Organizations that fall in this category have begun to learn the jargon and buzzwords found in the field and have typically become aware of how sustainable design is changing the industry. Phase Two organizations typically contain a mix of individuals, including those who might have a greater than Phase Two level of knowledge, but also many with only a Phase One understanding. Phase Two organizations often have leaders who give only mild support to sustainable ideas, or are early on their own learning curve.

Many times Phase Two organizations harbor individuals with little or no interest in sustainable design who have had to begrudgingly learn a few things about the subject because of the recent shifts toward green in the marketplace. In general, it takes an organization one to two years to move from a Phase One organization to a Phase Two organization with some effort, although an individual can move from the first phase in as little time as six months.

Phase Three–The Green-Green Phase

Phase Three organizations are categorized as those with moderate to serious interest and knowledge in sustainable design. Phase Three organizations have a working knowledge of how their specific field impacts the environment, basic knowledge of some solutions on how to minimize this impact and a beginning knowledge of the issues in other related disciplines. In general, Phase Three organizations still approach their process in largely the same way that they have always done, and attempt to apply sustainability as a layer (usually unsuccessfully) at the tail end of the project. For example, Phase Three mechanical engineering firms still make the same conservative assumptions about loads within a building and methods for providing comfort, but seek to specify more efficient equipment as the final solution. The overall environmental impact of projects that come out of Phase Three firms are typically not much less than conventional firms, due to the lack of systemic change that occurs to the process.

What is important to note is that when companies reach the Phase Three level, most begin to sell themselves as green businesses and tend to go after projects with this selling point as an angle. Phase Three organizations typically lack a high degree of technical knowledge about environmental performance, although a few technically skilled individuals may reside within the organization. Very few construction companies and engineers currently fit within the Phase Three category, although this number is changing rapidly. The largest group by far consists of architects and landscape architects. For most firms this phase serves as a type of ceiling because of the challenges of change within an organization and because of the amount time and resources it takes to progress to Phase Four. Depending on the organization and the resistance to change found within, the time to go from a Phase Two to a Phase Three firm can vary anywhere from two to five years. Since this is by far the broadest category, there are many shades of green or sub levels that could be identified within this group. Around the country, there has been an emergence of green teams in architectural and engineering companies, which for the most part tend to start in Phase Three firms.

Phase Four–The Dark Green Phase

Phase Four organizations are those with a high degree of interest in and knowledge of sustainable design principles and technologies and which have significantly modified their work process to adopt the holistic thinking process identified in Chapter Eight. Unfortunately, there are currently very few organizations that have reached the Phase Four level of knowledge. A Phase Four understanding requires years of technical research on both a broad and specific basis and practice trying to implement sustainable design principles. Inevitably it requires a willingness to throw out and relearn old professional habits. A Phase Four firm requires strong leadership as well as a consistent base of support to make sure that things do not slip back to the status quo. There are probably only a few hundred Phase Four individuals in the building industry today in the United States and Canada and only a couple of dozen organizations that would deserve the designation. Examples of some Phase Four Organizations[3] would be the Rocky Mountain Institute, The Center for Maximum Potential Building Systems, the Environmental Building News Team and Elements, the sustainable consulting division of BNIM Architects.

How Size Affects Green Change

In theory it is possible to green any organization regardless of size. However, in practice, the larger the organization the more difficult the process is to effect. Large organizations tend to have more levels of bureaucracy that fundamentally resist change. The larger the organization the more inertia there is and things tend to stay the way they are. Compounding this problem is the fact that, over time, organizations undergo substantial changes in personnel, most of whom come to the organization "green about being green."

What tends to happen is that larger organizations have smaller green teams within an office that hopefully are able to influence the larger entity, but usually these teams remain at the fringe of the organization. It is very possible for large organizations to have sub groups within that have reached a higher phase in the progress cycle than the organization as a whole. Many design firms now have green teams that contain Phase Three or Phase Four individuals surrounded by a sea of individuals at a Phase One or Two level. The amount of change that does occur has a lot to do with where these green teams emerge. An inspiring example is that of Ray Anderson, CEO of Interface Carpets, who "got religion" after reading Paul Hawken's book, *The Ecology of Commerce.* As CEO of Interface, Anderson was able to create sweeping changes within his company resulting in vastly reduced environmental impact per linear foot of carpet produced. More importantly, Anderson helped create change across the entire carpet industry as other carpet companies saw the marketing, operations and sales benefits of reducing waste, energy and water use and began their own journey to green change.

Change at the grassroots level and even the middle management level is also entirely possible, but more difficult. Most people are not willing to fight strongly for environmental issues if they perceive that their superiors will discourage change. It certainly is easier if the boss is on your side. The most effective change occurs when there is support at all levels. The leadership of an organization needs to send a strong message of support for change and a clear vision of direction. Middle management needs to ensure that the vision is being implemented at all levels, but particularly needs to enable changes to be pushed through from below.

It is doubtful that most organizations can progress beyond Phase Three without the major decision makers being in the Phase Four Category. To move beyond a Phase Two organization, the leaders of an organization need to, on many levels, give up being the expert and sometimes unlearn years of habits. For some it also involves accepting that the work done by the organization—work that they were responsible for in the past was not sustainable and may have been irresponsible. This is a hard thing to accept. Denial is easier. True leaders are those who realize that what they did in the past was likely the best they knew how to do at the time and now, with new information, there is no going back to the way things used to be. Another challenge for some leaders is to allow younger staff members who are better informed about sustainable design to become the experts.

Industry Trends – The Four Phases

Within a decade almost every organization involved in the building industry will have moved to a Phase Three level. With the increased adoption
of the LEED standard as a mechanism for change, and as a requirement in
many jurisdictions, most engineering and construction firms will complete
the transition from Phase One to Phase Two. Most architecture, interior
and landscape firms will complete the transition to Phase Three firms in
this time frame as well. By the end of the decade, sustainable design will
have completely emerged to the mainstream.

Ten years from now we will also see the emergence of a fifth phase of
development, The Phase Five firm. The Phase Five organization will be
defined as an organization that has honed its holistic, integrated design
abilities and has begun the process of consistently producing living buildings. While only a few organizations will have this capacity by 2015, by
2025 it will be more commonplace.

The attached diagrams show how various sectors of the building industry will likely undergo the change through the various phases.

Figure 1

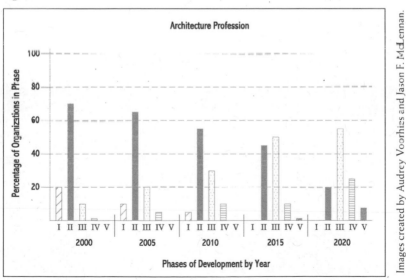

Fig. 1 shows how the architecture profession as a whole has progressed, or is
likely to progress through the five stages of development outlined in this chapter.
Note the emergence of the fifth phase by 2015.

Figure 2

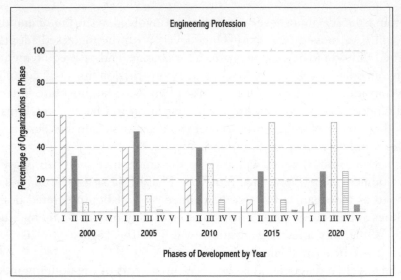

Images created by Audrey Voorhies and Jason F. McLennan.

Fig. 2 shows how the engineering professions are likely to progress.

Figure 3

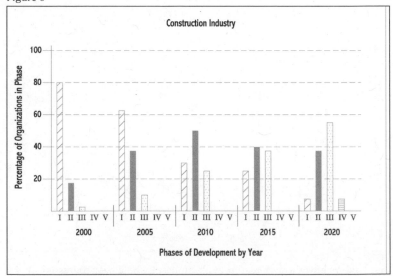

Fig. 3 shows a probable progression of the construction industry.

Step Two—Set Achievable, Measurable Goals

Once an organization has correctly assessed its current level of sustainability the next step is to set achievable, measurable goals for change. In order to set measurable goals the organization needs to have a good understanding of where it is today. How much environmental impact does the organization have? What things are working already? The process of setting goals for the future should not take on the tone that everything is terrible today. Rather, the process needs to recognize the good things that exist within an organization and then build on top of them. Goals that organizations set can take a variety of forms, but the important point is to find ways to measure progress and to set a series of targets that progress can be checked against.

For example, the City of Seattle has decided that all new city facilities will achieve a minimum of a Silver LEED rating. By using LEED, the city is allowing great flexibility in the strategies that individual design teams use to achieve the goal, and yet still require a very measurable method of assessing change. The Greater Seattle Area has adopted similar standards for all new buildings over two million dollars in construction cost. At the time of this writing, many other jurisdictions are exploring their lead. Still within the USGBC framework, many organizations are setting measurable goals based on the number of LEED accredited professionals in the organization. KEEN Engineering, a leader in green comfort engineering services, has set a goal that all employees in major decision-making roles (project managers and above) will have the accreditation. In less than two years they had almost completely achieved this goal.

Aside from LEED there are many other measurable benchmarks to explore. Some exist in other programs, such as participation in the DOE's Energy Star program or Spirit, the military's Green System. Many other goals do not involve a program per se, but they are no less powerful. Municipalities could set measurable watershed management goals, or goals for percentage of construction waste that is diverted from landfills. The possibilities are endless.

There are four main areas where an organization could set benchmarks or goals. These four categories are:

1. People
2. Facilities
3. Operations
4. Products

People–Since sustainability is concerned with the health and well-being of people, setting goals to improve well-being and productivity in an organization should be an important part of the goal-setting process. For example, organizations could set goals for reductions in absenteeism and sick days as part of their process for change. Or goals related to knowledge of sustainable practices. The process of setting goals could result in a better understanding of staff morale and team dynamics. How happy are people with their work environments? How productive are they? How could recruitment and retention be improved through the greening process?

Operations–Most businesses and institutions have an incredibly large ecological footprint. The amount of materials and energy required to keep them going can be onerous, and as a result, expensive. Setting goals for environmental change should include the operations of the organization. For example, according to a study by Sylvatica, BNIM and the Center for Maximum Potential Building Systems,[4] of all the embodied energy found within a typical new building at least ten percent can be attributed to the operational impacts of architectural and engineering services, (i.e. the amount of energy and resources it takes to keep the firms operating while working on the design of the project). Questions that should be asked include: What is the environmental impact of the operations of the organization? How much paper or related products are used? What waste products are created by the organization? Do people in the organization travel a lot (travel, especially airline travel, adds extensively to the footprint)? How much energy, water and materials does the organization consume over the course of a year? Once all of these factors are known the organization can set measurable benchmarks for change. Goals could include a transition to a paperless office, reducing solid waste produced by fifty percent and so on. On an operational basis, the organization could set important sub-goals related to profitability and marketing.

Facilities–Related to operations, but so important that it deserves its own category, are the facilities that an organization operates. In most cases this category has the largest direct environmental impact. Businesses would be wise to monitor and measure the amount of energy and resources it takes to operate their facilities over the course of a year and set targets for reducing these amounts. In many cases simple upgrades to lighting and mechanical systems can be made that reduce overall energy use by thirty to forty percent with incredibly short paybacks. With facilities the economic impacts are compelling. Simple goals could include setting targeted reductions in energy and water use to operate facilities.

Products—For companies that produce physical products, the environmental impact associated with manufacturing can dwarf all others. Understanding the implications of the manufacturing process and setting goals to reduce resource use per unit of product is essential. For the New Belgium Brewing Company in Fort Collins, Colorado, this meant purchasing all of its electricity needs from local wind farms—thus making this company the first wind-powered brewery in the world. Service–oriented organizations, while not directly having environmental impact, often have products that indirectly do. For example, design firms should question whether their services result in a positive or negative environmental impact and set goals to make positive change. Many architectural firms are in the process of greening their specifications and standard details, an action that can have wide-reaching positive implications. For universities, the question could be, "are we teaching our students what they should know about the environment?" Goals to address these types of questions should be identified in measurable ways just as if they were physical products.

Step Three—Understanding the Sources and Barriers to Change

Once an organization has correctly established its goals and assessed where it is in its overall journey, it is important to understand what barriers to change exist within the organization. For many organizations time and money are often major excuses for why change does not occur or occurs slowly, but this is usually a smokescreen for a different type of barrier that will be discussed. As long as goals for change are set based on realistic benchmarks at a reasonable pace and a clear vision for change has been crafted (either internally or with the help of a consultant) then fiscal and temporal barriers can usually be overcome.

The major barriers to organizational change in any type of organization are human-based barriers. It is these barriers that we will discuss. Understanding peoples' attitudes towards environmental change is important in crafting a strategy to create positive change. Within organizations there are individuals who can be grouped or typed as change resisters or change agents. Change for the sake of the environment alone usually enlists few dedicated individuals. Guilt is a poor motivator. Change that is shown to be in people's best interest on the other hand (higher profits, better work environment, etc.) attracts a lot of support. The problem is that, for the most part, when people see change they worry about all the potential negative ramifications that could result. Instead of looking for the potential positive spin-offs they focus on perceived negatives such as losing control of a situation, having to do more work, embarrassment or fear of inadequacy relative to potential new roles. The challenge is to help people see the benefits and the potential gains associated with the change.

This first group consists of people in the design professions who will try and find ways to undermine the process of greening an organization.

The Change Resisters

The Green Critics

For years, when sustainable design was still a fringe topic in the building industry, almost every organization had an army of Green Critics that resisted any attempt to move from conventional practice to one that was more respectful of resources and energy. Now, as the subject of green has moved more into the mainstream and become more accepted, the number of open Green Critics has declined dramatically. Green Critics can be defined as individuals who openly question the need for environmental concern and the appropriateness of changing organizational practices to lessen impact. Despite the drop in numbers (most have just changed tactics as we shall see), a significant number who view sustainable design as impractical and expensive still remain, typically on the construction side of the spectrum.

Green Critics are often older people within an organization who are used to being expert in all aspects related to their profession and who may view sustainability as being a threat to this position. At other times, the Green Critic may be an individual with an extreme dislike and distrust of environmental initiatives for political reasons. Regardless of the reason, the Green Critic will actively serve as a barrier to greening an organization, using his or her technical knowledge or seniority to discredit or hamper progress. When Green Critics occur in an organization it is very important to get to the root of their criticism and find technical ways to address their concerns. Sometimes their position is purely as a result of ignorance that can be adjusted with education. Most of the time however, the criticism is just a technically veiled smokescreen for an underlying fear of change. The organization should do what it can to educate and remove any fears that might exist within individuals of this type. Where technical excuses are used to block change, technical reasons to support change should be given. Wherever possible the tactic should be to identify and address the Green Critic's underlying concerns and find solutions that meet these concerns. However, if the critic cannot be converted, and the organization is serious about sustainable design, it must rid itself of all its internal Green Critics. This purging process should carry through within an organization to those who serve the organization down the supply chain. For example, if a green architect is working with a mechanical engineer who will not incorporate sustainable design principles into his or her design then the architect should pass the mechanical engineer over on the next job and refuse to work with this individual until he or she is willing to get on board. An owner who can not get the architect to do the right things should also find another architect. Sustainable design is challenging enough without people deliberately putting up roadblocks. Plenty of consultants (architects, engineers, etc.) now exist who are willing to change the way they design and build buildings. In most cases, the attitude is more important than the experience.

The Wolf in Green Clothing

Now that it is no longer politically correct to be an openly Green Critic, many of these individuals have found other ways to put up roadblocks without appearing to be difficult. The Wolf in Green Clothing describes these individuals who have not changed their base opinions, but have changed their tactics to maintain barriers to sustainable design. Because of the elusive nature of their tactics, this type of individual is much harder to address as a resister to change.

Indeed, the Wolf may be verbally supportive of sustainable design, but will find ways to avoid making change or make token changes as a diversion. This type of individual says all the right things but does nothing. In response to this type of individual the organization should request changes against measurable, predetermined goals over a set time period. If no acceptable change occurs by the set timeframe then the same purging invoked for the Green Critic should be adopted. Actions, as the saying goes, speak louder than words.

Another version of the Wolf in Green Clothing is the "Old Green Expert." This type of individual makes claim to already be practicing sustainable design and usually has been "doing this since the seventies." The real truth is that the individual has not done much, or was involved in one or two projects decades ago that did a few green things. Good technical understanding such as can be found in the 'Green Warrior' type described below can ferret out this individual for what he or she is—a wolf in green clothing.

The Designer with a Capital 'D'

Almost every architecture and interior design firm has a number of individuals who believe that the pure expression of their art is the highest ideal to be pursued. Environmental performance, indeed sometimes even the comfort of their clients, is secondary to the purity of their architectural concept. Like a page out of Ayn Rand's *Fountainhead*, these individuals believe in minimizing the number of issues that could provide obstacles to creating a great design in their mind. Usually the Designers with a Capital 'D' try to minimize or eliminate sustainable design concepts in their design process which they view as yet another barrier to their art. Usually these types of individuals take themselves much too seriously and through arrogance attempt to hide a deep-rooted insecurity about their own design abilities. The good news is that these types of individuals can often be approached through the language of design in order to show that sustainable design can provide opportunities to strengthen a parti (a parti is the architectural word for concept) rather than weaken it. As more and more talented designers embrace sustainable design and provide examples of how sustainable design has added meaning and richness to the design process, the less barriers will exist. For example, when talented design firms like Lake Flato Architects start preaching the virtues of sustainability, it does a lot to convert many Designers with a capital 'D' to at least begin to incorporate sustainable design principles into their buildings. Trying to convert these types of individuals by saying that "it's the right thing to do" never works. Only by speaking first to the issues important to them, and then providing examples of successful projects, can the individual be moved.

The Efficiency Engineer

Similar to the Designer with a Capital 'D', but found within engineering organizations exclusively is the "Efficiency Engineer." The Efficiency Engineer is used to describe engineers (mostly mechanical and electrical, but sometimes civil and structural) who resist making changes because they are either afraid to make changes to their set way of doing things or are afraid to be viewed as something other than the expert that they have been viewed. This type of individual can be extremely stubborn and will dig in and hide behind technical smokescreens to avoid the appearance of being wrong about something. For Efficiency Engineers efficiency is important but only within the spectrum that they are comfortable with. Their main fault is that they do not go far enough, and at the same time they think they are on the cutting edge. The Efficiency Engineers will often specify the right equipment, but will usually continue to grossly oversize a system with conservative assumptions. In the end these types of engineers produce more efficient systems at a premium and continue to believe that being green is always more expensive.

Their biggest concern is to remain the expert and to not look bad, and they typically hide behind a strong veil of jargon and technical data or experience in order to avoid change. It is particularly hard for clients and architects to challenge these engineers because of a lack of technical knowledge. Finding ways to widen their spectrum, without confrontation and in a way that empowers them is the most successful way of dealing with these individuals. Another effective way to deal with this type of individual is to tie suggestions to actual measurements in order to move the debate entirely out of the realm of the subjective. It is also good strategy to bring in an external green engineering consultant to question the engineer's assumptions. Good Efficiency Engineers will believe the numbers if they can be convinced to measure and monitor before designing a system. In the end, the Efficiency Engineers may welcome new opportunities to be even greater experts at what they do and become allies in the process.

The Change Agents

The Greens in Waiting

A majority of Americans today believe that environmental issues are important, yet most of these individuals are not willing to do much to change their own behavior. For them the environment is something that is very much external to their lives-important yes, but relevant—only barely.

The Greens in Waiting category presently sums up the vast majority of individuals within the design and construction world. They will do nothing to resist organizational change in this arena, but they will also not go against the more vocal protests of the Green Critics. Their passion and willingness to change lies dormant. Despite their seeming ambivalence, at heart they do support the issues and they are crucial to building momentum within an organization for change. They cannot be looked to for leadership or direction, but they can provide critical mass. With convincing enough arguments, good education and some inspiration a few can even be converted to Green Champions. Finding out who in the organization fits into this category and beginning a long process of education is important to creating organizational change. In time, the right way of doing things will become second nature to them.

The Green Champion

In almost every organization in the design and construction industry today there are a few individuals who feel passionate about the environment and are pushing to make positive change in as many ways as possible. These individuals are not always overly knowledgeable about green design, and often have little practical experience, but make up for these shortcomings with enthusiasm and persistence. This type of individual can be known as a Green Champion. Green Champions tend to be younger individuals within a firm with little clout until opportunities present themselves where the information that they know suddenly becomes useful to the organization (such as when a client requests that a project be green). Greening an organization requires the identification of Green Champions within the organizational structure and finding ways to promote or support them in their efforts. It is essential that Green Champions be given opportunities to educate themselves and spend time with individuals with greater sustainable knowledge than they possess. Uneducated Green Champions can sometimes do more harm than good by making unsubstantiated claims and by suggesting design and material changes that they do not completely understand. Green Critics often use the inexperience of Green Champions to provide more reasons to support the status quo rather than change. Despite this resistance, it is usually the Green Champions who begin change within an organization due to enthusiasm and often, youthful exuberance.

The Green Warrior [6]

After several years of hands-on learning and research in the sustainable design world and with exposure to the right teachers, Green Champions can become Green Warriors. The Green Warrior is a Green Champion who has developed a high degree of technical competence in the issues that underlie the sustainable design process. The metaphor of the warrior was chosen to symbolize the extensive knowledge and skill that is present in this type of individual. Unfortunately, there are very few true Green Warriors in the country today (although a lot of individuals think they fit the bill). Out of all the individuals within an organization, Green Warriors have the most ability to affect change because they can back up sustainable design ideas with technical knowledge essential in solving problems that arise and competently address issues raised by critics.

It typically takes five to ten years at a minimum, fully immersed in sustainable design projects to become a Green Warrior, although time alone does not bring people to this level of understanding. The Green Warrior is one who understands the interconnections between various aspects of the sustainability umbrella and has internalized the holistic thinking approach to design and problem solving. An essential part of the definition of these individuals is their awareness of what they do not know about sustainable design. In other words, they know their limitations and are able to prioritize impacts based on a thorough understanding of the issues.

Wherever possible, an organization wanting to make change should hire Green Warriors to help to make change happen. An organization may start with Green Champions who learn on the job but this approach takes more time and often results in a non-linear path towards the ultimate goals. Hiring a Green Warrior as a consultant or as an employee in charge of making change will be more helpful in achieving goals than anything else.

Step Four–Making a Plan for Change

Change of any type requires a roadmap. After an organization has set goals and determined where its staff and organization as a whole sits relative to these goals, a plan for change needs to be crafted. Again, these goals need to be set with measurable benchmarks along a realistic schedule. The roadmap needs to be flexible to account for changes of direction and pace along the way. The speed of travel is less important than the direction. The good news is that once people start moving in the right direction seldom do they move back. Who wants to revert back to practices that are irresponsible, polluting and immoral?

While every organization is different, there are a few common strategies that can be used to set a framework for making change. Nine of these are listed below:

1. Seek Help
2. Start an Education Program
3. Build a Library
4. Build Incentives for Change
5. Change Standard Practices
6. Allow for Research
7. Change Hiring Practices
8. Weed Out Resisters
9. Change Marketing

Seeking Help

Making change within an organization frequently requires outside help. Often, the organization in question does not possess the knowledge and experience to implement a shift towards sustainability. The first part of making a plan for change should be to enlist qualified consultants who can provide direction and information. A growing list of individuals is available nationally who can provide this support. While LEED Accreditation is no guarantee for true sustainable knowledge, the US Green Building Council is a good source for this type of information, as is the American Institute of Architects Committee on the Environment. Care should be taken to find individuals with true experience with sustainable design and not just theoretical knowledge. Be wary of the new crop of green "experts" who have little knowledge or experience. Even if an organization contains individuals with knowledge and experience in sustainable design it is still usually wise to enlist outside help. There is a strange part of human nature that listens better to outside experts than inside experts. Even though individuals within an organization might possess the same information as the outside expert, having it presented by the outside consultant is often more effective.

Start an Education Program

The answer to many problems rests with good education. An organization wishing to make change must find a way to educate its people about sustainable design strategies. An education program could incorporate a series of monthly presentations by both outside and inside experts, participation in green building conferences, or even required readings. At BNIM Architects for example, Phaedra Svec, a member of the Elements consulting division, created an intensive program for greening the whole firm. The heart of her program centers on a monthly presentation series called: It's Elemental. It's Elemental features speakers from within the office presenting on topics ranging from daylighting to green material selection. When outside consultants come to the office for project work, some of them are enlisted as guest speakers. Svec's program continues through a series of focus groups containing interested individuals from a cross section of the firm who discuss sustainable design concepts and strategies. The training program has been highly successful. BNIM also sends many of its employees to conferences to continually add new information to the firm's knowledge base.

The essential part of an effective education program is that it must be continuous. A single conference or presentation does little to move an organization over time, as the inertia of the status quo is quite taxing. Education towards a sustainable organization must be viewed as a long-term effort with frequent sessions to be effective, and at all times information must be presented in a way that is relevant to the audience. The appendix in the back of this book contains a list of some of the best sustainable design conferences in the country.

Build a Library

Related to building an education program is the importance of giving people access to sustainable design information. Every organization hoping to make change should build its own green library and make the collection accessible and highly visible. The library should consist of more than just books and include green material samples, videos and graphics. The appendix in the back of this book contains "The Green Warrior Reading List", a collection of books that read together over time can provide a compelling background. Also in the appendix is a collection of useful websites that provide sustainable design information. The single best source for sustainable design information continues to be the resources put out by *Environmental Building News* in Vermont. Its monthly newsletter is well worth a subscription for any organization directly in the building industry. An even better deal is their back-issues integrated with green product listings and case studies in the online Building Green Suite.

Provide Incentives for Change

Providing incentives for change is crucial to getting broad participation within an organization. Incentives could include promoting green champions within an office or rewarding motivated employees with opportunities to travel and participate in green conferences in exciting locations. Sometimes all the incentive that is needed is to make sure that the climate for change is encouraged. Leaders within an organization need to send a strong message that actions to promote sustainability will be encouraged and all others met with disapproval.

Change Standard Practices

The Achilles heel for many organizations relative to sustainable design is often the standard practices or rules of thumb that guide how an organization does its business. When standard practices are not green, each use of them is a step in the wrong direction. Many times standard practices are not changed simply because this is how it always was done. For design firms, standard practices would include a firm's typical specifications or standard details. For engineers it might consist of rules of thumb for sizing equipment. An organization wishing to make change should begin by examining its standard practices. When these are improved, changes ripple through each project that the organization is involved with.

Allow for Research

Successful organizations are often those that realize that it is important to invest in research to keep new information flowing in. Because of the speed at which new technologies are changing in the sustainable design world, investing in research becomes critical.

Change Hiring Practices

It is counter productive to hire Green Critics. Over time an effective way of creating organizational change is to hire individuals who have experience with sustainable design. This hiring strategy is an effective way to jump-start the change process. Failing that option, the organization should look for individuals who have knowledge about and a good attitude towards sustainability. Changing hiring practices to include candidates who are university graduates with these credentials has the added bonus of influencing the schools that they come out of. Most universities are still not teaching enough about sustainability, but this will change as the marketplace demands candidates with certain skill sets in this area.

Weed Out Resisters

As mentioned earlier in this chapter, once all avenues have been exhausted in trying to motivate reluctant employees towards sustainable practice, an organization must rid itself of these individuals if it is sincere about creating change. Other businesses down the supply chain should also be given opportunities to reform, and then they too should be let go until they change their practices. Practicing with integrity at all levels means that organizations will also fire their clients if they continually refuse to make improvements in the right direction. Be wary, however, of making the perfect the enemy of the good. Do not hold people to impossible standards.

Change Marketing

The last thing an organization should do in its quest for sustainability is to change its marketing. Too many organizations now exist that claim to be green before they have actually done anything to change their behavior and impacts. Making claims to be a green organization should only be done after considerable progress has been made.

Green Economics

By the time the design for most human artifacts is completed but before they have actually been built, about 80-90% percent of their life cycle economic and ecological costs have already been made inevitable.

—Joseph Romm

Green Economics

Few things in the sustainable design arena are as misunderstood as the economic implications behind designing and building sustainably. And yet, perhaps the most often asked question by designers and clients alike is "how much does it cost to build green?" The perception by most in the building industry is that sustainable design costs considerably more than conventional building construction and is appropriate only if the budget can support the added costs. Because of the perceived added cost, some shy away from sustainable design altogether and many more merely try to incorporate a few token green features that can make affordable substitutes for conventional materials and systems.

While the belief that sustainable design is always more expensive than conventional construction is ultimately incorrect, as we shall explore, it is founded in a great deal of historical truth. In the early days of the movement, sustainable design was almost always more expensive. Most design teams had minimal experience with sustainable strategies and the resolution of these ideas seemed to always cost more money and time. Green materials, such as they were, were always more expensive than their conventional counterparts due to smaller economies of scale, and the lack of competition within this new niche market willing to pay more because of ethical beliefs. A huge problem was often the invisible "green mark-up" (which still exists today but is shrinking) tacked on by builders unfamiliar with the new technologies and techniques and unwilling to take any risks. Since some of the new green products had been tested less over time than their conventional counterparts, there was indeed good reason to worry about how they would stand up to conventional criteria. A few defective products further clouded the issue within the industry. For example, some of the earliest "healthy paints" did not stand up to the same durability tests as conventional paint and required additional coatings for the same level of finish, greatly increasing the cost. The inexperience of design teams further compounded the price problem, as less efficient equipment was swapped for more efficient equipment on a one-to-one basis, rather than investigating the costs in a more integrated, holistic way. By way of illustration, a more efficient and expensive pump would be used to replace a less efficient one, without first seeing if, through careful design, a smaller pump could be used that would offset the incremental increase in efficiency and cost.

At the same time, many of the national green experts continued to claim that sustainable design did not have to cost more, which helped counter the increased expense perception, but in most cases added to the confusion. So to the present, the economics of green remains one of the burning issues facing the movement. How much does green cost and how does it compare to conventional construction? Such a reasonable and straightforward question deserves an equally reasonable and straightforward answer. And yet, this type of answer is impossible to give. The real answer is **that it depends.**

In chapter eleven, we learned about the significant potential economic benefits of sustainable design linked to the effect on human health and productivity. Many people are now realizing that for these reasons alone, sustainable design makes a compelling economic case. Productivity gains in green buildings often make up or exceed any additional upfront costs of green building within the first year or two. In addition, several other related benefits occur. According to the Rocky Mountain Institute: "Green Buildings typically sell or lease faster, and retain tenants better, because they combine superior amenity and comfort with lower operating costs and more competitive terms. The resulting gains in occupancies, rents, and residuals all enhance financial returns." The Institute also reports, "Better indoor air quality can improve health and productivity and reduce liability risks. The EPA estimates that building related U.S. illnesses account for $60 billion of annual productivity lost nationwide, and a wider study valued that loss as high as over $400 billion."[1] For many people, the arguments described above are too esoteric. They require a more direct, easily proven link between cause and effect. For these individuals discussions of payback and economic trade-offs are unimportant.

Many in the building industry just want to know the bottom line—how much will it cost upfront? The answer to traditional economic questions depends on a host of factors, some of which include:

1. How Green is the Team?
2. Where is the Site and What is the Project Type?
3. What is the Economic Criteria or Baseline that the Costs are Being Compared Against?
4. How Green is the Project?

This chapter will examine these four questions as they relate to sustainable design costs.

How Green is the Team?

As with a lot of things in life, experience counts. Teams that have little experience with sustainable design end up producing solutions that invariably cost more than is necessary. There is a cost associated with learning on the job. For the design or engineering firm this may mean accepting a lower profit in order to pay for the additional training and research time, or higher fees to accomplish the job. For the owner or developer the inverse is true; a willingness to pay more to train their consultants, or a willingness to accept what they get—which is usually a much lower level of performance than is possible for the same economic outlay with a more experienced team. While Phase One firms (as described in the previous chapter) would not even attempt it, Phase Two firms are usually not capable of producing a high performing green building that is not significantly more expensive than their conventional product. For them, it is usually critical to hire sustainable design consultants (bringing the experience in from the outside) in order to avoid making costly mistakes in terms of performance and cost. A client wanting a green building should pay for a design team that has experience, or be prepared to pay a lot more for the final product. For Phase Three and Phase Four firms, the costs tend to come down significantly, and in some cases there is considerable cost savings.

Efficiency expert Joseph Romm points out that while "upfront building and design cost may represent only a fraction of the building's life-cycle costs, when just 1 percent of a project's up-front costs are spent, up to 70% percent of its life-cycle cost may already be committed. When 7 percent of project costs are spent, up to 85% of life-cycle costs have been committed."[2]

Mistakes made by inexperienced design teams in the beginning of the project are hard to make up later. The authors of *Natural Capitalism* elaborate by saying "that first one percent is critical because, as the design adage has it, all the really important mistakes are made on the first day."[3] The experience and knowledge of a design team have a significant effect on cost. Understanding the cost of green involves an accurate assessment of the knowledge and skills of the team pursuing the work. As reported in *Natural Capitalism*, "Economic Dogma holds that the more of a resource you save, the more you will have to pay for each increment of saving...however, if done well, saving a large amount of energy or resources often costs less than saving a small amount."[4] Done well, in this sense, means thinking holistically and finding ways to tunnel through the cost barrier that is usually self-imposed by a particular way of thinking. The more creative the team, the less chances that team members will fall trap to the "green is always more" syndrome. *Natural Capitalism* describes several examples of whole-system thinking including piggybacking on existing improvements to pay for upgrades in other areas, doing things in the right order (the order of operations) and looking at improvements as part of a system rather than in isolation. These strategies are all discussed in the next chapter—Holistic Thinking.

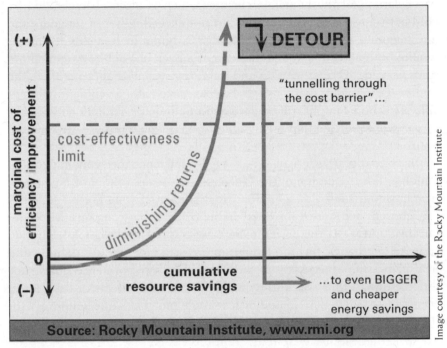

Image depicting the concept of 'tunneling through the cost barrier' as described in the groundbreaking book *Natural Capitalism*.

Where is the Site and What is the Project Type?

The answers to the economic questions posed vary greatly depending on where the building is located, the nature of the site and the nature of the building and its size. Broad generalizations across categories and locations do not work. The reason why some people believe green is more expensive while others think it is the same or less is that they are usually not comparing "apples to apples", which can be very difficult in buildings on a national scale. Unlike cars, no two buildings are exactly alike. Climate can play a large role in a building's cost due to the systems required to keep the occupants comfortable. In a mountain climate, for example, it may be possible to design a house with no mechanical heating and cooling system, instead relying on solar heat gain in the winter and natural ventilation in the summer. Eliminating these systems might result in a high performance house that is equal to or less expensive than a conventional house. The particularities of the mountain climate, which is often characterized by cold but sunny winters and warm, but not exceedingly hot summers and low humidity allow for this. In contrast, a home in Kansas City might require both a heating system (at least as a back up) due to extended periods of cold, overcast weather and a cooling system that can remove the oppressive humidity that for several weeks make natural ventilation untenable. This home might still be designed to allow for natural conditioning in acceptable weather but the design response would not save any money upfront.

On a micro-scale, the actual site may also influence the economics of the building. For the design of the University of Texas School of Nursing, a benchmark green building in Houston, a site with a long north-south axis was chosen. Because of the unfavorable orientation (long facades facing due east and west) the design team was required to design an elaborate series of overhangs, fins and atriums in order to meet the daylighting and heat gain criteria necessary to meet the client's performance goals. Additional design time was also required to study the effects of daylight in the space to avoid glare caused by low angle sun. The same building, with the same performance goals, would have been cheaper if a site had been available that was oriented in the right direction.

Beyond the site and climate, the other important variable is that of the building itself. Some building types lend themselves to greater cost reductions than others, although the specific cost reductions change as the buildings grow or shrink. Returning to the first example reveals an instructive lesson. A passively conditioned house in a mountain climate depends on a proper balance between thermal mass and glass. As a house grows the relationship must also adjust. A house that grew too big might make it impossible to rely on passive heating and cooling systems and the addition of mechanical systems would start to bring the cost up. Similarly, in the same climate a large auditorium accommodating large numbers of people might make the use of natural ventilation inadvisable for occupied modes but certainly useful for pre-heating or cooling the structure.

So the answer to how much green costs is still "that it depends". Generalizing costs based on such a complex mix is nearly impossible. Ultimately, the most accurate way to address the question is to simply find out how much an existing building with comparable qualities and performance costs to build in that region. As shown above, the comparison building should be in the same climate, with similar site conditions and with a very similar program and size.

What is the Economic Criteria or Baseline that the Costs are Being Compared Against?

Trying to answer the question of how much a building is going to cost compared to a conventional building also raises a series of compelling issues. The first is understanding what is meant by conventional. For some spec developers, the baseline is often the cheapest building that can legally be built. Green Buildings typically have a difficult time competing on a first-cost basis with this type of building as it usually suggests a certain level of quality that just would not be found in the lowest common denominator. For others, the baseline might be of a much higher quality. A university, for example, might establish a baseline comparison to the last building that was built on campus. In this case, the economic baseline may not end up being any lower than the green building, because once a certain level of quality and durability in construction is reached it is often the design response that makes the most difference in which building would be more expensive or efficient.

The questions pertaining to cost also raise the issue of what costs are compared. Will the comparisons take into account untraditional methods of comparing value such as productivity or marketing benefits? Is the comparison on a first-cost basis (as with spec developers and some homeowners) or on some sort of life-cycle basis? Cost may also differ greatly depending on what numbers are included in the comparison. A lot of green buildings have difficulty competing on a first-cost basis with their traditional counterparts (designed to externalize their costs first) but quickly show an advantage over a few years. Looking at cost in this manner is known as life-cycle costing. Deciding on the basis for the investment and its payback usually makes a big difference. For example, requiring a two-year payback on all systems within a building may make it difficult to improve environmental performance greater than twenty percent on a large office building. Extending the accepted payback to five to seven years on the other hand tends to open up a lot more options in terms of specifying equipment and systems that perform well but cost more upfront. A payback of fifteen years effectively captures any technology available on the marketplace in the green arena. In general, it is in the best interest of any property owner who plans to hold on to a building for a long time to accept longer paybacks on materials and systems. Another important question is whether the comparison is between construction costs or soft costs or both? (Soft costs refer to the non-building related fees such as architecture and engineering fees, and permits) A comparison of soft costs only might reveal greater expenses on the green building due to higher design fees and yet, combined with the construction costs, this increase might be negligible, or even reduced, if the design team managed to reduce the construction costs more than the increase in its fees.

While the payback argument is a powerful one for sustainable design, it has at the same time hurt it on a few occasions. In some ways the desire to see a payback on any green substitutions has gone too far, with some clients expecting to see payback calculations for any material that is considered green. Most traditional materials are not subject to this analysis and yet green ones are.

How Green?

In Chapter Seven we discussed the various shades of green that exist in the industry based on the LEED rating system's four levels. We also discussed the addition of a fifth level of sustainability, a level that is called **The Living Building**. It is the living building, which is to provide a vision for the future of architecture. In addition to these five levels it is possible to envision a preliminary level that we can call the market level that describes the average low end, first-cost basis building that is so often built. Looking at the economic implications of each of these levels would likely reveal a difference in cost even if all other variables remained the same. The level of sustainability matters when it comes to economics.

In 2001, the David and Lucille Packard Foundation, a charitable foundation based in Los Altos, California, hired a team of sustainable design experts[5] to design its new headquarters building. The Foundation has a history of funding environmental and conservation projects worldwide and wanted its new building to be an example of environmental responsibility. At the same time, however, it wanted to produce a green building that could be used as a model for other institutions, and not something that was too futuristic and possible only because of the Foundation's substantial resources. With this as a goal, the relationship between cost and performance became a major part of the project's definition. The design team was faced with the same challenges that have been previously outlined in this chapter. How does the level of sustainability change its cost? How does one define replicability? And on what time frame? How would the site and climate and program affect performance and cost? Based on the unknown nature of some of these questions, the Foundation hired the design team to answer its own questions, reasoning correctly that the knowledge gained would be useful to the whole sustainable design movement and not just for its own purposes.

The result, after a year of work and a rigorous peer review process, was the groundbreaking Packard Sustainability Matrix and Report that can be found at the David and Lucile Packard Foundation website. The matrix is the first holistic study of the economic implications of the various shades of green in the industry. To produce the study, the team designed six different buildings on a schematic level. The six buildings were all designed on the same site and with the same program—the major variable being the level of performance achieved. Each level of performance resulted in different responses in form and materials and systems specified. The lowest level of performance was the Market building, which was based on the typical speculative office buildings being built in the area. The next four levels were comprised of the four levels of sustainability found within the LEED rating system. The final level was that of the Living Building. After the team had designed the six buildings, energy models of each were built to calculate energy usage, the resulting pollution and operating costs. An independent cost estimator with experience in the region was hired to estimate the construction costs of each of the five levels in order to determine first costs. In addition, the design team investigated possible impacts to the construction schedule, design time and design fees.

Once results from the energy model and construction estimates were known, the team was able to show how the buildings would do economically over thirty, sixty and one hundred years (which was one of the goals

for the project—to produce a building that would last one hundred years).
The team also showed the amount of pollution that would be generated
over twenty years in NO_x, CO_2, SO_x and PPM[10] and the resulting "external costs to society" calculated very conservatively from a Harvard study
linking pollution to external health care costs. The results proved to be
a compelling case for the strength of sustainable design. Over time the
highest levels of environmental performance proved to also be the best
economic performer, and the lowest level, the Market building, proved to
be the least sound economically. The jump from Market to Certified alone
represented almost a fifty percent reduction in pollution, yet with no additional design costs or schedule impacts and only a ten percent first-cost
premium over the lowest common denominator.

An important point to make about the Packard study is that while the
actual numbers are useful, it would be a mistake to try and apply them
wholesale to other projects unless that project happened to be an office
building of similar size in Los Altos. As we have already learned, a great
number of things ultimately influence cost in a green building. What is important are the general trends that the study sheds light on. For example,
since actual costs can vary, it should be assumed that achieving a certified
level of performance is not necessarily any more expensive in first-cost
dollars than a conventional building. Depending on the quality of construction in a comparison building, it is likely not any more expensive to
build to the silver level either. In most cases, however, a gold building will
bring additional upfront costs to a project. The Packard study also solidi-
fied the idea that over the life of an institution like a university, munici-
pality, or foundation, the wisest economic choice would be to produce a
living building or platinum-level building. To view the complete Packard
Sustainability report and Matrix, visit the website.[7]

Now that the major variables affecting cost have been discussed, can
any useful generalizations be made? The answer to this question is yes.
With a healthy dose of caveats it is possible to lay out some rules of thumb
about the economic costs of sustainability.

Areas of Design and Construction Typically Unaffected by Cost Premiums or Savings

Structural Systems– In general, there are few premiums or savings associated with the structural systems in a green building. On a case-by case

scenario a green building may have either a lower or higher first cost than a conventional project depending on the design response but no overarching generalizations seem to apply.

Interior Systems–Generalizing about the cost premiums of interior systems (furnishings and fixtures) is incredibly difficult due to the wide variety of options available. In the past this category was typically more expensive in green buildings than in conventional buildings but much of this discrepancy has diminished because of the proliferation of green building materials in the market. Better alternatives for carpet, paints and furniture systems are now readily available at no real premium. The cost premiums or savings in interior systems that do remain are more typically the result of design rather than intrinsic cost premiums. Expect either no premium, or only a small one.

Areas of Design and Construction with Reduced Costs

Site Design and Infrastructure—In many instances, sustainable site design results in lower upfront and maintenance costs. In general, the philosophy argues for less parking, less site disturbance, fewer curbs and narrower streets. Landscape design typically relies on indigenous plantings that require less water and less maintenance costs as well.

Mechanical Systems–The principle of rightsizing, providing the size of mechanical system that is needed rather than grossly overcompensating (which is typical) usually means that mechanical system design is less expensive in green buildings than in conventional ones. In many green buildings mechanical systems can be eliminated or downsized significantly due to the adoption of passive heating and cooling strategies and a greatly improved building envelope. It should be noted that green buildings usually have some more expensive controls such as motion sensors, daylight dimming and carbon dioxide monitors than their conventional counterparts. Additional commissioning also has the potential to increase the upfront costs of the mechanical system, albeit with very attractive paybacks.

Areas of Design with Increased First-Costs

Design Fees–How cost affects design fees is a big issue in the sustainable design arena. In theory, achieving lower levels of performance should require no additional design fees compared to conventional design. However, as the level of performance rises, so too should the design fee. To achieve a high performance building requires greater collaboration among disciplines. The result is a better product, but higher fees. For less experienced teams the amount of time for research also increases. Cross-referencing the levels of experience of design firms with the design time might reveal the following relationships.

> **Phase One**–Higher Design Fees required to achieve any shade of green
>
> **Phase Two**–Higher Design Fees required to achieve a silver or higher rated building
>
> **Phase Three**–Higher Design Fees required to achieve a gold or higher rated building
>
> **Phase Four**–Higher Design Fees required to achieve a platinum or higher rated building

What this referencing says to potential clients is that it makes sense to pay for firms further ahead on the sustainable design spectrum and not to scrimp on design fees or the desired level of performance will likely not be reached.

Envelope Design–The amount of money spent on the envelope of the building, its glazing, insulation and exterior materials is almost without exception higher in a green building than in a conventional building. Green buildings typically have more expensive glass, a greater attention to reducing infiltration losses through caulking and sealing the building and more insulation. Green building envelopes also typically include more external shading devices that add first cost. The good news is that these premiums, since they deal with energy usage, come with some sort of payback.

Lighting Design–Lighting design in a green building is usually slightly higher than in a conventional building. Sometimes this increase is due to fixtures that offer better distribution but with increased first cost, or to lighting controls that adjust the amount of light. Typically, improvements in lighting design offer short (two to four year) paybacks and remain great investments in any building type.

Green Buildings Add Value

By building green a developer may in fact increase the property value of the building compared to a conventional building because of its significantly lower operating costs over time. Since the expenditures per square foot are lower than a comparable building of the same size when capitalized the value per square foot rises significantly—very helpful when it is time to resell the building. In one example, provided in *Environmental Design and Construction* magazine, a one hundred and forty-five thousand square foot building saw an eleven percent increase in its value due to its significantly lower energy costs.[8] Since utility bills are reduced developers can either pass on savings to their tenants, which will help make any building more attractive, or they could increase the rental rate to increase profits while keeping the overall rate comparable to the market. Either way, more value is added.

With the focus on indoor air quality and occupant comfort in most green buidings there is also the potential to attract more people who value being in a healthy work or living environment. In other words, in a corporate environment a green building can become a marketing tool to attract and retain good employees and also be, for developers, a way to distinguish their building from others in a real estate market.

Conclusion

As can be seen in this chapter, the economic argument in support of sustainable design is impressive. Green design, when done properly, does not necessarily cost more and in some cases is less expensive than conventional construction. For many projects the costs still do come in higher than conventional construction, but with paybacks and fringe benefits that quickly make a difference in making up the premium. The final word on the economics of sustainability is that the answer really depends on how the question is framed, and what variables are considered in the equation. Viewed in isolation, the relative costs of sustainability will vary greatly depending on the level of performance achieved, the building type, size and site, and the make-up and experience of the team. When viewed holistically, sustainable design is the most economically successful option available to designers and their clients.

Why build green?
- Improved marketing potential
- Improved productivity of inhabitants
- Improved retention and recruitment of staff
- Reduced litigation potential of occupants
- Increased property value
- Higher rental rates potential for owners

CHAPTER FOURTEEN

Photo courtesy of Jason F. McLennan

The Sustainable Design Process–
Holistic Thinking

*"Instead of seeing the rug being pulled out from under us,
we can learn to dance on a shifting carpet"*

Thomas F. Crum

Defining Traditional Design

While architectural design is by its nature an iterative process, it is not a particularly inclusive one and often involves only a narrow field of specialists who perform their work in relative isolation. Architects, engineers, contractors, and other building professionals often do little to understand the interconnectedness and interdependency of the issues that affect each other. Nor do they try to understand the ways in which they could improve each other's performance by altering their own process. Instead, many seem stuck in the inertia of "the way things have always been done."

The design process has often been described as a cyclical one. Designers test concepts and work back and forth through various solutions arriving at the one that seems like the best fit for the given set of issues analyzed. Traditionally, these issues tended to be centered on cost, functionality and aesthetics, with little attention paid to the possible wider implications of design. The notable exception is often urban design issues, which architects in particular think a lot about. However, with typical project schedules and tight budgets this cyclical process is very quickly abandoned for a more linear one. Architectural solutions are layered with mechanical, structural and electrical solutions rather than integrated. Often the only real discussions about their integration occurs when there is a significant conflict among the various professions involved in a project. As long as things are working adequately then the project proceeds forward.

The Sustainable Design Process

Sustainable design requires a change in the typical design process in several fundamental ways.

1. It implies a willingness to do things differently than what is conventionally done
2. It requires expanded collaboration between disciplines and a greater focus on process
3. It requires adhering to a green design methodology or Order of Operations
4. It requires the use of a holistic thinking process by key decision makers on the project.

The result of these four changes in the design process is outlined in detail below.

Doing Things Differently

Sustainable design requires doing things differently. It typically spells the end to boilerplate solutions that do not change from building to building and place to place. It often requires more change to design process than to changes in materials or technologies (although these changes are also made). And sometimes, conventional materials and technologies used in unconventional ways can have a dramatic effect on performance.

Change is difficult for people, especially in areas where it means changing old habits and thought patterns. It is far easier to merely substitute a green material for a conventional one than it is to change process. Sustainable design demands a willingness to unlearn and relearn things as fundamental as simple problem solving skills. Because of this demand, many architects and engineers feel that sustainable design can be a burden to the design process, forcing them to deal with more issues than they should reasonably handle. They also fear that the demand will short-change the traditional issues that are still deemed more important by them. This is an unfortunate and uninformed conclusion.

Like many assumptions, this one is merely an excuse to not have to learn another set of skills and a discomfort with being in a position of learning instead of being an expert. It is difficult for many who have spent a lot of time in a position of knowledge to suddenly feel like a student again. For some individuals there is also a feeling that to change invalidates previous work and creates a defensive reaction. "If I have to do something completely different than I did before, does that mean that everything I did up until now was wrong?" In fairness, the answer to this question should probably be "no", but the next response should be, "but if you do it again it will be!" Innocence can be rightfully claimed with ignorance, but once informed a lack of action can only be regarded as irresponsibility.

Sometimes the problem is not with the profession itself, but with the way professionals are taught. Green design is still not taught in most architecture or engineering schools. And in most schools where it is taught it is usually presented as something separate from design and unrelated to the "real" craft of architecture. Engineering colleges teach efficiency, but really preach sufficiency and boilerplate solutions. Until this changes, this process- related barrier will limit the wholesale adoption of the sustainable design principles.

Nevertheless, it is fair to admit that green design is perhaps more difficult than conventional design, as it involves an expanded set of issues that must be considered often in the same time frames as conventional projects. At first glance, it does seem to create potential constraints to the process. And yet, good architecture has always been about creatively solving design problems involving limitations and restraints. Sustainable design is no different. Under talented hands even the most restrictive of circumstances can be turned into a work of art. Indeed, it is often the limitations and the idiosyncrasies that lead to the most ingenious and beautiful solutions. Not being able to rely on tried and true solutions in all cases, designers are forced to think, and in the process thoughtful solutions are achieved. Forcing this process is good for the design profession, for individual designers and for those who occupy their buildings. Sustainable design can add layers of interest and meaning to designs so often lacking purpose. In essence, it arms a good designer with more tools. Sustainable design should never be viewed as actively interfering with good design, nor should design sacrifice environmental performance. Doing things differently means continuing to rework an idea until an artful solution that does not sacrifice performance is achieved.

Expanded Collaboration

Sustainable design requires a greater amount of collaboration between disciplines than does the traditional design process. As the list of issues is expanded, so too must the expertise and the participants in the process. These participants must begin the process early and stay with the project through completion. The number and types of collaborators is also increased in a sustainable design project in order to integrate building science into the design to ensure performance. This means that design projects, where warranted, should include other specialists such as in daylighting, regional material usage, and indoor air quality in addition to architects and engineers, a hurdle that the sustainable designer must overcome is the often-strained relationship or mistrust that occurs between architects, engineers and other building professionals. This mistrust usually stems from a lack of understanding and lack of respect for what the other does. This ignorance is precisely the result of a design process that is not collaborative. Increased collaboration has the result of minimizing mistrust and posturing on design teams as each contributes to the spirit of the larger goal and along the way "walks in the other's shoes." When the architect has to play mechanical engineer and the engineer plays architect, a greater respect grows. This mutual respect is essential, because no high performance building can be designed without the architect giving the mechanical engineer input into his or her systems and the mechanical engineer helping with the design of the building and envelope. This spirit of collaboration is vital to achieving high levels of environmental performance. Collaboration consists of more than just sitting in a room together. It suggests cultivating an attitude towards each other that is very different from the traditional process. Bob Mann, director of the environmental non-profit Bridging the Gap, in Kansas City[1], calls this process "thinking like a partner." When we truly think of our engineers, architects, clients, contractors and other design professionals as partners, rather than consultants, sub consultants or owners, then the nature of the relationships change. Trust grows, ideas flow and performance increases exponentially.

An off-shoot of the need for increased collaboration on sustainable design projects is the need for intense eco-design charrettes. The eco-charrette is one of the most effective ways that design teams can ensure that collaboration and a diversity of information is considered on a design project. Charrettes are basically intense design brainstorming sessions that look to solve a particular design problem by quickly generating multiple schemes (solutions) through the input of various team members. The word "charrettes" is derived from the French for cart, and describes the process of collaboration that existed in eighteenth century Paris as designers competed for projects assigned by the king. In these early competitions, strict time limits were given and a man in a large cart would come by and collect competition drawings to be brought to the judges. As the cart was slow, those who had their drawings collected last had significant advantages over those that were collected first, and so these early designers soon learned that if they jumped on the cart they could continue to work on their drawings throughout the route. Over time those who jumped on first began to share information and supplies and collaborated with their competitors, quickly modifying drawings over this intense trip—hence the name charrette.

Eco-charrettes are typically done over a period of one to three days involving a host of individuals who have input valuable to the design process. The need for collaboration on sustainable design projects means that charrettes are critical and the players often more numerous than in typical charrettes. Over the life of a typical sustainable design project a few charrettes are often necessary to generate integrated design solutions and to check progress by all stakeholders at key points. The first charrette can sometimes be the most important as it sets the tone and standard for all the others. BNIM architects calls the first charrette the visioning charrette. This charrette establishes measurable goals that will be checked throughout the project, but more importantly solicits buy-in from all of the participants whose co-operation will be critical for high performance. Results from visioning sessions should be captured in a continually updated design intent document, which can then be used as a checkpoint to measure progress and ultimately become part of a commissioning manual to make sure the building is operating as designed.

A hard lesson to learn on sustainable design projects is that teams can often only be as collaborative as the leader of the team is collaborative. For clients, this is a critical thing to understand when requesting project managers and decision makers on projects. However, clients should also be advised that this greater collaboration almost always leads to better services, a better product and less overall cost for a given level of performance due to the integrated nature of the problem solving. Progressive clients learn that it is worth paying higher design fees (soft costs) for this process.

A key component of collaboration within the sustainable design process is the open access to information. Project managers on sustainable projects need to rid themselves of the need to control information and must maintain open access to process and information. With sustainable design it is appropriate to assume that everything is relevant in some way to every team player. All things are connected. Meaningful communication is challenging and takes an immense, conscious effort to keep the access and channels of information open and dialogue flowing.

The Elements Green Design Methodology–The Order of Operations

Another change to the traditional design process is that sustainable design requires an understanding not only of the principles and components of the philosophy, but also the order in which things are examined and included.

In mathematics, this idea is called the Order of Operations. Consider a simple mathematical equation

$$(4+4) \times 3 + (10\text{-}7) = 27$$

The order of operations demands that the numbers in the brackets be treated first and that multiplication precedes subtraction and addition. The correct answer is 27.

If the rules were not followed, many different and incorrect answers would appear, such as;

$$4 \times 3 = 12 + 4 = 16 + 7 = 23 - 10 - 13$$

$$4+4 = 8 \times 3 + 7\text{-}10 = 0$$

Sustainable design has its own order of operations in order to be effective. Without this hitherto unwritten order of operations, the cost of implementing the strategies increases and the effectiveness of the strategies decreases. In some cases, by ignoring the order of operations the result can often do more harm than good.

The Order of Operations or Elements Green Design Methodology[2] is as follows:

1. **Understand Climate and Place**
   Designers should first understand the place in which they are designing. What effect does the climate have? Temperature, humidity, diurnal temperature swings, precipitation amounts and distribution, snowfall, wind speed and direction, air quality, landscape features, vegetation, surrounding obstructions, etc. must all be understood.
2. **Reduce Loads**
   Designers should then analyze what loads or system requirements there are in the design and seek to systematically reduce them or accurately define them rather than inflate them.
3. **Use Free Energy**
   Designers should then look to use free sources of energy to further minimize loads and dependence on mechanical systems such as using the sun for heat and natural ventilation to cool where appropriate.

4. **Use The Most Efficient Technology Possible**
Only after each of the other steps has been done should the designer look to mechanical or technological solutions to design problems. At this point the designer should specify the most efficient and elegant solution possible.

Understanding this process is essential to achieving sustainable design solutions that are environmentally effective and cost effective. A good example of the need for the Green Design Order of Operations is the use of Building Integrated Photovoltaics (BIPV) for generating electricity. Photovoltaic panels generate electricity directly from solar radiation without producing any unwanted byproducts, making it one of the most important, and yet underutilized technologies today. The problem is that PV is still rather expensive, with costs between seven and eight dollars per installed watt. This price makes it difficult for many projects to afford, and any investment needs to be maximized. For example, if a typical homeowner desired to take his or her house off the grid or provide one hundred percent of its power through photovoltaics on an annual basis without following the **order of operations**, the owner may need to spend anywhere between twenty-five to thirty thousand dollars to do so because the typical American home is incredibly energy wasteful. The owner or installer may also make some poor decisions as to the placement of the panels which may render them less effective than anticipated.

However, following the Order of Operations has a dramatic effect on the outcome. If such homeowners first examine their climate and place they would better understand where exactly to position the solar panels and at what angle to maximize its harvest and reduce the payback of the system. They would also be less likely to locate the panels in a place that might receive shade for parts of the day, further decreasing the panels' effectiveness. Following the Order of Operations, the individual homeowner would then examine the entire home's electrical loads and seek to reduce them. The homeowner might decide to switch all interior lighting to compact fluorescents and to replace the refrigerator and water heater with highly efficient models at an additional first cost of three to four thousand dollars. There is much more the homeowner could do but this would provide a dramatic load reduction by itself. The next step would be to use free energy wherever possible which might include understanding when to open windows for natural ventilation to reduce summer cooling loads and providing external shades to further block heat gain. After all of these things are done, the homeowner, by following the Order of Operations, is finally ready to purchase solar panels. To his or her surprise the owner would likely find that the new cost to achieve the same goal of providing one hundred percent of power from PV had dropped from twenty-five to thirty thousand dollars to between ten and twelve thousand dollars with an incremental investment of only four thousand dollars for the efficiency upgrades. A net reduction of between nine to sixteen thousand dollars!

The book, *Natural Capitalism*, provides another outstanding example of this design methodology in the chapter entitled Tunneling Through The Cost Barrier. Its focus is on holistic thinking applied to green economics.

For example, if people were going to retrofit their lights and air conditioner, they would do the lights first so they could make the air conditioner smaller. If they did the opposite, they would pay for more cooling capacity than they need after the lighting retrofit, and they would also make the air conditioner less efficient because it would either run on part load or cycle on and off too much.[3]

Using the Order of Operations applies not only to energy solutions, but to almost all aspects of sustainable design. Efforts to improve indoor air quality should also follow the same methodology. For example, to improve air quality in a building, the designer should first understand the ambient outside air conditions and sources of pollutants and allergens. The designer should also understand how the local climate is going to affect the air quality in the building due to humidity, prevailing breezes or other environmental factors. Using free energy might mean looking to natural ventilation to provide fresh air. Finally, the designer might look at extensive filtration equipment to purify air and air quality sensors that monitor carbon dioxide. In addition, reducing loads in this case might mean preventing dirt track-in through careful entryway design, specifying materials that do not off-gas harmful chemicals and selecting materials that also do not collect pollutants or need extensive cleaning with chemical cleaners. Not understanding the Order of Operations has led to many of the misconceptions that still exist in reference to green building; in particular, that green buildings always cost more money than conventional buildings.

Holistic Thinking

Sustainable design differs from traditional design not only in its results (environmental and human impact), its rationale (the six principles), but also its process. Successful sustainable design requires a shift in status quo thinking about how things are put together, how they are operated and how they are maintained. If the sustainable design process had a single name it would be holistic thinking.

If design can be described as the art of problem solving, then holistic thinking is the Tao of problem solving. Successful sustainable designers (green warriors) are those who have internalized the philosophy while mastering its methods and techniques and holistic thinking. The process of holistic thinking is one of constant work, for once achieved it does not guarantee to linger, as human nature, ignorance and motivations often get in the way. Instead, it is something to always strive for, like the intellectual equivalent of an athlete being in the zone. Like anything worthwhile, perseverance is necessary.

Holistic thinking does not require that we know and understand everything we are dealing with, but rather that we acknowledge what we know and understand and what we do not. It involves working with people who might, in fact, know all the information needed to solve a particular design problem, but who need help conceiving of the ideas and seeing the linkages. This piece of holistic thinking is called acting as a Maieutic teacher, from the root maia meaning midwife (discussed by Daniel Quinn in the Story of B). A Maieutic teacher is "one who acts as a midwife to pupils, gently guiding to the light ideas that have long been growing inside of them." [4]

By its very nature, holistic thinking is not easily defined. It naturally encompasses more than words can describe, and surely, more than what can be described by any single essay or any single author. Holistic thinking is a way of thinking that attempts to widen the circle of understanding in order to comprehend the connections that exist between all things and, more specifically, to aspects of the design process and the built environment. It acknowledges that it always fails in some capacity, as the circle can never be widened to infinity. And yet despite this, the holistic thinker strives to get to the fundamental essence of any problem to understand what is at the core of decisions and results and, where possible, make changes at the source that ripple outward to improve the health of our buildings, communities and environment.

Holistic thinking strives for clarity and simplicity but it does so by embracing diversity and sometimes seeming chaos in order to uncover a closer approximation of truth. This approach is in contrast to the traditional western reductionist scientific process, which also draws circles around things in order to define the problem and eliminate variables. However, as we have seen, this type of science misses things because it does not first attempt to widen the sphere of the known, as holistic thinking does, uniting the intuitive with the empirical.

A classic example of this failure is described in the book *Natural Capitalism*. It tells the incredible story of how and why the World Health Organization and the British Air Force in the fifties parachuted fourteen thousand live cats into Borneo. This crazy mission was started at first in response to the need to combat malaria in rural villages. The chemical DDT was sprayed extensively there to kill the mosquitoes that caused the disease, as it was done all over the world—because of how safe it was deemed (DDT's toxic legacy still exists with us today). And then, as the book describes,

> an expanding web of side effects started to appear. The roofs of people's houses began to collapse, because the DDT had also killed tiny parasitic wasps that had previously controlled thatch-eating caterpillars. Meanwhile, the DDT–poisoned bugs were eaten by geckoes, which were eaten by cats. The DDT invisibly built up in the food chain and began to kill the cats. Without the cats, the rats multiplied. The World Health Organization, threatened by potential outbreaks of typhus and sylvatic plague, was then obliged to parachute 14000 live cats into Borneo![5]

Holistic thinking reminds us that all things are connected. This extreme example of the limits of the reductionist process is not meant to disprove its value, but rather to show its limits. The scientific process is still a major tool of holistic design. Instead of drawing a tight boundary around what is relevant, it acknowledges this boundary and then attempts to expand it until it can not any longer, and then and only then zooms in on potential. The result, surprisingly, is often more efficiency as well as more clarity and long-term success. Fewer mistakes are made as more is considered.

Very few people are holistic thinkers naturally. In fact, it probably does not occur naturally, as human nature compels people to quickly draw limits around what they know, to seek comfort in what can be easily defined and quickly described. It takes perseverance and practice to overcome these tendencies. A holistic thinker, by necessity, is a life-long learner because, as the cliché goes, "the more you know, the more you realize you don't know." Edward Land once described the process as a "sudden cessation of stupidity." [6]

Holistic thinking involves asking questions. Holistic thinking applied to sustainable design is about striving for win/win solutions for people and the environment. The process involves testing assumptions and asking many questions in order to get to the root of the problem. In every case, the real cause is revealed by asking "Why?" This process of asking questions can be called the Five Why's to problem solving because usually the root of every problem can be traced back to its origins by asking "Why?" Five times.

On the EpiCenter Pilot building, designed by BNIM Architects for Montana State University, this methodology was used to find ways to reduce pressure drop (resistance) in the air delivery system, a feature that traditionally hampers the performance of laboratory buildings. The team closely examined fans, pumps, valves, filters, duct design and equipment, and carefully disassembled conventional thinking and reassembled what the team believed was the most efficient laboratory system ever designed. At each stage the team asked questions like, "what is causing resistance and how can this resistance be reduced or eliminated?" Through the holistic design process, given the name "Plus Ultra Design" by Bob Berkebile, optimal solutions were reached and final barriers identified such as:

- How to select building materials that transform the local waste stream to new, durable products that improve the local economy and the environment
- How to design a closed-loop water and waste system while balancing human health concerns
- How to design a flexible structural system to allow for the lowest possible pressure drop in the building's mechanical systems

In a short amount of time, working in synergy across disciplines, the team was able to develop integrated, elegant solutions that removed the barriers in the way of achieving the project goals.

Bob Berkebile selected the term "Plus Ultra" to serve as the guiding spirit for this holistic thinking process of decision-making and design. Plus Ultra means "more, beyond" in Latin and was not only a vision statement for the EpiCenter, but was also a methodology, repeatable in the steps necessary to attain it. The methodology that the project team used to define Plus Ultra had three simple steps applicable to any process, technology, or field of study:

- Identify state of the art in any field, system, or technology
- Identify the barriers to moving beyond state of the art
- Remove the barrier and redefine state of the art

With the Plus Ultra methodology as its guide, the EPICenter project became an opportunity to create new products, technologies, and processes that would provide the building industry with a new benchmark against which to measure environmental health and economic performance. The Plus Ultra methodology was also an opportunity to turn convention on its head and begin the course correction necessary to protect the health of the environment for future generations. But, most importantly, this philosophy provided an opportunity to prove that this course correction was not only necessary but also attainable.

Holistic thinking requires much of us. To begin with, it requires that we check our own assumptions and preconceived notions at the door. To be successful, it involves undoing what Don Miguel calls the "domestication of humans" which is that we are taught what to think and how to think from a general cultural perspective, and yet as Einstein reminds us, "no problem can be solved by the same manner of thinking that created it."

Some further lessons on the pre-requisites to holistic thinking are embedded in the Toltec teachings of Don Miguel in his book *The Four Agreements*. This book reminds us that most of our limitations are self-imposed, that almost all of our energy is spent in keeping silent agreements we make with ourselves about any number of things such as what we know, what we do not know, what we are good at, and what we can achieve. All of these things limit our potential as holistic thinkers and limit our ability to affect the outcome of our projects. And yet, "each time you break an agreement all the power you used to create it returns to you." [7] The more open we can be with ourselves the more open we can be to true collaboration with others and to good ideas and integrated design solutions when they present themselves. Most of the true barriers to sustainable design are in fact human-based barriers based on fear, self-doubt and insecurity, and not technological or economic barriers.

Don Miguel suggests four new agreements that people make with themselves that replace the old self-limiting ones. These four agreements are:

1. **Be Impeccable With Your Word**–Which means, in a nutshell, to be positive about how you talk to yourself, about yourself. You will only receive a negative idea if your mind is fertile ground for that idea.
2. **Do not Take Anything Personally**–Which means developing a harder shell about what other people say or do, as nothing other people do is truly because of you, but rather, based on their own silent agreements. Sustainable design is about change, and change is hard for people. People's insecurities are often brought to light with the sustainable design process and this new agreement is essential.
3. **Do not Make Assumptions**–Basing decisions on assumptions has killed many green projects. We make assumptions to feed our need to know and to replace our need to communicate. And yet sustainable design requires communication and collaboration. An assumption is only good for generating questions that then *must* be asked.
4. **Always Do Your Best**–This new agreement is fairly self-explanatory, but also means accepting that your best is not always the same in every situation. It is not about demanding perfection.

The four agreements are essential, because to create change in the outer world we must begin that change in our inner world.

Integrated Design

The end result of the holistic thinking process, collaborative design and the Order of Operations are buildings that achieve high levels of environmental, economic and social performance. In the end, what is produced are examples of integrated or nested design solutions. Integrated design solutions are those that simultaneously solve several problems within the one solution and embody the work and requirements of multiple disciplines. Nested, integrated solutions should increase efficiency, increase health and well-being, increase durability and increase economic viability. For the EpiCenter, the integrated design process meant improving daylighting and electric lighting to the point that the mechanical systems could be greatly reduced. This integrated design, in turn, meant smaller

Computer rendering of the atrium design at the MSU EpiCenter by BNIM Architects. This image shows the celebration and integration of mechanical systems into the design of the building.

transformers and smaller emergency generators that more than paid for the incremental cost of the lighting and control improvements.

Integrated design safeguards against the value engineering process, which is not engineering and does not add value. Value engineering is the process whereby projects are brought on budget by removing design features and often quality from the building (called vision assassination by one knowledgeable green consultant). Sustainable design features are often the first to go in the value engineering process, unless they are the result of an integrated design process. Performance features identified through this process that simultaneously serve several other critical needs are difficult to remove. Truly sustainable buildings are achieved only by this integrated design process.

CHAPTER FIFTEEN

Photo courtesy of Jason F. McLennan

The Aesthetics of Sustainable Design

In anything at all, perfection is finally attained, not when there is no longer anything to add, but when there is no longer anything to take away.

—Antoine De Saint Exupery

The Aesthetics of Sustainable Design

It is surprising for some to learn that aesthetics and beauty must play a significant role in the sustainable design philosophy. For ultimately, if sustainable design is going to become the dominant approach to the design process, then it must inspire and motivate people as much as any great architecture has done throughout history. For sustainable design to be successful it must have models that captivate the imagination equal to any architecture or design component that has been completed using more traditional ways.

Most architects and design professionals are drawn to the industry because of a desire to make a contribution to society and practice their craft, or to have a creative outlet in the most durable and grandiose of the arts, architecture. Few individuals become designers for the pure reason of trying to champion environmental issues. While a growing army of designers now see the importance of balancing environmental concerns with the pursuit of their profession, for many the social and aesthetic issues are far more important to them. This chapter will explore the aesthetic side of the argument.

Unfortunately, when it comes to aesthetics, many designers still cling to the belief that it is difficult or impossible to achieve a high degree of environmental performance without sacrificing the quality of design. For sustainable design to become the dominant paradigm in architecture, landscape architecture and the allied arts, this perceptual barrier must be removed. Sustainable design must allow practitioners to continue to push boundaries in design meaning and design quality at the same time that environmental concerns are elevated. The sustainable design movement must not brush aside the importance of aesthetics to its practitioners or take a purely moral high ground that performance alone is enough. With sustainable design neither aesthetics nor environmental performance are subjugated. Solutions must be found that meet the satisfaction of both the design community and the environmental community.

To get at these issues a few questions must be explored:
- Why is there a belief that sustainable design and aesthetics are mutually exclusive? Is it true?
- Is there a sustainable design aesthetic?
- How can these issues be balanced?
- Why is it important to maintain aesthetic beauty in sustainable design?

Green is Ugly

So why is there a belief by many that sustainable design and beauty are at odds? Too many people have beliefs that green is ugly, because the earliest examples of environmentally responsible design were often not beautiful. First impressions go a long way in forming people's lasting opinions. Many of the earliest models of sustainable design focused little on anything other than performance. Traditional aesthetic concerns such as proportion, balance, color and context were relegated to a much lower position. This was understandable for a new movement struggling to figure itself out, but problematic if long ranging and wide ranging appeal was desired. Many of the first green buildings, then known as energy conserving buildings, were truly experiments. Some worked better than others. If a building needed to have a sunspace for passive solar gain then it did, regardless of whether contextually this made sense or whether it could be detailed in an appealing way. Technologies such as photovoltaics were tacked on to the south sides of buildings with little regard to the architectural implications.

Part of the reason for these results occurred because many of the earliest adopters and pioneers of the sustainable design movement from the early seventies to the late eighties, while often brilliant and technically proficient, were not always the most talented of designers. The early adopters tended to be techno-engineering types more so than artistic ones. This recognition is not to diminish the importance and intelligence of the early pioneers, but rather to point out a consistent shortcoming that held back the movement's broad appeal. In fairness, many of the most talented designers had a lot to learn from the innovation and creativity of these early green pioneers. Regardless, with focus spent almost solely on inventing or reinventing building systems and adapting new technologies, the buildings' final appearance was often left wanting.

Another reason for the aesthetic failure was that training in designing for new technologies, materials and systems was not available. Until recently, design schools did not teach sustainable design issues and sustainable design principles were learned on the job, sometimes with favorable results, but many times with results that were unattractive to most designers and the public. Early solar buildings from the seventies were often ungainly and poorly detailed, fitting perhaps for prototypes but not suitable as models to emulate. Sometimes these projects suffered from low budgets and a few failed to perform as well as promised, further eroding the idea that the movement was an improvement over conventional ways. At the dawning of the new century, almost every architecture school in the United States and Canada has at least one course related to sustainable design, with a few schools such as the University of Oregon and Arizona State University providing many courses to prepare future designers in balancing environmental and aesthetic concerns. This trend will continue to grow.

Despite this advance, even today, the stereotype that green buildings are less attractive gets some credence as many of today's sustainable design practitioners ignore or diminish the importance of aesthetics while trying to meet environmental goals. Sustainable designers can not be content to produce buildings that are only good environmental performers. They can not be complacent in the development of their craft and rationalize that they are exempt from the need to create beauty in the built environment because of altruistic concerns. Beauty is a requirement in the success of the sustainable design philosophy. And yet, is this possible? Or is sustainable design inherently ugly?

The answer is a resounding no. Sustainable design is no more or less likely to be ugly than any other approach to design. As with any approach to design, what matters most in achieving a good aesthetic result is an understanding of the approach, its technologies and design talent. Since the movement is young, misunderstanding of many of the principles and technologies of sustainable design has perhaps limited its success aesthetically. An example of this would be a designer who feels forced towards a less desirable design resolution in order to achieve a high level of environmental performance because of a lack of awareness of other options that would balance the two. Thankfully, the issue of design talent within sustainable design is being resolved. Many of the field's most talented designers are now adopting the principles of sustainable design into their everyday practice. Talented designers such as Overland Architects, Miller Hull Partnership, James Cutler, Richard Rogers and Glenn Murcutt are redefining early perceptions of sustainable design. Green can now be beautiful as well as ugly depending on the design skills of the individuals involved.

As the sustainable design field matures, more and more successful models of greener buildings will emerge that combine high performance with beauty. There is an opportunity for the next generation of sustainable designers to bridge the rift between environmental responsibility and beauty and produce an architecture that is truly worthy of enduring through the ages.

The Green Aesthetic

A second problem that emerged in the aesthetic realm was that many people began to believe that sustainable design always produced a similarly predictable aesthetic result. This belief (that there was a green aesthetic) was potentially more problematic than the first, as the movement could then be easily dismissed if a certain aesthetic or style was desired that seemed different than what the green aesthetic would deliver. Even if sustainable design could be beautiful, unless we were trying to achieve the green aesthetic we had to do something different. Green buildings have been type-caste by many people, designers and laymen alike, who believe that sustainable design results in a particular style and that its practitioners will produce a predictable and, in many cases, less than desirable structure. People still think of quirky solar panels when they think of sustainable design despite the wide array of successful sustainable design case studies now present, including beautiful buildings with some incredible usage of building integrated photovoltaics.

So, is there a sustainable design aesthetic or style? Can sustainable design be practiced within any particular style? For many designers there is a belief that with the practice of sustainable design comes a prescribed style or green aesthetic, which, depending on the architect can be either a deterrent or an attraction to the movement. While this view is incorrect, (remember that sustainable design is not a stylistic endeavor but a philosophical approach to design) it is understandable, because early green projects often had certain stylistic attributes in common. The primary reason for this tendency was that until only very recently (the late nineties) the menu of green materials and systems was quite small. Designers had fewer responsible options to choose from and, like a painter with only two colors, the images had a similar resonance in green buildings. Likewise, since the movement is so young, there were fewer models to provide aesthetic inspiration of how to express new materials, approaches or technologies. The only right way to install a new material might be that imagined by the manufacturer. Just as rock music could not have evolved without blues, the more aesthetically mature buildings produced in the last decade could not have been conceived without the first buildings produced in the seventies. Developing a favorable aesthetic expression of new technologies and new approaches takes time and, as the sustainable design movement has matured, designers are finding ways to do just that. Interestingly enough, the idea that there is a green aesthetic has been purposefully clouded by the fact that many practitioners of the movement have cultivated a green aesthetic. This is the second reason for the green aesthetic myth.

Over the last two decades, beyond energy efficiency, the only way that green building designers and their clients had to prove that their building was green was if enough overt symbols or icons of sustainability were included in the design. The movement and the market as a whole were not yet sophisticated enough to realize that the external package was not important to the environment. We might care about aesthetics, but nature does not. Green roofs, solar panels, greenhouses, above-ground cisterns and biological waste treatment centers have graced many green buildings, some which deserve the designation, and some which do not. While each of these technologies are, in fact, positive components of buildings that do tend to lower environmental impact, their mere presence do not a green building make. A tiny photovoltaic array placed prominently at the entrance of an energy hog of a building might give a certain appearance or serve as an icon, but its true environmental impact would say otherwise.

The negative flip-side to this phenomenon is that some designers who want to appear to be green have used this idea to their advantage by tacking on a few green features at the end of the design process in order to make a nod to the growing demand for sustainable buildings. These designers have not changed their design approach or true attitudes. Without a way of scientifically documenting performance of buildings, many individuals erroneously link icons or features directly to performance. This is an incorrect assumption to make, especially because the true environmental performance of a building often lies within parts of the design that are invisible and not iconic. A building with the right orientation will have a much lower environmental impact than the exact same building facing due east-west. Same design, different impact. Much of its environmental performance is due, not to anything that is visually different, but to how it is put together and how it is sited. As we shall explore in a moment, this is an important reason why green buildings do not intrinsically have an aesthetic and can be designed in any style.

Interestingly enough, this invisible nature sometimes has been a problem. Many people want to see something different, even those who know that a green icon is not necessary. We have become a features society. To many, if it looks the same, acts the same, yet requires a different schedule, a different budget, or a different anything, then something is wrong. If people pay for a green project they want to be able to point to things that make it so, things they can see! They demand to see the differences. In a world of marketing, it is still the features that sell. Hopefully over time, with education in the marketplace, this need will disappear, as ultimately the only difference that people should see physically is a more direct response to climate and orientation but not necessarily a different aesthetic expression.

The US Green Building Council's LEED rating system has begun the process of debunking the green aesthetic myth, by firmly tying the greenness of a project to a series of performance related environmental standards rather than overt prescriptive features. While not intentional, this may turn out to be one of the Council's greatest gifts to the architectural profession. As more and more certified green buildings get built all over the country, in all styles and building types, the need for visual greenness should disappear completely, thus opening up the philosophy to a wider and wider group of individuals. When this change has truly occurred and sustainable design principles are fully internalized, architects can once again focus on the artistic side of their craft while ensuring responsibility and respect for the six principles of sustainable design. The desire to make buildings look green will be replaced by buildings that are authentically green. Until recently, when someone asked, "How green is the building?", the reply might be a laundry list of technologies that were included. Soon it will be a statement of the project's LEED rating, the amount of BTUs per square feet per year consumed or some other performance metric.[1]

The third and final reason for the belief in a green design aesthetic is the one with the most truth in it. As mentioned, many sustainable strategies and technologies such as proper orientation and site response have no visible impact on the design of buildings. Many other examples of sustainable technologies exist such as healthier paints and finishes that look like traditional paints, invisible coatings on glazing that improve performance, and careful detailing within wall construction that reduces heat loss and gain. Despite this lack of visible impact there are a few approaches and technologies of the sustainable design philosophy that do influence the design of buildings. It is the consistent expression of these approaches and technologies in green buildings that lend some credibility to the argument for a green aesthetic. For example, some of the technologies and strategies described in the *Components of Sustainable Design* chapter are form-givers, where their application requires modifications to the design of the building form. On a micro level, sustainable design performance requirements sometimes dictate the location of programmatic elements such as copy centers in locations with dedicated exhaust to enhance indoor air quality or service zones placed in areas so as not to block daylight to frequently inhabited spaces. And yet, while these issues do affect design, their impact on style and appearance is minimal.

On a macro level, and much more significant, green buildings tend to require the fine-tuning of facades based on orientation in order to maximize daylighting while controlling heat gain and glare. This produces buildings that are sometimes very different on one side of the structure than the other. The amount and distribution of glazing is often changed from façade to façade, as is the need for adequate shading devices such as overhangs and fins whose use changes by orientation. Green buildings also tend to dictate the depth of floor plates to allow more people access to daylight and views to the outside. Uniform facades, with no response to sun, wind and light are generally outlawed by the tenets of the philosophy. Sustainable design, when taken to the level of urban design, also imposes form-giving attributes in terms of street orientation, landscaping and rules for solar setbacks that ensure an equitable distribution of light to all future buildings.

Aesthetically, these differences can be addressed but it does require a great deal of attention in certain building styles. What it amounts to is a strong acceptance of a bioregional approach to design regardless of the aesthetic expression desired. The philosophy of sustainable design argues for contextual design at least in terms of climate if not in the more traditionally considered cultural and architectural contexts that inform most building design. It requires that designers respond to the movement of the sun, to prevailing breezes and the adaptation of form to rain, heat and cold. It requires that designers build with materials close at hand rather than from far away. It argues that designing for context means learning from nature to provide comfort wherever possible, before relying on our own less perfect systems. The philosophy of sustainable design argues that if a designer is in touch with a place, then beauty is more likely to result.

An interesting spin on this discussion is that eventually this form-giving process will diminish to some extent with the improvement of technology. In the early seventies when the first solar houses were built, solar designers had to rely on bulky contraptions for night insulation in order to make up for the poor thermal performance of glass at that time. These systems

became an icon for performance during this time period but have sub-
sequently gone away. This insulation would often take the form of giant
shutters or thermal blankets that would roll down in front of the windows.
In some cases insulation would be blown into a cavity in the window and
then sucked out the next morning, often leaving bits of styrofoam stuck in
the glazing. As glazing technology has improved, the need for these form-
giving insulation products has disappeared. As technologies continue to
improve many more green form givers might also disappear. For example,
Solera, a British company, has just released a new product that may make
the iconic light shelf obsolete. The Solera product reduces glare by bounc-
ing light up towards the ceiling as do light shelves, through the design of
internal reflectors in the glazing assembly. The Solera product could be
used where architectural concerns make light-shelves unattractive, thus
balancing performance concerns in buildings of any style.

The continued development of cost-effective super windows provide
another example. In residential designs in mixed and cold climates it makes
a great deal of sense to minimize north-facing windows as they are net
energy losers for the building and add to the energy intensiveness of the
structure (comfort is also affected). As R-values increase beyond R-7 even
north facing windows become net energy providers (more heat added
through radiation than lost through conduction) for the same house,
changing the rule of thumb. For the time being, it is still a good idea to
minimize north windows and maximize south windows. In the future the
amount of glass might remain constant while the invisible properties of
the glass are varied to achieve certain results such as less glare. The visible
presence of photovoltaics might also diminish with the proliferation of
transparent photovoltaic cells and cells in other colors beyond the ubiquitous blue or black under development.

Given the fact that there are certain form givers with sustainable design,
are there architectural styles that lend themselves better to the sustainable
design philosophy than others? As we have discussed earlier, sustainable
design can be practiced in any design style, but it may in fact be harder in
some than others. For example, in its efforts to reduce embodied energy
and material use, sustainable design tends to discourage ornamentation
without direct function, and in this sense allies itself with modernist thinking as opposed to classical or postmodern. Ample beauty and ornamentation can often be found through the expression of structure, lighting and
materiality and frivolous decoration is not needed. It is better to do with-

out and build with the minimum of materials than to apply meaningless ornamentation. According to Jonathan Hale, "To please the spirit is not a frill. To play is not a diversion. Architecture uses decoration, but architecture is not decoration."[2] Building on this notion is the idea of *structure as finish*. This idea encourages the celebration of structural elements (often to the delight of structural engineers who for too long have had their work covered up and ignored). This attitude in material thriftiness often has the secondary benefits of enhancing indoor air quality because reducing finishes within a building usually eliminates a good portion of the VOCs (volatile organic compounds) typically found within buildings.

Again, this perspective does not say that classical or postmodern structures cannot adhere to the principles of sustainable design, only that architects must somehow reconcile these issues in their design process and select materials for ornamentation that are healthy and have a low embodied energy. Rigid stylistic rules such as those from classical architecture that govern proportion and symmetry might also be difficult with a philosophy that requires responses to local conditions and variations based on façade orientation. While this perspective does suggest that it is easier to build green buildings in a more modern style, it is important to remember that in many ways the philosophy of the modernist movement is responsible for much of the environmental problems caused by the built environment. Sustainable design rejects some of the earliest ideas of its first proponents such as Le Corbusier and Mies Van Der Rohe. In particular, the idea that buildings can and should be built the same regardless of climate, culture, orientation and available local materials is in opposition to the sustainable design approach. In addition, the sustainable design philosophy casts out the machine as metaphor for buildings and replaces it with the metaphor and model of natural systems—biomimicry.

This approach in no way means that green buildings must look organic—sustainable design is not the same as organic architecture pioneered by Frank Lloyd Wright. Indeed, when many people think of a green aesthetic the image of an organic building comes to mind. Whether a building has organic forms is not important. What is important is its impact on human and natural systems.[3] Buildings may still look like machines, but they must now *act* more like living things, in turn providing habitat for us. In this way modernism as style is more congruent with sustainable design than modernism as philosophy.

So in essence, there is no reason why, under skilled hands, green buildings can not be built of any type from a historic classical style to the most minimalist modernist building. Each architectural style merely contains its own challenges in integrating this philosophy into its expression. Indeed, from a stylistic and aesthetic standpoint, sustainable design should be highly attractive to the profession because there is still a lot of opportunity to break new ground in designing and detailing the emerging green technologies and finding relevant ways to express the ideas of the philosophy in wood, stone and concrete.

Why is Beauty Necessary to Sustainable Design?

If sustainable design can be built in any style and appeal to any person regardless of aesthetic preferences, then why is there a need to discuss aesthetics and beauty with the philosophy?[4] The reason is that there is a hidden practical meaning to the need for beauty that directly impacts the environmental performance of buildings. Most of the buildings being built today have life spans that are considerably less than their counterparts of one to two hundred years ago. Sustainable buildings must reverse this trend and look to the idea of permanence on the scale of the great buildings of the past. This means creating places that will endure because people want them to endure. It is critical to remember that beautiful designs—whether they are simple objects like a tea pot or complex ones like a cathedral usually receive better care, and last longer than counterparts that have less aesthetic value. What is the environmental impact of buildings like the great cathedrals that have endured through the ages due to their beauty, construction quality and meaning? Pro-rated over the centuries their embodied energy is non-existent.

Taking care of a building and respecting the resources and energy that went into creating it is one of the most important tenets of sustainability. Beautifully designed buildings that elicit an emotional response are likely to be respected in their use, and be maintained and repaired as necessary. It is the most beautiful of buildings that typically gets saved from the wrecking ball. While this is not always the case, as we know, it tends to help in sometimes significant ways. The Historic Preservation movement arose as a reaction to the wholesale destruction of beautiful historic works of architecture that was occurring around the country. The preservation movement has done wonders to preserve a cultural and artistic legacy as well as preserving the embodied energy inherent in the structures while preventing the need for new buildings to be built in their place. Something that has been carefully designed and built is also more likely to be re-used when its original functional life is over, even if it does not have historical value. The thousands of brick warehouses and factories all over America that have been converted to office buildings and high end residential lofts are prime examples. As opposed to many of the warehouses that are being built today, these buildings were built at a time when beauty, form and attention to detail were important even in a warehouse. Beauty does not always have to be expensive, but it does require care. Just about every family can point to things that have been handed down from previous generations either for their beauty, their utility, a family story or some combination of the three. As the utility and family significance fades, it is often only the beauty of the object that keeps it cherished and passed on.

The need for beauty in sustainable design provides other examples. Many technologies have been developed over the last few decades that have had the potential to lower environmental impact, and yet have failed because the products in question have been aesthetically unacceptable to potential users. The previous example of the bulky night insulation products provide a good example. Used properly, the product can greatly reduce heat loss with a relatively short payback. However, almost no one produces the product because it fails to sell. Similarly, in the nineties a growing list of recycled content products made from plastics and tires entered the market. Many of these products had less than desirable aesthetic appeal and have made little impact in the market. Thankfully, recycled content products are now being manufactured that have aesthetic value equal to their traditional counterparts. These products are selling well and making a difference.

The most environmentally friendly technology in the world is useless if it is not *used* in place of its more polluting counterparts. To be used it must appeal on all levels. The sustainable principles of reduce, re-use and recycle rest firmly within the construct of whether the object in question is worth re-using or recycling to people. Accepting inferior products merely because they are recycled content or salvaged might be a valiant attempt at responsibility, but if they will simply be discarded, poorly maintained or quickly damaged, then likely more harm than good is being done in the first place.[5] If we want the sustainable design movement to be successful than we must accept that appearances do matter to people. As was discussed in the beginning, it is the aesthetic shortcomings more than the technical that kept many people away from green buildings for so long.[6]

On a more positive note, beautiful buildings become sources of peda-gogy for individuals, a result that is essential to the sustainable design phi-losophy that must teach people how to reconnect to their environment. A building that is in tune with its context, the changing of the seasons, the sun's path through the sky and the vagaries of wind, snow, sleet and rain while being beautiful can not help but connect people with these pro-cesses as well. Beauty inspires us to dream and seek solutions to problems that have yet to be solved. The old discussion of form and function can be restated to say that sometimes form can reinforce function, in that beauty can increase the functionality of an object or building. Attraction and care can compel people to learn more about the places we inhabit and in this way can be a handmaiden to helping people connect to their surround-ings, and even their larger context within nature and community. There is even emerging evidence that we have an innate biological need for beauty in our lives. Neurological science is showing increasing evidence of the role beauty plays in stimulating the brain. There appears to be a need for proportion, texture and shapes that are pleasing to the eye for mental health. If this proves true, we will have ultimately proven that the cities of the twenty-first century have been contributing to our stress and our poor health in ways never originally imagined.

As a society, we are slaves to the idea of quantity instead of quality, an at-titude that the philosophy of sustainable design firmly rejects. Because of this attitude, and the lack of respect for good design and craft, there is an impoverishment of beauty in the built environment, at least in most places built since World War II. As Jonathon Hale documents in *The Old Way of Seeing,* "we have put what we thought was practicality first, and everywhere is the result."[7]

Sustainable design must inspire and elevate our spirits. It should argue for beauty in all settings and at all scales. If we do not put care into the de-sign of our homes, streets and offices then why should we extend care out-ward, to our farms, forests and fields? We accept billboards, parking lots and strip malls as being aesthetically acceptable in the same breathe that we accept clear-cuts, factory farms and strip mines. Sustainable design, and its built-in care for the quality of the built and natural environment, is a movement that seeks to solve the impoverishment of the environment and the impoverishment of beauty. The goal of architecture is to create shelter for human activities that lift the spirit and the philosophy of sustainable design maintains this focus while balancing environmental responsibility. Sustainable design demands responsibility to both environment and people.

CHAPTER SIXTEEN

Photo courtesy of Bob Berkebile.

The Future of Architecture

*It is horrible to see everything that one detested in the past
coming back wearing the colors of the future.*

Jean Rostand

The Future of Architecture

And so, this book ends in the same manner that it began, with a chapter told in the first person. Predicting the future is risky business, and unless the information is taken from some psychic source, it is guaranteed to produce many errors. Which is why I take sole responsibility for the ideas, predictions and trends that are laid out here. This chapter is not meant to be an objective review of the facts, but rather a prediction of what will likely unfold through the next few years and decades. It seemed inappropriate to end with the present when the movement has so much future ahead of it. Indeed its greatest tests are yet to come. Bob Berkebile often says "we are at a unique moment in human history." I think he is right. In the next few decades we will see whether the principles of Sustainable Design will resonate strongly enough with humanity and begin to redefine how all buildings and communities are designed, built and operated.

In the seventies Paul and Ann Ehrlich[1] made bold predictions about an environmental catastrophe that generated a great deal of criticism, primarily because their predictions did not prove as timely as they thought. Changes to the global economy in general and the green revolution in particular delayed or reduced the effects of substantial population growth. Many thought scientists should stay out of the prediction business entirely and labeled them Malthusians after Thomas Malthus, the first person on record to predict environmental collapse due to the stretching of resources. And yet a great deal of the trends and issues the Ehrlich's highlighted would show to be true in varying degrees. In their case, it was a good thing that their predictions were off base in severity. The world continues to avoid the kind of suffering that uncontrolled population growth can bring.[2] The real power of their predictions resulted in the debates and discussions that followed, and also from the policy changes made by some governments that realized that they had to find ways to control population in their own backyards. While I do not have any pretenses about my predictions generating as much waves as theirs did, I do hope that they engender discussion among people in our industry, and that we continue to find ways to improve the way we design and build our buildings.

At the time of this writing the planet has been shown to be under powerful and sustained attack on all its primary systems. The world is creaking under the weight of our technologies, appetites and population growth. In the next few decades the burden will only worsen as more and more individuals strive to survive and thrive and countless millions will seek to emulate the lifestyle that we in the west have enjoyed for the last century. By any measure the road ahead looks to be a tough one. Our children and grandchildren will be exposed to a world much poorer than we were blessed to have known. They will grow up knowing many animals only through pictures in books rather than see them running in fields. The effects of global climate change will disrupt and weaken our world's economy and the health of many ecosystems. An increasing number of conflicts will occur over resources such as water, topsoil, food and biodiversity that we once wasted because of their seeming abundance. With increased population will come greater levels of starvation, war and disease than we have experienced for quite some time. Clean water and healthy topsoil in particular will become precious to many. And through it all the life support systems on this magnificent blue rock will continue to be strained.

The question is not whether the earth will survive. It would take more firepower than we could imagine to destroy it. The question is not about destroying all life on earth either. The earth has gone through multiple periods of mass extinctions and each time has rebounded back with an amazing diversity of life. What is at stake is the survival of our own species. It remains to be seen whether a tall, erect ape with a big brain turned out to be a species that had a long or short history on the planet. The challenges that face us are immense, the questions to be answered daunting. Can we become the first species in history to self regulate before the system regulates us? And so, what is the role that architecture will play in this future? What is the future of architecture and sustainable design? The truth is that as long as we live on this planet we will need shelter. Architecture, and the communities we build, will continue to be the largest single artifact we will leave to the future. And in the end, it will have to be a sustainable architecture that is the future. So how will we get there?

The Next Ten Years 2005-2015

- Over the next decade there will be a continued doubling of support for Green Building initiatives around the United States and Canada. However, even at this rate this will still represent only twenty to thirty percent of the buildings being built each year. By 2015 the sustainable design movement will be mainstream, but will still have a lot of room to grow.

- A growing number of local and state jurisdictions will adopt green building practices as their base standard. Near the end of the decade stricter standards such as California's Title 24 Energy standards will become commonplace in all states.

- The USGBC will continue to grow in influence in the first half of the decade through its LEED rating tool. However, a growing backlash will occur by individuals interested in sustainability but who do not want to use the USGBC's tools due to cost and complexity. The US-GBC will have to find ways to reinvent itself and resist bureaucratic complacency to continue with its success. Competitors to LEED will emerge by the end of the decade.

- Almost every architecture school will develop curriculum specifically centered on sustainability. Engineering schools, reacting to pressure from the industry, will also begin sweeping changes to how their students are taught.

- The architecture profession will begin to build incredible buildings that combine environmental performance with beauty and trend-setting design. Many of the perceived aesthetic barriers to green will be lifted.

- The era of the generalist sustainability consultant will diminish to be replaced by individuals with both highly technical knowledge and a holistic grasp of the issues.

- By the end of the decade most design firms will have a few green projects built, thus beginning to diminish the distinction between green firms and non-green firms.

- Alternatives to PVC products, ubiquitous today, will appear on the market and meet with immediate widespread useage.

- The US Green Building Council will completely redesign its LEED tool and near the end of the decade will significantly raise the bar for performance. The Platinum level of performance will then be the same as the Living Building.

- Many of the economic barriers to green will continue to be removed by the end of the next decade further accelerating the adoption of green building strategies.

- A majority of contractors and developers will now be familiar with green building practices and will start to reduce their resistance to sustainability ideas and principles.

- A growing number of zero-energy homes will appear on the market with demonstrations of the living building occurring in a few locations.

- The United States and Canada will create a widespread national database of materials that helps make it easier to select environmentally preferable products.

- Product manufacturers will, almost without exception, be marketing the environmental advantages of their products and many will make great strides to reduce the embodied impacts of their products. More companies will adopt the Natural Step and other sustainability frameworks as part of their operating principles.

- PVC will be banned from production and lawsuits similar to the tobacco industry's litigation history will ensue. Other toxic chemicals will be banned as ingredients to consumer products.

- Near the end of the decade we will see the emergence of technologies that will soon change many aspects of our built environment. The first fuel cell cars will be released to the public and the beginnings of a hydrogen infrastructure will be tested. More buildings will also begin to include fuel cells and photovoltaics, which will continue to slowly drop in price. Green power from wind farms will soon be readily available to almost all consumers. Smart glazing will be introduced and will see limited demonstrations in buildings.

- Energy costs will rise throughout the decade making alternative energy more cost effective, further accelerating its acceptance.

- The environment will continue to see widespread decline and the beginnings of climate change effects will be confirmed.

- War, conflict and new diseases will increase throughout the world due primarily to resource scarcity.

Twenty Years From Now 2015-2025

- The green building movement will finally emerge into its adult stage and become the dominant paradigm of architecture and development in the West. Twenty years from now what was the gold level of performance in LEED will be the standard level of performance for all buildings in the United States and Canada. Multiple examples of the living building will exist, further raising the bar to performance. Most buildings will use forty to fifty percent less energy than their counterparts today. The best buildings will use eighty to ninety percent less energy than their counterparts today and use fifty percent less water.

- A national labeling standard for green building materials and products will be created based on the database created in the previous decade. This label will become a mandatory part of any product sold in the United States and Canada similar to the nutrition labels found on all foods. Consumers will demand to know what is in the products they buy and all ingredients will be listed. There will be a backlash against materials containing known carcinogens, mutagens and teratogens.

Environmental Impact Rating Unit Size - 1 ft2	
Overall Weighted Rating 7.7*	
Water Consumption 3.4 gallons	
Energy Consumption 18 000 BTU	
Criteria Air Pollution Score 87	
NOX	82
SOX	78
PPM	90
CO2	96
Criteria Water Pollution Score 52	
Toxicity Rating	46
Life Expectancy	7-9 yrs
Recycleable	NA

* Based on weighting by the Environmental Protection Agency

Contains: Straw, water, linseed oil, formaldehyde, g-Terpinene, ethyl acetate, camphor, benzyl acetate

- Biomimicry will emerge as a vibrant specialization in the economy.

- The national park system will double in size to protect the few unde-veloped areas left in the continent. A world-wide effort at ecosytem sanctuaries will gain momentum.

- The United States will finally adopt the metric system!

- Studies linking productivity and well-being to the built environment will finally transform the market. Building owners will now engage productivity experts to review designs and suggest ways to improve buildings.

- Resource scarcity will start to become a serious problem in a large part of the world. Resource based conflicts will erupt in the third world on an increasing scale. The effects of global climate change will weaken the agriculture and food production systems of the world. The public at large will finally understand the connection between their lifestyles and the effect on the environment. Political parties will start to be influenced to a greater extent by environmental groups.

- The rising costs and safety concerns of aging nuclear power plants and spent fuel will spell the end to that industry. Most western countries will dismantle their remaining plants because of citizen pressures and the result of a few spectacular failures in safety. Hundreds of thou-sands will be exposed to unhealthy levels of radiation during this time period.

- Traditional energy costs will rise more, but will be stabilized in the West by the continued emergence of renewable energy. Wind power will be the cheapest form of energy available. By the end of the second decade photovoltaics will drop to the point that this power source will be competitive with conventional power sources. The amount of photovoltiacs and wind turbines will quadruple in use and will start to become a noticeable part of the landscape. Much of the third world will begin to leapfrog over the mistakes of the West.

- All design and engineering schools will teach the principles of sustainable design as a central part of their curriculum. A new generation of designers will emerge that will take the design of our buildings and communities to a whole different level of performance.

- The hydrogen economy will become a proven component in many countries around the world. Fuel cells will start to become as ubiq-uitous as the television is today, further transforming society. The major automakers will stop making the internal combustion engine near the end of the second decade as the hydrogen infrastructure is completed.

The Next Half- Century 2050 - 2100

Despite the predictions of science fiction in the twentieth century, human-ity will not create new colonies on the moon or on distant planets. Indeed, the rising difficulties on earth will capture most resources away from space travel and the folly of human space conquest. The focus instead will be on keeping this planet fit for life. Population numbers will peak fifty years from now, kept in check by the availability of resources, disease and war. Almost every country in the world will see some sort of population stabilization or decline due to the enactment of population policy, manda-tory education regarding birth control options and resource scarcity.

The effects of global climate change will be difficult for even the richest countries to adapt to. Great changes to society will emerge. The world will be a much poorer place from a diversity standpoint, both in the diver-sity of natural systems and species, but also in terms of cultural diversity and language. Future generations will scorn the excesses and arrogance of the people of our generation. And yet, finally, through it all will emerge a truly sustainable society, transformed scarcely fifty to seventy-five years from today. The level of the living building will become the baseline for all buildings in the future. Our communities will produce no pollution through energy use and no waste from things they create for use. A true eco-economy will have emerged that balances the use of resources with the earth's capacity to handle its harvest. While we will continue to suf-fer from effects of the nineteenth and twentieth centuries in a multitude of ways, in the end, despite hardships not seen since the middle ages, I believe we will endure. I think we will prove smarter than the bacterium, even though we have not yet proven so? Our true intelligence will be displayed, not by creating additional earths or crazy schemes to inhabit other planets, but by living peaceably on our own blue rock. And when we look back we will see the efforts of many great people, sustainable design philosophers and regular folks, an army of individuals who realized that they needed to do things differently. Perhaps this army includes a few who will read this book.

Along the way fundamental belief systems must change to reconcile with our true place in nature. We will finally learn that our economy is a subset of natural systems, not the other way around. People will make the shift from the short view to the long view of the world. They will shift from the promotion of technology for the sake of itself to technologies that enhance life of all kinds, for all time. They will make the paradigm shift to the realization that we are wholly dependent on an intricate web of life for our survival. They will even shift the metaphors and language that they use to describe themselves and their relationship to nature. They will realize once and for all that their place in the world is no higher, or no lower than any creature on the planet, and that all are part of the same act of creation.

Our biggest challenges will be to overcome the inertia of the status quo and the cult of inevitability. We will have to say no to certain types of progress, and insist, as citizens of a democracy, on other kinds of progress that benefit us. We must find ways to foster co-operation among the citizens of all nations and insist on ideals as important as universal standards of living and the rights of all species to survive in dignity. We must, as Linda McQuaig writes, rekindle "the notion that we can collectively achieve great things, indeed, that we can achieve even basic things that were regularly achieved centuries ago—like providing work, shelter and food for everyone in the community."[3] In this case, it must be the world community. We must also abandon the 'cult of the individual' that produces a race to the bottom for society, we must abandon our blind worshiping of the market just as strongly as the belief by some that government can save us.[4]

In other words, we must take responsibility for our actions, our appetites and our mistakes. We must push our leaders to set examples and hold them accountable, and find a way, a system that rewards us for self-restraint. We must push for the adoption of revolutionary ideas, not just slow evolutionary ideas. The future we desire requires a culture of peace and forgiveness, rather than a rhetoric of war and punishment. We must help the developing world skip over a century and a half of polluting technologies and industrialization that we created. We must fight for universal equality rights, for the disparity we have today is shameful and contributes to a multitude of problems for all of us. We must find ways to slow and stabilize population growth and promote the well-being and education of women and children. And from this day forward we must save everything we can through a system of conservation and stewardship unparalled in history. No small order. But we can do it.

And through it all our architecture will continue to be a critical part of what makes us unique along with the other habitat builders. The future of architecture will remain the same as before in many ways, while being completely different in others. Architecture will continue to play its role as our protector, sheltering us from the elements and giving us comfort. It will continue to play its role as a manifestation and expression of our culture and ideals and inspire us to dream and create. But in the future our architecture will also reconnect us to the natural world and, indeed, become part of it, restoring and enhancing the places where we build. The future of architecture is bound inextricably to the future of living buildings. The future of architecture is sustainable.

Photo courtesy of Jason F. McLennan

Appendix A
The Green Warrior Reading List

"Writers are at their best as terrorists—Sometimes social terrorists, sometimes political, sometimes terrorists of the heart. If a writer is good, he will be all three at once. His weapons are words well used to disturb and to clarify thought, emotion and action."

—John Ralston Saul

Some Thoughts

I have long believed that the written word has the power to create paradigm shifts in individuals more than any other medium. Yet, as Mark Twain reminded us, "those who do not read, have no advantage over those that who cannot." Too many individuals do not spend time reading anything beyond newspapers or magazines, or do not read anything at all, which is unfortunate because good books inspire ideas, and great books inspire change.

The Green Warrior reading list is a collection of books that have served me well in my own quest for understanding how to make positive environmental and social change, and it is my hope that some of the books will serve others equally well. This list is important, I believe, because if we want to make change, we must be properly armed, which is to say that we must be educated. We must understand the interconnections between politics, economics, biology, physics, engineering, philosophy and architecture in order to make headway in this era of compartmentalization and specialization. We must put aside our notions that some subjects are not interesting or important and realize that within every discipline there is both beauty and power. This list, while having a consistent theme, approaches the challenges we face today from a variety of standpoints. As in nature, solutions spring forth from diversity.

The Green Warrior reading list is a collection of great books whose sole purpose is to inspire change among readers. Some of the books are great because of the power of the prose, some for the information and connections presented, others simply for the power of their ideas. The list is by no means comprehensive, nor is it complete. Indeed, it is a living document that I hope will be continually expanded for years to come.

Western Culture

Ashphalt Nation: How the Automobile Took Over the Nation and How We Can Take It Back
Jane Holtz Kay, University of California Press 1998

A Better Place to Live: Reshaping the American Suburb
Philip Langdon, University of Massachusetts Press 1997

Bowling Alone: The Collapse and Revival of American Community
Robert Putnam, Simon & Schuster 2000

Geography of Nowhere: The Rise and Decline of America's Man-Made Landscape
James Howard Kunstler, Touchstone Books 1994

Home from Nowhere: Remaking Our Everyday World for the Twenty-First Century
James Howard Kunstler, Touchstone Books 1998

My Ishmael
Daniel Quinn, Bantam Books 1998

The Next American Metropolis: Ecology, community, and the American Dream
Peter Calthorpe, New York. Princeton Architectural Press 1993

The Story of B
Daniel Quinn, Bantam Books 1997

The Unconcious Civilization
John Ralston Saul, Free Press 1997

The Unsettling of America
Wendell Berry, San Francisco: Sierra Club Books, 1977.

Voltaire's Bastards: The Dictatorship of Reason in the West
John Ralston Saul, Vintage Books 1993
What Are People For?
Wendell Berry, North Point Press 1990

The Environment and the State of the World

Becoming Native to this Place
Wes Jackson, Counterpoint Press 1996

Diet for a New America: How Your Food Choices Affect Your Health, Happiness and the Future of Life on Earth
John Robbins, H.J. Kramer 1987

Gaia: A New Look at Life on Earth
James Lovelock, Oxford University Press, 2000

The Garden of Unearthly Delights: Bioengineering and the Future of Food
Robin Mather, Plume 1996

The Sacred Balance: Rediscovering our Place in Nature
David Suzuki, Amherst, New York: Prometheus Books 1998

A Sand County Almanac
Aldo Leopold, Ballantine Books 1991

State of the World 1999-2001
Lester Brown, Christopher Flavin, Hilary French et al. New York: W.W. Norton World Watch Institute 2001

State of the World
Lester Pearson et al

Stuff: The Secret Lives of Everyday Things
John C. Ryan and Alan Thein Durning, Northwest Environment Watch 1997

Vital Signs 1999
Lester Brown et al, WorldWatch Institute, New York: W.W. Norton 1999
Economy, Trade and the Environment

Biopiracy: The Plunder of Nature and Knowledge
Vandana Shiva, South End Press 1997

The Cult of Impotence: Selling the Myth of Powerlessness in the Global Economy
(out of print) Linda McQuaig

Downsize This!
Michael Moore, Harperperennial Library 1997

The Ecology of Commerce: A Declaration of Sustainability
Paul Hawken, New York: HarperBusiness 1993

Home Economics: Fourteen Essays
Wendell Berry, North Point Press 1987

The Post-Corporate World: Life After Capitalism
David C. Korten, Berrett-Koehler Pub 2000

Sex Economy Freedom and Community: Eight Essays
Wendell Berry, Pantheon Books 1994

Small is Beautiful: Economics As If People Mattered: 25 Years Later...With Commentaries
E.F. Schumacher, Hartley & Marks 1999

When Corporations rule the World: Second Edition
David C. Korten, Kumarian Press 2001

Social Inequity and Government

Defending the Left: An Individual's Guide to Fighting for Social Justice, Individual
Rights, and the Environment
David E. Driver, Noble Press 1992

The Essential Trudeau
Pierre Elliott Trudeau, McClelland & Stewart 1999

The Greening of Conservative America
John R. E. Bliese, Westview Press 2001

Keeping the Rabble in Line: Interviews With David Barsamian
Noam Chomsky, Common Courage 1994

Profit Over People: Neoliberalism & Global Order
Noam Chomsky, Seven Stories Press 1998

The Prosperous Few & The Restless Many
Noam Chomsky, Odonian Press 1993

What Uncle Sam Really Wants
Noam Chomsky, Odonian Press 1992

Human Nature and Philosophy

Biophilia
Edward O. Wilson, Harvard University Pr 1986

Consilience: The Unity of Knowledge
Edward O. Wilson, Random House 1999

The Healing Earth: Nature's Medicine for the Troubled Soul
Phillip Sutton Chard, Northword Press 1999

The Magic of Conflict
Thomas F. Crum, Touchstone Press 1987

The One Minute Manager
Spencer Johnson, Berkeley Publishing Group 1993

The Tao of Pooh
Benjamin Hoff, Viking Press 1983

Tao Te Ching
Lao Tzu, Harpercollins 1999

The Te of Piglet
Benjamin Hoff, Penguin USA 1993

Your Money Or Your Life: Transforming Your Relationship With Money and
Achieving Financial Independence
Joe Dominguez, Penguin USA 1999

Designing a New Future

Biomimicry, Innovation Inspired by Nature
Janine M. Benyus, New York: William Morrow and Co. 1997

Cool Companies: How the Best Businesses Boost Profits and Productivity by Cutting Greenhouse Gas Emissions
Joseph J. Romm, Washington, D.C.: Island Press 1999

Ecological Design
Sim Van Der Ryn and Stuart Cohen, Washington D.C: Island Press 1996

Factor Four: Doubling Wealth, Halving Resource Use
Ernst Von Weizsacker, Amory Lovins, and L. Hunter Lovins, London: Earthscan Publications Ltd 1997

Natural Capitalism: Creating the Next Industrial Revolution
Paul Hawken, Amory Lovins, and L. Hunter Lovins, Boston: Little, Brown and Company 1999

The Sand Dollar and the Slide Rule Drawing Blueprints from Nature
Delta Willis, Reading, Massachusetts: Addison-Wesley Publishing Company, Inc. 1997

Green Design Resources

Cold Climates
Joseph Lstiburek, The Taunton Press 2000

Climatic Building Design: Energy Efficient Building Principles and Practices
Donald Watson and Kenneth Labs, McGraw Hill 1993

Deep Design: Pathways To A Liveable Future
David Wann, Island Press 1996

Design With Nature
Ian L. McHarg, John Wiley & Sons 1995

Environmental Building News Magazine
Building Green, Inc.

Environmental Resource Guide CD ROM
Green Building Advisor Software
Environmental Building News

Green Development: Integrating Ecology and Real Estate
Rocky Mountain Institute, John Wiley & Sons, Inc. 1998
Green Development CD ROM

Greening the Building and the Bottom Line: Increasing Productivity Through
Energy-Efficient Design
William D. Browning and Joseph J. Romm, Rocky Mountain Institute 1994

The HOK Guidebook To Sustainable Design
Sandra F. Mendler and William Odell, New York City: John Wiley & Sons, Inc.
2000

LEED Reference Guide & Technical Manual
US Green Building Council 2000

Mechanical & Electrical Equipment for Buildings
Benjamin Stein and John S.Reynolds, New York: John Wiley & Sons, Inc. 2000

Mixed Climates
Joseph Lstiburek, The Taunton Press 2000

A Pattern Language: Towns, Buildings, Construction
Christopher Alexander, Oxford University Press 1977

Photovoltaics in the Built Environment
Solar Design Associates et al, US DOE 1997

Sun, Wind & Light
G.Z. Brown and Mark DeKay, New York City: John Wiley & Sons, Inc. 2001

Sustainable Building Technical Manual
Public Technology, Inc

A Primer on Sustainable Building
Dianna Lopez Barnett and Bill Browning, Rocky Mountain Institute 1998

Tips For Daylighting
Lawrence Berkeley National Laboratory

Appendix B
Who's Who in Green Design

Who's Who in Green Design

Every movement has its leaders, both people and organizations whose ideas and work shape the development of dozens and sometimes thousands of others who march onward to create change. The sustainable design movement is no different. This appendix shows a partial list of people and organizations that have been influential in shaping the development of the sustainable design movement through the ideas, buildings or teachings that they are responsible for.

The challenge was not so much in making this list, but in figuring out how to limit it. How do you limit the enormous contributions of so many talented individuals to just a few? The sustainable design movement is blessed with so many who have done so much. For this list, individuals or organizations were selected because they embody a diverse array of the most important principles and ideas. For each person highlighted there are three or four others, perhaps just as deserving, whose name does not appear here. The omissions are the sole mistake of the author.

Some of the individuals, like Pliny Fisk, Amory Lovins, Bill McDonough and Bob Berkebile would likely appear on any person's list who has knowledge of sustainable design. Others are less well known but bring an incredible amount to the field. In many cases where individuals are singled out, it is essential to remember that there usually is a wealth of talented people who support and build upon the ideas created by these individuals. Without their contributions much less would be accomplished.

Educators and Schools

Arizona State University

Each year Arizona State turns out a crop of talented graduate students related to sustainable design. Professor Harvey Bryan is behind a lot of them.

Harvey Bryan
State of Arizona
School of Architecture, College of Architecture and Environmental Design
P.O. Box 871605
Tempe, AZ 85287-1605
www.asu.edu/caed

California Polytechnic State University

While I know much less about the programs at Cal-Poly, with gifted educator Rob Pena now teaching there, sustainability will definitely become ingrained with many students.

Rob Pena
California Polytechnic State University
San Luis Obispo, CA 93407
www.calpoly.edu

Carnegie Mellon

Some of the most exciting and innovative research in the field of architecture today is produced at Carnegie Mellon. Professor Vivian Loftness is behind much of this research. Make the effort to check them out.

Vivian Loftness
Carnegie Mellon University
School of Architects
5000 Forbes Avenue
Pittsburgh, PA 15206
www.cmu.edu

University of Kansas

Each year this school slowly builds more capacity in teaching sustainable design to its students. Mike Swann, Shannon Criss and Nils Gore are behind much of this initiative. Look to this school to be a leader in the next few years.

Michael Swann
The University of Kansas
School of Architecture and Urban Design
Lawrence, KS 66045
www.saud.ku.edu

University of Oregon

For years the University of Oregon was the nation's strongest school related to environmental performance and is still strong today. Enrol, or look for good graduates. Retired U of O professor John Reynolds is one of the most gifted educators in the country—read his books and learn. Look for work by G. Z. Brown as well.

> John Reynolds
> University of Oregon
> 5225 University of Oregon 476C
> Lawrence Hall Department of Architecture
> Eugene, OR 97403-5225
> www.uoregon.edu

Architects

BNIM Architects

Led by Bob Berkebile, one of the founders of the Green Design movement in the US, and backed up by a host of dedicated green designers, BNIM is a firm to watch.

> Bob Berkebile
> BNIM Architects
> 106 West 14th St., Suite 200
> Kansas City, MO 64105
> www.bnim.com

Croxton Collaborative

Early leaders in sustainable design with a mix of interesting and efficient projects.

> Randy Croxton
> Kirsten Childs
> Croxton Collaborative
> 475 Fifth Avenue
> New York, NY 10017
> www.croxtonarc.com

HOK

A large firm that mostly does conventional building design harbors some incredibly innovative individuals and projects. Look for Sandy Mendler's work in particular.

> Sandy Mendler
> Canal House
> HOK Architects
> 3223 Grace Street, NW
> Washington, DC
> www.hok.com

Jersey Devil
Not your typical architects; look to them for unique ideas.

Steve Badanes
Jersey Devil Architecture
115 Architecture Hall
Box 355720
College of Architecture & Urban Planning
University of Washington
Seattle, WA 98195-5720
www.washington.edu

Lake Flato Architects
Consistently unique and elegant work with a regional focus and a growing emphasis on sustainability. Check them out.

David Lake
Lake Flato Architects Inc.
311 3rd St.
Suite 200
San Antonio, TX 78209
www.lakeflato.com

Matsuzaki Wright Architects
This firm is responsible for a strong body of green work in Canada.

Kiyoshi Matsuzaki
Matsuzaki Wright Architects Inc.
2410 1177 West Hastings St.
Vancouver, British Columbia
Canada, V6E 2K3
www.hinetbc.org

Mithun Architects
Combining solid regional design with good sustainable design principles, Mithun is a firm to watch.

Mithun Architects
Pier 56 1201 Alaskan Way
Suite 200
Seattle, WA 98101
www.mithun.com

Overland Partners Architects
Beautiful regional work with a focus on environmental performance. Check them out.

Overland Partners Architects
5101 Broadway
San Antonio, TX 78209
www.overlandpartners.com

Peter Busby & Associates
This office is responsible for some exciting work coming out of Canada. Check them
out.

Peter Busby & Associates
1220 Homer Street
Vancouver, British Columbia
Canada V6B 2Y5
www.busby.ca

Siegel & Strain
Siegal and Strain is beginning to turn many heads. Look for their work.

Siegal& Strain Architects
1295 59th Street
Emeryville, CA 94608
www.seigelstrain.com

Susan Maxman
Another pioneer in the green design movement. Check out their projects.

Susan Maxman & Partners
1600 Walnut Street
Second Floor
Philadelphia, PA
www.maxmanpartners.com

Van Der Ryn Architects
Led by Sym Van Der Ryn, who is one of the founders and thought leaders of the sustain-
able design movement, the firm consistently produces thoughtful designs at a small scale.
Check them out and read all of Sym's books.

Sim Van Der Ryn
Van Der Ryn Architects
245 Gate Five Rd.
Sausalito, CA 94965
www.vanderryn.com

William McDonough & Partners

Led by its namesake and sustainable design visionary, this firm each year produces great examples of sustainable design. Look for McDonough's book *Cradle to Cradle* and listen to him speak—he is perhaps the most eloquent presenter in the industry.

William McDonough
Michael Braungart
William McDonough & Partners
410 E. Water St.
Charlottesville, VA 22902
www.mcdonough.com

Engineers

Arup

Internationally recognized as a leader in engineering solutions, Arup is consistently good. The west coast office has strong skills in façade engineering, which brings a new dimension to their work.

Alisdair McGregor
Maurya McClintock
Arup
901 Market St., Ste. 260
San Francisco, CA 94103
www.arup.com

Clanton & Associates

Led by Nancy Clanton and her partner Dave Nelson, Clanton and Associates is an authority on sustainable lighting design. Give them a call for efficient lighting solutions.

Nancy Clanton
Dave Nelson
Clanton & Associates
4699 Nautilus Court South
Suite 102
Boulder, CO 80301
www.clantonassociates.com

Eley & Associates
More than engineers and modelers but also developers of green building programs and modeling tools. Check them out.

Charles Eley
Eley & Associates
142 Minna Street
San Francisco, CA 94105-4125
www.eley.com

KEEN Engineering
One of the most innovative engineering firms in North America. Look to them for a variety of mechanical engineering needs. Look for an opportunity to talk with their engaging CEO, Kevin Hydes—but watch out for the kilt!

Kevin Hydes
Keen Engineering Co. Ltd.
116-930 West 1st St.
North Vancouver British Columbia
Canada V7P 3N4
www.keen.com

Rumsey Engineers
A small, innovative engineering firm in California with perhaps the most talented mechanical engineer in the country—Peter Rumsey. Hire them!

Peter Rumsey
Rumsey Engineers, Inc.
99 Linden St.
Oakland, CA 94607
www.rumseyengineers.com

Steve Winter & Associates
Innovative firm led by veteren Steven Winter. Check them out.

Steven Winter
Winter & Associates
50 Washington St.
6th Floor
Norwalk, CT 06854
www.swinter.com

SuperSymmetry USA

A one-man mechanical engineering genius by the name of Ron Perkins. Hire him only if you want your engineering solutions solved in unique ways with maximum efficiency. Ron is the best.

Ron Perkins
Super Symmetry USA
4509 Evergreen Forest Lane
Navasota, TX 77686
www.supersym@supersymmetry.com

Solar Design Associates

Led by the solar visionary Steve Strong, Solar Design Associates is an international leader in the integration of Photovoltaics into architecture. Read Steve's book and hear him speak when you can.

Steve Strong
Solar Design Associates
P.O. Box 242
Harvard, MA 01451-0242
www.solardesign.com

The Weidt Group

Energy efficiency and modeling experts in the north United States.

The Weidt Group
5800 Baker Rd.
Minnetonka, MN 55345
www.theweidtgroupenergy.com

2020 Engineers

Led by two soft-spoken and brilliant young civil engineers—call them to help make your sites more sustainable.

Mark Buehrer
Christopher Webb
2020 Engineers
700 Dupont St.
Bellingham, WA 98225
www.2020engineering.com

Scientists

Dr. John Todd
The 'inventor' of the living machine, John has a wealth of green knowledge on biological systems. Read his books.

John Todd
Living Machine Inc.
10 Shanks Pond Road
Falmouth, MA 02540

Michael Braungart
Working with architect Bill McDonought, Braungart is a chemist with a passion for creating the next generation of eco-friendly products. Check out their book *Cradle to Cradle.*

William McDonough & Partners
410 E. Water St.
Charlottesville, VA 22902
www.mcdonough.com

Judy Heerwagen
Social scientist
A pioneer in the field of productivity analysis. Look for opportunities to hear her ideas.

J.H. Heerwagen & Associates
2716 N.E. 91st Street
Seattle, WA 98115
j.heerwagen@worldnet.att.net

Dr. Janine Benyus
Green Consultants
Authors of the groudbreaking book Biomimicry, Janine is teaching architects and engineers countless lessons in how nature leads hte they way.

Janine Benyus
2813 Caribou Lane
Stevensville, Montana 59870
benyus@montana.com

Green Design Consultants
David Eisenberg
One of the pioneers in the green building movement and alternative building techniques, David is a treasure trove of information. Currently working on the critically important issue of greening the codes.

David Eisenberg
Development Center for Appropriate Technology
P.O. Box 27513
Tucson, AZ 27513
www.dcat.net

Elements
A subset of BNIM architects, one of the most innovative sustainable design and consulting teams in the country. Look to them for help with architectural projects, daylighting and materials.

Elements
106 West 14th St., Suite 200
Kansas City, MO 64105
www.elementsbnim.com

Ensar Group
Led by the pioneer Greg Franta, Ensar is an international leader in sustainable design with a solid focus on daylighting.

Ensar Group Inc.
2305 Broadway
Boulder, CO 80304
www.ensargroup.com

Gail Lindsey
A knowledgeable pioneer in all aspects of sustainable design.

Gail Lindsey
Design Harmony, Inc.
16 North Boylan Avenue
Raleigh, NC 27603

Hal Levin
An international expert in indoor air quality and healthy building design.

Hal Levin
Building Ecology Research Group
2548 Empire Grade
Santa Cruz, CA 95060

Kath Williams, Ed.D.
A passionate spokeswoman for sustainable design with heavy involvement in the USGBC.
Kath can lend particular support to green-building owners.

Kath Williams & Associates
P.O. Box 1191
Bozeman, MT 59771-1191

Keen Green
A subset of Keen Engineering, this small team specializes in energy and natural ventilation modeling.

Jennifer Sanguinetti
116-930 West 1st St.
North Vancouver British Columbia
Canada V7P 3N4
www.keeneng.com

Marc Rosenbaum
Marc is an extremely knowledgeable engineer and designer of energy efficient buildings.

EnergySmiths
Marc Rosenbaum
PO Box 194
Meriden, NH 03770
www.oikos.com/companies/rosenbaum.html

Natural Logic
With Gil Friend and Bill Reed a good resource for sustainability.

Gil Friend
Bill Reed
Natural Logic, Inc.
P.O. Box 119
Berkeley, CA 94701-0119
www.natlogic.com

Robert Kobet
Bob is a great source of green building ideas and a talented presenter. Give him a call to learn.

Robert J. Kobet
Sustainaissance International
5140 Friendship Avenue
Pittsburgh, PA 15224
www.usgbc.org Organizations

Organizations

AIA Committee on the Environment
A branch of the American Institute of Architects, with a focus on sustainable design. Look for their annual Top Ten Green Awards Program.

Joyce Lee
Dan Williams
AIA Committee on the Environment
1735 New York
Washington, DC 20006-5292
www.aia.org

American Solar Energy Society
Providing invaluable information on all aspects of passive and active solar design since the seventies. Look for their conference and their magazine *Solar Today*

American Solar Energy Society
2400 Central Avenue, Ste. G-1
Boulder, CO 80301
www.ases.org

Athena Sustainable Materials Institute
Athena is a research institute based in Canada that is producing some of the most useful LCA materials tools in the industry. Check out their website and try their products.

Wayne Trusty
Athena Institute
28 St. John Street
PO Box 189
Merickville, Ontario
KOG INO
Canada
www.athenasmi.ca

California Integrated Waste Management Board
Check out their website—a large amount of useful information from the most innovative state in the country.

> California Integrated Waste Management Board
> 1001 I Street
> PO Box 4025
> Sacramento, CA 95812-4025
> www.ciwmb.ca.gov

Center for Maximum Potential Building Systems
Led by team geniuses, Pliny Fisk and Gail Vittori, this small Texas think-tank is a organization to follow. For thirty years they have been the source of green building ideas consistently ahead of their time. Support them and learn from them any way you can.
> Pliny Fisk
> Gail Vittori
> Center for Maximum Potential Building Systems
> 8604 FM 969
> Austin, TX
> www.cmpbs.org

City of Seattle
The first city to adopt LEED as its standard and arguably the most innovative in the country related to sustainability. Check out the Seattle's green building websites and look to them for continued leadership.

> Tony Gale
> Lucia Elena Athens
> Lynne Barker
> Amanda Sturgeon
> City of Seattle
> Architecture Engineering and Space Planning Fleets & Facilities Dept.
> Mail Stop 15-14-02 618
> 2nd Avenue, Room 1400
> Seattle, WA 98104
> www.cityofseattle.net

Environmental Building News
Hands down the single best source for green building information in the industry. Buy and read everything they have. You can not go wrong.

Alex Wilson
Nadav Malin
Environmental Building News-Building Green
122 Birge Street, Suite #30
Brattleboro, VT 05301
www.buildinggreen.com

Florida Solar Energy Center
A great research group located in the south.

Florida Solar Energy Center
1679 Clearlake Rd.
Cocoa, FL 32922
www.fsec.ucf.edu

Global Green USA
Part of a network of green think tanks. For architecture, contact Lynn Simon.

Lynn Simon
227 Broadway Street, Suite 302
Santa Monica, CA 90401
www.globalgreen.org

Jocelyn Castle Institute
A good resource for green building information. The leader, Cecil Stewart, provides inspiration for the movement.

Cecil Stewart
Jocyln Castle Insititute
3902 Davenport St.
Omaha, NE 68131
www.joslyncastle.com

Lawrence Berkeley National Laboratory
Each year the lab turns out a great deal of innovative research incredibly useful to the sustainable design world – much of the most exciting work centers around daylighting and lighting. Check out their website and read their reports- pay attention to the excellent work by the individuals highlighted.

Michael J. Siminovitch
Steve E. Selkowitz
Elenoar Lee
Konstantinos Papamicheal
Lawrence Berkeley National Lab
Environmental Energy Tech 1 Cyclotron
Road Mail Stop 46-125B
Berkeley, CA 94720
www.lbl.gov

Rocky Mountain Institute

The leading think-tank on sustainability perhaps in the world, founded by Guru Amory Lovins and backed up by an incredible staff of talented young greenwarriors, RMI will always be looked to as a leader. Under the direction of Bill Browning, their green building team is especially talented. Search their website, buy their books and cd's and donate money if you can. They are worth it.

Amory Lovins
Hunter Lovins
Bill Browning
Jen Uncapher-Seal
Rocky Mountain Institute
1739 Snowmass Creek Rd.
Snowmass, CO 81654
www.rmi.org

SouthFace Institute

A great resource for sustainable design in the south.

The SouthFace Institute
241 Pine St.
Atlanta, GA 30308
www.southface.org

US Green Building Council

The premier organization on sustainable design in North America. Become a member, get accredited, order their resource guides and get your projects LEED certified.

US Green Building Council
1015 18th Street, NW, Suite 805
Washington, DC 20036
www.usgbc.org

World Build Technologies
Led by USGBC founder David Gottfried, look to Worldbuild for trendsetting ideas in
green building.

David A. Gottfried
World Build Technologies
2269 Chestnut St., Suite 981
San Francisco, CA 94123
www.worldbuild.com

Developers

John Knott
The first and foremost developer to make the list thanks to John's vision, passion and intel-
lect. Check out Dewees Island and look for opportunities to hear John Speak.

John Knott
Ray Anderson
Noisette Company
Old Naval Base Complex
1360 Truxtun Ave., Bldg. 7, Ste. 100
North Charleston, SC 29405
www.noisettesc.com

Melaver Inc.
A small but highly committed development-company based in Savannah Georgia
Melaver is beginning the process of transforming all of its projects to a high degree of
environmental performance.

Martin Melaver
114 Barnard St.
Suite 2b
Savannah, GA 31401
www.melaver.com

Appendix C
The Phases of Green Design

The Five Green Phases of Firms

Phase One–The Brown-Green Phase

Phase One organizations are defined simply as those organizations that have zero to little interest in or knowledge of sustainable design. Needless to say, most petrochemical and automotive companies would fit in this category. Unfortunately, the same could also be said for most organizations involved in the building industry, although this is changing at a phenomenal rate. Just a few years ago, most architecture firms fell into the Phase One category alongside their counterparts in engineering and construction. However, most architecture and design firms have now moved beyond this phase, leaving engineering and construction firms behind. Many Phase One firms exist, not because they are against environmental stewardship per se, but rather, until recently, they did not understand the connection between their work and its impact on environmental health. The Phase One organizations can be summed up by describing these organizations as being "green" about "green."

Phase Two–The Light Green Phase

Phase Two organizations are those with a mild interest and beginner's knowledge in sustainable design. Organizations that fall in this category have begun to learn the jargon and buzzwords found in the field and have typically become aware of how sustainable design is changing the industry. Phase Two organizations typically contain a mix of individuals, including those who might have a greater than Phase Two level of knowledge, but also many with only a Phase One understanding. Phase Two organizations often have leaders who give only mild support to sustainable ideas, or are early on their own learning curve.

Many times Phase Two organizations harbor individuals with little or no interest in sustainable design who have had to begrudgingly learn a few things about the subject because of the recent shifts toward green in the marketplace. In general, it takes an organization one to two years to move from a Phase One organization to a Phase Two organization with some effort, although an individual can move from the first phase in as little time as six months.

Phase Three–The Green-Green Phase

Phase Three organizations are categorized as those with moderate to serious interest and knowledge in sustainable design. Phase Three organizations have a working knowledge of how their specific field impacts the environment, basic knowledge of some solutions on how to minimize this impact and a beginning knowledge of the issues in other related disciplines. In general, Phase Three organizations still approach their process in largely the same way that they have always done, and attempt to apply sustainability as a layer (usually unsuccessfully) at the tail end of the project. For example, Phase Three mechanical engineering firms still make the same conservative assumptions about loads within a building and methods for providing comfort, but seek to specify more efficient equipment as the final solution. The overall environmental impact of projects that come out of Phase Three firms are typically not much less than conventional firms, due to the lack of systemic change that occurs to the process.

What is important to note is that when companies reach the Phase Three level, most begin to sell themselves as green businesses and tend to go after projects with this selling point as an angle. Phase Three organizations typically lack a high degree of technical knowledge about environmental performance, although a few technically skilled individuals may reside within the organization. Very few construction companies and engineers currently fit within the Phase Three category, although this number is changing rapidly. The largest group by far consists of architects and landscape architects. For most firms this phase serves as a type of ceiling because of the amount of time and resources it takes to progress to Phase Four and the challenges of change within an organization. Depending on the organization and the resistance to change found within, the time to go from a Phase Two to a Phase Three firm can vary anywhere from two to five years. Since this is by far the broadest category, there are many shades of green or sub levels that could be identified within this group. Around the country, there has been an emergence of green teams in architectural and engineering companies, which for the most part tend to start in Phase Three firms.

Phase Four –The Dark Green Phase

Phase Four organizations are those with a high degree of interest in and knowledge of sustainable design principles and technologies and which have significantly modified their work process to adopt the holistic thinking process identified in chapter eleven. Unfortunately, there are currently very few organizations that have reached the Phase Four level of knowledge. A Phase Four understanding requires years of technical research on both a broad and specific basis and practice trying to implement sustainable design principles. Inevitably it requires a willingness to throw out and relearn old professional habits. A Phase Four firm requires strong leadership as well as a consistent base of support to make sure that things do not slip back to the status quo. There are probably only a few hundred Phase Four individuals in the building industry today in the United States and Canada and only a couple of dozen organizations that would deserve the designation. The epitomy of Phase Four Organizations would be the Rocky Mountain Institute, The Center for Maximum Potential Building Systems, the Environmental Building News Team and Elements, the sustainable consulting division of BNIM Architects.

Phase Five – Living Green Phase

Ten years from now we will see the emergence of a fifth phase of development, The Phase Five organization. The Phase Five Organization will be defined as an organization that has honed its holistic, integrated design abilities and begun the process of producing living buildings consistently.

Appendix D
The Elements Green Design Methodology

The Elements Sustainable Design Methodology

1. **Understand Climate and Place**
   Designers should first understand the place in which they are designing. What effect does the climate have? Temperature, humidity, diurnal temperature swings, precipitation amounts and distribution, snowfall, wind speed and direction, air quality, landscape features, vegetation, surrounding obstructions, etc. must all be understood.

2. **Reduce Loads**
   Designers should then analyze what 'loads' or system requirements there are in the design and seek to systematically reduce them or accurately define them rather than inflate them.

3. **Use Free Energy**
   Designers should then look to use free sources of energy to further minimize loads and dependence on mechanical systems such as using the sun for heat and natural ventilation to cool where appropriate

4. **Use The Most Efficient Technology Possible**
   Only after each of the other steps have been done should the designer look to mechanical or technological solutions to design problems. At this point the designer should specify the most efficient and elegant solution possible.

Appendix E
The Principles of Sustainable Design

Principle 1
Respect for the Wisdom of Natural Systems–The Biomimicry Principle

Respect for the wisdom of natural systems is centered on the idea that we should use nature as a mentor and model for all of our designs. In fact, the source of all of our innovations can be traced back to nature itself. Where technologies have been misapplied, they are usually examples of forgetting the lessons inherent all around us. In order to return to a path of true sustainability our communities and built environment need to emulate natural systems.

Principle 2
Respect for People–The Human Vitality Principle

Sustainable design endeavors to create the healthiest, most nourishing places possible for people without diminishing the ability of nature to provide nourishing places for the rest of creation and for our own species in the future. Respect for people reminds us that sustainable design is about creating healthy habitats—for us and the rest of creation.

Principle 3
Respect for Place–The Ecosystem/Bioregion Principle

Sustainable design is built on the idea of regionalism. It honors the differences that exist between places, both on the macro level, with climate regions, and on the micro level, with topographical and biological differences. The philosophy of sustainable design rejects the notion that our buildings should look the same and be built the same in any region regardless of whether we have the technological know—how and resources to do so. Indeed, it demands that our buildings respond to place in fundamental ways—from the level of the site to that of climate and bioregion.

Principle 4
Respect for the Cycle of Life–The "Seven Generations" Principle

In nature, all waste products are useful to other organisms as food. Respecting the Cycle of Life involves eliminating things wherever possible that are toxic to people and the environment so that the environment is safe "to all people, for all time" [1] Following this principle also means that there should be an appropriate fit between the life expectancy of an object and its use, be it an appliance or a whole building.

Principle 5
Respect for Energy and Natural Resources–The Conservation and Renewable Resources Principle

Simply put, we live in a finite world but treat our resources like they are infinite. This principle starts out by recognizing that all of our natural resources have intrinsic and foundational value in their natural state. It is a principle that recognizes that our whole industrial economy is but a mere subset of the natural economy and that we have a responsibility to use as little of any resource as is necessary for a given job.

Principle 6
Respect for Process–The Holistic Thinking Principal

It is not possible to build for a sustainable future using the same design and construction processes that have created the environmental burdens in the first place.

Its major message can be summed up by a single sentence; if we want to change a result, we must first change the process that led to the result. Respect for Process has six sub-principles.

The Sub-Principles of the Respect for Process

1. A Commitment to Collaboration and Interdisciplinary Communication
2. A Commitment to Holistic Thinking
3. A Commitment to Life-long Learning and Continual Improvement
4. A Commitment to Challenging Rules of Thumb
5. A Commitment to Allowing for Time to Make Good Decisions
6. A Commitment to Rewarding Innovation

End Notes

Preface

[1] smelting is the process by which raw ore is turned into metal.
[2] *Sudbury, Rail Town to Regional Capital*, Wallace and Thomson, pg. 258
[3] Ibid, pg. 275
[4] From the *Geography of Nowhere*, pg. 166
[5] See the Green Warrior Reading List in Appendix A.
[6] From a speech at EnvironDesign 2001

Chapter One

[7] Unfortunately, many make false claims about the true environmental performance of their products, which is known as green wash. Be wary of manufacturer claims.
[8] The definition is from the Microsoft Word Dictionary. Note: the word did not even appear in the Webster's New World Dictionary.
[9] As was proposed by Sim Van Der Ryn in his book of the same name.
[10] From Through the Looking Glass by Lewis Carroll. Actual quote is

"when I use a word," Humpty Dumpty said in rather a scornful tone, " it means just what I choose it to mean—neither more nor less. Quote taken from Spicyquotes.com.

[11] John Stuart Mill's quote appears to be adapted from an earlier quote by Arthur Schopenhauer who said " Every truth passes through three stages before it is recognized. In the first it is ridiculed, in the second it is opposed, in the third it is regarded as self-evident." Taken from *The most Brilliant Thoughts of All Time*, John M. Shanahan, Cliff Street Books 1999 New York.

[12] This topic will be discussed in greater detail in Chapter Fifteen—The Aesthetics of Green Design.

[13] This is discussed in Chapter Ten—Shades of Green

[14] From *Ecological Design*, pg. 9

[15] From the *Sustainable Design Primer*, pg. 2

[16] These principles and more are described in Chapters Three to Eight—The Principles of Sustainable Design.

[17] Vitruvius was one of the first individuals to have written about architectural theory and did so in Ancient Rome before the birth of Christ. He was the author of the famous treatise 'De architectura' which was highly influential in architectural thought for centuries.

[18] From a speech at the EnvironDesign Conference, 2001

[19] Burke's quote has appeared in numerous publications and speeches referencing sustainable design. This version of the quote came from the website, SpicyQuotes.com.

[20] *The Doubter's Companion*, pg. 231

Chapter Two

[1] From *Naked Ape to Super Species*, pg. 6

[2] From *Naked Ape to Superspecies*, pg. 219

[3] As described by J. Scott Turner, Associate Professor of Biology at the State University of New York College of Environmental Science and Forestry in Syracuse, New York, a leading authority in termite behavior in a telephone conversation with the author.

[4] *The Sacred Balance*, David Suzuki, pg.22

[5] It could be argued that we are the only habitat builder that doesn't consistently build ecotones-defined as a biologically rich transition area be-

tween two dissimilar ecosystems, and so the net result is not an improved ecosystem, but a degraded one.

[6] One of the best, and most interesting accounts of this history can be found in the Cartoon Guide to the Environment listed in the bibliography.

[7] From the *Ecology of Architecture*, pg. 14

[8] David Suzuki, From *Naked Ape to Super Species*, pg. 46

[9] Population projections can be risky business. Far ranging estimates have often proved to be wrong. A variety of factors will determine where exactly the earth's population will indeed level off, but the range is consistently between 9-12 billion people. For up to date information look to the World Watch Institute. www.worldwatch.org

[10] Regionalism can be defined as; 'designing in response to local or regional environmental, climatological and cultural conditions.'

[11] From, *Racing the Antelope*, pg.8

[12] There are exceptions to every rule of course, but historical evidence does not suggest that fear of ecological collapse motivated early civilizations—at least until it was likely too late.

[13] From, *Something New Under the Sun*, pg.235

[14] Mega fauna refers to giant animals such as the wooly mammoth, bears and rhinoceros. North America once had a host of such animals before mankind arrived.

[15] From a great history that can be found in the *Ecological Indian*.

[16] From *Guns, Germs and Steel*.

[17] For several decades between the twenties and the eighties the leading architects of the time dismissed regionalism in favor of an intensely modern international style and brutalist architecture.

[18] Bacon's ideas have been highly influential in modern thought. This quote was taken from a paper by Oakley E. Gordon entitled, 'From a Brief History of Psychology' published on the University of Utah website. Many similar themes can be found in Bacon's original writings.

[19] From Le Corbusier, *Towards a New Architecture*, translated from the French for " machine a habiter".

[20] From *Sex, Economy, Freedom and Community*, pg. 150

[21] From *Something New Under the Sun*, pg. 72

[22] Ibid pg. 67

[23] Ibid, pg. 109

[24] The smokestack at 381 meters is taller than the Eiffel tower at 324 meters.

[25] By 'cleaning' we mean scrubbing of pollutants out of the air stream

before they are released. Unfortunately, the cleaning process is never a complete process.

[26] CFC's stand for Chlorofluorocarbons. Thankfully, CFCs have been phased out and replaced by the less damaging HCFCs and HFCs.

[27] From *Something New Under the Sun*, pg. 113

[28] Ibid, pg. 73

[29] From *Truth Against the World*, pg. 67

[30] Wright's Broadacre City was a prelude to suburban sprawl, with large distances separating tall buildings. People got around by automobile.

[31] The Union of Concerned Scientists group that signed the document in 1993 contained the signatures of 157 scientists from 69 countries.

[32] Quoted from the author Loucks in *The Sacred Balance*, pg. 28

[33] Source from the Union of Concerned Scientists and the Worldwatch Institute

[34] From the *Consumers Guide to Highly Effective Choices*, pg. 5

[35] From *Natural Capitalism*, pg. 51

[36] From the *Consumers Guide to Highly Effective Choices*, pg.17-18

[37] Famous quote generally attributed to Rogers a humorist and Actor who lived between 1879 and 1935.

[38] *Environmental Building News*, May 2001

[39] This point is argued in more detail in Chapter Twelve—The Aesthetics of Sustainable Design.

[40] See the Who's Who list in Appendix B to find out who some of these individuals are.

[41] Although ASES was around in other forms for quite a bit longer.

[42] This was a postmodern critique of modernist Mies Van Der Rohe's opinion that "less is more" in the design process.

[43] The LEED rating system is explained in more detail in Chapter Ten—Shades of Green.

[44] This idea is also explored further in Chapter Ten—Shades of Green.

[45] Statistics provided by the US Green Building Council.

[46] See Chapter Ten - Shades of Green

[47] Awarded in 2003

Chapter Three

[1] From the *Tao Te Ching*, Chapter viii
[2] From a speech by Bill Browning in 2000
[3] From *The Sand Dollar and the Slide Rule*, pg. 41
[4] From a NPR report in 2002
[5] The spider silk data is from Biomimicry.
[6] From *Biomimicry*, pg. 135
[7] From *Medicine Quest*, pg. 40
[8] Also from *Medicine Quest*, pg. 40
[9] These technologies will be described further in Chapter Nine—The Technologies and Components of Sustainable Design.
[10] Some are already taking this message to heart; the engineering firm Arup has designed a skyscraper in Zimbabwe that operates like the insides of a termite mound, harnessing natural ventilation for comfort. For more information contact Arup Engineers.
[11] From *Biomimicry*, pg. 23

Chapter Four

[1] From the *Greening of Conservative America* pg. 21
[2] Ibid pg.23
[3] Again, this is an unfortunate misconception, as most of the early green pioneers were incredibly concerned about the well-being of their fellow man and woman.
[4] *Earth in the Balance*, pg. 368
[5] See Chapter Thirteen—Green Economics for more information.

Chapter Five

[1] From *Design With Nature*, pg. 80
[2] This quote shows up in several green books as well as architecture books. People like to quote Churchill...and so do I!
[3] From *Truth Against the World*, pg. 232
[4] "coolth" is an actual term used in the engineering world that means to provide cool air.

[5] From conversations with Eng Lock Lee.
[6] Statistics from *Asphalt Nation*
[7] Statistics from the University of Texas, School of Public Health
[8] From *Design With Nature*, pg. 55
[9] See the bibliography for the Restoration Economy.
[10] Paraphrased from numerous conversations with Berkebile between 1997-2004

Chapter Six

[1] There are many ancient prophecies and legends from North American Indian tribes about Seven Generations. In one of them, seven generations from first contact with Europeans it was predicted that all the elm trees would die and other terrible things would happen such as animals being born deformed and birds falling from the sky. Eventually, it was predicted that man would grow ashamed of the way he had treated his mother and provider, the earth. The lesson that is often taught, is that we have a responsibility to think not only of ourselves with our actions, but how are actions will affect others in the present, but also in the future, seven generations from now.
[2] From *the Prophet*, pg. 24
[3] From *Cradle to Cradle*, pg. 92
[4] From *Design with Nature*, pg. 56
[5] From *Biomimicry*, pg. 126
[6] From a speech by McDonough in 2001
[7] From a speech by McDonough in 2001
[8] From *Design With Nature*, pg. 55
[9] From *Biomimicry*, pg. 97
[10] *Silent Spring*, pg. 6

Chapter Seven

[1] From the National Renewable Energy Lab Website www.nrel.gov/
[2] From *Eco-Economy* pg. 103
[3] Of course we used to when we actually walked places!!
[4] Our greatest people-moving invention is actually the bicycle, which moves people farther per calorie of energy than anything we've come up

with. Forty times more efficient than the car and three times more efficient than a person walking!

[5] From *Natural Capitalism*, pg. 24

[6] See the HyperCar project at Rocky Mountain Institute—www.rmi.org

[7] For more on Fuel Cells see Chapter Nine—The Technologies and Components of Fuel Cells.

[8] Rocky Mountain Institute, presentation by Bill Browning and Jen Uncapher—2000

[9] 1 quad = 10 to the 15th BTU

[10] *Mechanical and Electrical Equipment for Buildings* (MEEB), pg. 11

[11] Renewables account for just a fraction of the US economy's energy mix-about 1%.

[12] Not to mention the health effects of coal mining to the miners.

[13] A parasitic load is energy use that comes from appliances that draw energy even when off. The TV for example, always draws electricity when plugged in, in order to keep the 'tube' warm so that it turns on quicker

[14] If we got serious about efficiency we could easily eliminate our need for foreign oil—true homeland security.

[15] The US currently spends about 4-5% of its GDP on the military and an additional 4-5% on education. If half of the military expenditures were redirected to education (or any other worthy sector) it would have a transformative impact on our society...and yet the United States would still have the largest military in the World. For example, in 2001 the United States spent 300 billion (now closer to 400 billion) on its military—compared to $30 billion for Britain.

[16] From *The Sacred Balance*, pg. 23

[17] Ibid

[18] With Canada not far behind in per capita resource consumption.

[19] From *Natural Capitalism*, pg. 85.

[20] From *Silent Spring*, pg.39

[21] From *Natural Capitalism* pg. 220

[22] *Something New Under the Sun*

[23] *Natural Capitalism*, pg. 220

[24] Elements (BNIM) study on water usage for the City of Seattle.

[25] For more information on these water saving technologies see Chapter Nine.

[26] Three such tools include: BEES (http://www.bfrl.nist.gov/oae/

software/bees.html) Athena (http://www.athenasmi.ca/) and Baseline Green (www.cmpbs.org)

Chapter Eight

[1] A large part of architectural education occurs within a studio, which operates as a laboratory for learning to design. In a studio, a small class of students each take on the same design assignment and work progressively towards a design solution with interaction with a studio instructor and fellow students. The studio is an incredibly intense part of an architect, landscape architect or interior designer's education and is the single most important setting for learning the process of design and decision-making.

[2] From *Home Economics* by Wendell Berry.

[3] From a speech at the 2001 EnvironDesign Conference.

[4] From the *Doubter's Companion*, pg. 181

[5] From the *Doubter's Companion*, pg. 15

[6] This quote has appeared in numerous locations in many variations.

[7] The *TE of Piglet*, pg. 152

[8] The *TE of Piglet*, pg. 69

[9] *Consilience*, pg. 13

[10] *Cult of Impotence*, pg 157.

Chapter Nine

[1] From the USGBC

[2] Over 3 stories and the toilet stack becomes too tall to properly function.

[3] Typically ten to fourteen percent efficient at converting sunlight into electricity.

[4] Typically five to seven percent efficient.

[5] This is the author's opinion—not fact

[6] Even if BP is supposedly going 'Beyond Petroleum'.

[7] ONSI, now owned by UTC Fuel Cells a United Technologies Company.

[8] Source from the US Green Building Council

Chapter Ten

[1] Austin Green Builder Program—http://www.ci.austin.tx.us/greenbuilder/

[2] AIA Committee on the Environment—http://www.aia.org/cote/

[3] Canada has just set up its own Canadian Building Council based on the USGBC and many other countries are following suite under the umbrella of the newly formed World Green Building Council.

[4] The Green Building Challenge website is: http://www.iisbe.org/iisbe/gbc2k2/gbc2k2-start.htm

[5] The BREEAM website can be found at: http://www.breeam.com/

[6] Based on LEED 2.1—USGBC Website www.usgbc.org

Chapter Eleven

[1] From *Cool Companies*, pg. 4

[2] From *Greening the Building and the Bottom Line*

[3] *Cool Companies*, pg. 98

[4] *Greening the Building and the Bottom Line*, pg...

[5] *Greening the Bottom Line*

[6] *Greening the Bottom Line*

[7] *Cool Companies*, pg. 89

[8] *Cool Companies*, pg. 4

[9] From a conversation with Judy in 2003

[10] From a conversation with Peter in 2003

[11] From a conversation with Nancy in 2003

[12] From American Lung Association educational literature

[13] From the EPA website, www.epa.gov

[14] *The Healing Earth*, pg. 14

[15] *The Healing Earth*, pg. 20

[16] *A Better Place to Live*, pg. 207

[17] The author would submit that Kahn understood these lessons exactly. His great works such as the Salk Institute and Kimble Library are both austere and life-filled.

[18] See "The Living Building," *The World & I*, October 1999, pg. 160

Chapter Twelve

[1] paraphrased from a famous quote generally attributed to Geothe.

[2] From a speech given by Knott at the Melaver Symposium, 2002

[3] The author's opinion only—not fact.

[4] A report for the University of Texas Health Science Center on Embodied Energy-unpublished.

[5] From *Truth Against the World*

[6] Some might think that the term 'warrior' is a strange choice of words because it has certain violent connotations. The truth is, that in many cultures, a true warrior is one who is incredibly disciplined, centered and effective. A warrior is one who embraces conflict while avoiding violence at all costs. Change, which is what this book is all about, requires the willingness to embrace conflict and to transform negative energy into positive action.

Chapter Thirteen

[1] *Green Developments*, pg. 343

[2] *Cool Companies*, pg. 53

[3] *Natural Capitalism*, pg. 11

[4] *Natural Capitalism*, pg. 114

[5] BNIM Architects, KEEN Engineering, Tipping Mar + associates, Scott Lewis

[6] Nitrogen Dioxide, Carbon Dioxide, Sulphur Dioxide and Particulates under 10 microns in size respectively.

[7] BNIM Architects, www.bnim.com, KEEN Engineering, http://www.keen.ca/home.cfm, David and Lucile Packard Foundation, http://www.packard.org/

[8] Green Leases and the Speculative Office Market–EDC Magazine –2001

Chapter Fourteen

[1] Bridging the Gap is a local non-profit organization dedicated to making environmental change in the Kansas City region. http://

www.bridgingthegap.org/

[2] This Order of Operations Methodology was developed by McLennan for the Elements team at BNIM in order to quickly teach sustainable design concepts to new clients.

[3] From *Natural Capitalism*, pg. 122

[4] From *The Story of B*, pg. 70

[5] From *Natural Capitalism*, pg.286

[6] Source from Polaroid Camera's website

[7] From *The Four Agreements*, pg. 23

Chapter Fifteen

[1] BTU's/sf/year is a common metric used to compare the amount of energy used in a building. BTU stands for British ThermalUnit and is a standard measure of energy.

[2] The *Old Way of Seeing*, pg. 190

[3] This is not to say that organic buildings cannot be green. No style, even the 'organic' style that many associate with green buildings, is inherently green or not green.

[4] By beauty we mean something that has been carefully designed and executed, and made of quality materials with attention to detail.

[5] In no way should we suggest that salvaged or recycled content products are inferior. Indeed, they are often superior, but these attributes are not by themselves enough.

[6] That and cheap energy.

[7] From *The Old Way of Seeing*, pg. 100

Chapter Sixteen

[1] From *The Population Bomb*.

[2] Although millions do suffer and die each year from a lack of resources.

[3] From *The Cult of Impotence*, Linda McQuaig, pg. 282

Appendix F

1 From a speech by McDonough

Bibliography

Alexander, Christopher, *Oregon Experiment* (New York: Oxford University Press, 1975)

Alexander, Christopher, *A Pattern Language: Towns, Buildings, Construction* (Oxford: Oxford University Press, 1977)

Alexander, Christopher et al, *The Timeless way of Building,* (Oxford: Oxford University Press, 1979)

Benyus, Janine M., *Biomimicry* (New York: Quill William Morrow, 1997)

Berkebile Robert J. and McLennan, Jason F., *The World and I,* 1999 issue *Biomicry in Architecture*

Berkebile, Robert J., Williams, Kath and McLennan, Jason F. et al, *The Nist Report,* (2000)

Berry, Wendell, *Home Economics: Fourteen Essays* (New York: North Point Press, 1987)

Bliese, John R. E., *The Greening of Conservative America* (Boulder, Colorado: Westview Press, 2001)

Boldt, Laurence G., *Zen and the Art of Making a Living* (New York: Penguin Books, 1999)

Brown, Lester, *Eco-Economy: Building an Economy for the Earth* (New York: W.W. Norton & Company, 2001)

Browning, William and Lopez Barnett, Diana, *Sustainable Design Primer–RMI* (Rocky Mountain Institute, 1995)

Browning, William D. and Romm, Joseph J., *Greening the Building and the Bottom Line: Increasing Productivity Through Energy-Efficient Design* (Rocky Mountain Institute, 1994)

Calthorpe, Peter, *The Next American Metropolis: Ecology, Community and the American Dream* (New York: Princeton Architectural Press, 1995)

Carroll, Lewis, *Through the Looking Glass* (New York: Dover Publishing, 1999 edition)

Chard, Philip Sutton, *The Healing Earth* (Minnetonka, Minnesota: Northword Press, 1994)

Cohen, *Trudeau's Shadow: The Life and Legacy of Pierre Elliot Trudeau–Canada:* Vintage Books, 1999, Toronto

Crum, Thomas F., *The Magic of Conflict: Turning a Life of Work into a Work of Art* (New York: Touchstone, 1998)

Diamond, Jared, *Guns, Germs and Steel. The Fates of Human Societies* (New York: W.W. Norton and Company, 1999)

Elkington, John, *Cannibals with Forks, The Triple Bottom Line of 21st Century Business* (New Society Publishers, 1998)

Exupery, Antione de Saint, *Wind, Sand and Stars* (New York: Harcourt, 2002)

Gonick, Larry, *The Cartoon History of the Universe* (New York: Doubleday, 1990)

Gore, Al, *Earth in the Balance* (Boston: Houghton Mifflin Company, 1992)

Hale, Jonathan, *The Old Way of Seeing* (New York: Houghton Mifflin, 1994)

Hasse, Betty and Heerwagen, Judith, *Phylogenetic Design: A New Approach for Workplace Environments* (unpublished article)

Hawken, Paul, *The Ecology of Commerce* (New York: Harper Business, 1993)

Hawken, Paul; Lovins, Amory and Lovins, L. Hunter, *Natural Capitalism: Creating the Next Industrial Revolution* (Boston: Little, Brown and Company, 1999)

Heerwagen, Judith H., *Design, Productivity and Well Being: What are the Links?*, research paper, American Institute of Architects Conference on Highly Effective Facilities 1998

Heerwagen, Judith H., *Green Buildings, Organizational Success and Occupant Productivity*, Building Research and Information Vol. 28 (5) 2000:353-367 (London, UK 2000)

Heinrich, Bernd. *Racing the Antelope—What Animals Can Teach us About Running and Life* (New York: Bernd Heinrich Cliff Street Books, 2001)

Hoff, Benjamin, *The TE of Piglet* (New York: Penguin Books, 1992)

Jacobs, Jane, *The Nature of Economies* (Toronto: Random House, 2000)

Kunstler James Howard, *The Geography of Nowhere, The Rise and Decline of America's Man-Made Landscape* (New York: Simon & Schuster, 1993)

Kunstler, James Howard, *Home from Nowhere: Remaking our Everyday World for the 21st Century* (New York: Touchstone Books, 1998)

Krech III, Shepard, *The Ecological Indian, Myth and History* (New York: W.W. Norton & Company, 1999)

Langdon, Philip, *A Better Place to Live–Reshaping the American Suburb* (Boston: University of Massachusetts Press, 1997)

Le Corbusier, *Towards a New Architecture* (New York: Dover Publications, 1986)

LEED Reference Guide, 2001 Paladino and Associates, US Green Building Council

Lovelock, James, *Gaia: The Practical Science of Planetary Medicine* (Oxford: Oxford University Press, 2001)
McDonough, William and Braungart, Michael *Cradle to Cradle: Remaking the Way We Make Things* (New York: North Point Press, 2002)

McDonough, William, *The Hannover Principles* (New York: 1992)

McHarg, Ian, *Design With Nature* (New York: John Wiley & Sons, 1995)

McKibben, Bill, *The Age of Missing Information* (New York: Plume, 1993)

McNeill, J.R., *Something New Under the Sun–Environmental History of the Twentieth Century World* (New York: W.W. Norton & Company, 2000)

McQuaig, Linda, *The Cult of Impotence: Selling the Myth of Powerlessness in the Global Economy* (New York: Viking Books, 1988)

Ming-Dao, Deng, *Everyday Tao–Living with Balance and Harmony* (San Francisco: Harper San Francisco, 1996)

O. Wilson, Edward. *Biophilia* (Cambridge: Harvard University Press, 1986)

O. Wilson, Edward, *Consilience, the Unity of Knowledge* (Random House, 1999)

Paladino & Associates, *USGBC–LEED Reference Guide* (Seattle: 2001)

Plotkin PHD., Mark J., *Medicine Quest–In Search of Nature's Healing Secrets* (New York: Penguin Book, 2000)

Quinn, Daniel, *The Story of 'B': An Adventure of Mind and Spirit* (New York: Bantam Books, 1996) ·

Ray, Paul H., *The Cultural Creatives* (New York: Three Rivers Press, 2000)

Rocky Mountain Institute, *Green Development: Integrating Ecology and Real Estate* (John Wiley & Sons, Inc., 1998)

Romm, Joseph, *Cool Companies* (Covelo, CA and Washington DC: Island Press, 1999)

Ruiz, Don Miguel, *The Four Agreements* (San Rafael, California: Amber-Allen Publishing, 1997)

Ryan, John C. and Durning, Alan Thein, *Stuff, The Secret Lives of Everyday Things* (Seattle, Washington: Northwest Environmental Watch, 1997)

Saul, John Ralston, *The Doubter's Companion–A Dictionary of Aggressive Common Sense* (New York: The Free Press, 1994)

Sierra Club magazine–July 2000 Issue–Bears of the Yellowstone

Stein and Reynolds, *Mechanical & Electrical Equipment for Buildings,* (New York: Stein and Reynolds, 2000)

Strong, Steven J., *The Solar Electric House: Energy for the Environmentally-Responsive, Energy-Independent Home* (New York: Chelsea Green Publishing Company, 1994)

Suzuki, David, Dressel, Holly, *From Naked Ape to SuperSpecies, A Personal Perspective on Humanity and the Global Eco-Crisis* (Ontario, Canada: Stoddard Press, 1999)

Suzuki, David, *The Sacred Balance: Rediscovering Our Place in Nature* (Amherst, New York: Prometheus Books, 1998)

Todd, Kay CEO of the Oklahoma American Lung Association, Interview, 2001

Turner, J Scott. *Architecture and Morphogenesis in the Mound of Macrotermes michaelseni in Northern Namibia*, (Cimbebasia 16:143-175, 2000) Paper

Turner, J Scott *The Extended Organism. The Physiology of Animal-Built Structures* (Cambridge, Massachusetts: Harvard University Press, 2000)

Tzu, Lao, *The Tao Te Ching* (Penguin Books, 1963)
Tzu, Sun, *The Art of War: A New Translation* (Boston: Shambhala Publications, Inc., 2001)

USGBC–LEED Reference Guide and US Green Building Council Website at usgbc.org

Van Der Ryn, Sym and Cohen, Stewart, *Ecological Design* (Washington D.C.: Island Press, 1996)

Venturi, Robert, *Learning From Las Vegas-Revised Edition: The Forgotten Symbolism of Architectural Form* (New York: MIT Press, 1992)

Wallace, CM and Thomson, Ashley (edited by), *Sudbury, Rail Town to Regional Capitol* (Toronto: Dundurn Press, 1993

Willis, Delta, *Sand Dollar and the Slide Rule, Drawing Blueprints from Nature* (Reading, Massachusetts: Addison Wesley Publishing Company, 1995)

Williams, Kath, Berkebile, Robert J., and McLennan, Jason F., et al, *The NIST Report for the MSU Epicenter*, Washington DC: National Institute of Standards and Technology 2000 In Proceedings of the Second International Green Buildings Conference and Exposition, EDS. K.M.Whitter and T. B Cohn, National Institute of Standards and Technology (NIST) Special Publications 888, Gaithersburg, MD

Wright, Frank Lloyd, *Truth against the World: Frank Lloyd Wright Speaks for an Organic Architecture* (New York: Preservation Press, 1992)

Zeiher, Laura C., *The Ecology of Architecture—A Complete Guide to Creating the Environmentally Conscious Building* (New York: Whitney Library of Design, 1996)

Zeiher, Laura, *The Ecology of Architecture, the Complete Guide to Creating the Environmentally Conscious Building* (New York: Whitney Library of Design, 1996)

The Sustainability Report—David and Lucile Packard Foundation—BNIM Architects, HPS Architects and KEEN Engineering, Unpublished 2001

Index